THE MODERN THEATRE

Volume Six

THE

MODERN THEATRE

Volume Six

Edited by

ERIC BENTLEY

Five Plays

LORENZACCIO

SPRING'S AWAKENING

THE UNDERPANTS

A SOCIAL SUCCESS

THE MEASURES TAKEN

GLOUCESTER, MASS.

PETER SMITH

1974

The Anchor Books edition is the first publication of *The Modern Theatre,* Volume 6, edited by Eric Bentley.

Anchor Books edition: 1960

ACKNOWLEDGMENTS

Among those who helped to make this volume possible were:

Mrs. Kadidja Wedekind Biel
Mr. Martin Esslin
Dr. Manfred George
Mr. Theodore Hoffman
Mr. Richard Howard
Dr. Hugo Schmidt
Mr. Eric Vaughn

E. B.

CONTENTS

AFTERWORD TO THE MODERN THEATRE
VOLUMES I–VI

. . . we live in a period of social passions. The tragedy of our period lies in the conflict between the
individual and the collectivity, or in the conflict
between two hostile collectivities in the same individual.

—Leon Trotsky, in
Literature and Revolution

In the early and middle Forties, I had the experience of doing
a little theatre work and a little teaching of modern drama,
and finding unavailable in book form most of the plays I
wanted to use. An immigrant to the do-it-yourself country, I
decided to try and fill part of the gap myself and in 1947
embarked on a project which has only now in 1959 reached
its termination—I will not say completion. My hope was to put
between covers enough of the missing modern repertory at
least to suggest what riches existed if only people wished to
tap them.

The first volume I planned was rejected by all the New York
publishers I approached except one. That one would have
accepted it on condition that I destroy its identity and make
it resemble the anthologies already in print. I was unable to
find a publisher east of the Rockies, but found one in a dis-
tinguished supporter of (financially) lost causes, Mr. Alan
Swallow, who at that time was Director of the University of
Denver Press. Having published the second of my volumes,
this press went under. *From the Modern Repertoire* became
a three-volume set only when Indiana University Press, under
the directorship of Mr. Bernard Perry, took it on; they have
kept it steadily in print ever since.

In the Fifties came paperback books. There was nothing
new about paper bindings, of course, nor even about the publication of good books bound in paper. It had been known for

a long time that you could sell certain kinds of good books in
cheap editions. A Tolstoy novel, for example, was known to
be something that would sell. The point proved by Anchor
Books—and no doubt by the other "lines" of quality paper-
backs that followed Anchor—was that the book that *won't* sell
will sell. My anthologies stood high in the ranks of books
that won't sell, and were accordingly of interest to Mr. Jason
Epstein of Anchor Books. Hence the present series, of which
this volume is the sixth and last.

The starting point was *From the Modern Repertoire*, but
The Modern Theatre is not a reprint, for my plan was not to
supplant the earlier collection, but to have both in the book-
shops simultaneously. There are thirty plays in each collection, and only two scripts (*Woman of Paris* and *Electra*) have
been taken over bodily from the one to the other. *Fantasio*,
Danton's Death, and *La Ronde* appear in both anthologies
but in different translations. To set forth certain foreign plays
in more than one English dress had been a long-standing wish
of mine, and here at last was the opportunity. One translation
is in no way displaced by the other, but, rather, stands as a
second interpretation resulting from a second approach. Another subject of importance for any student of the theatre is
that of revision—or "rewrite" as the commercial theatre calls it.
Seldom does the outside world get to see successive stages of
revision, and I was happy to show to whoever was interested
two degrees of revision in *The Threepenny Opera*. In view of
such facts, it is not seriously inaccurate to state that my nine
volumes contain sixty plays.

What is the range of these plays? It is easier, first, to say
what their range is not. Excluded on principle are the seven
most highly regarded modern playwrights: Ibsen, Strindberg,
Chekhov, Shaw, Pirandello, O'Neill, and García Lorca. These
authors already have their place on the shelves of every theatre person and every student of drama. I wish I could say that
I was free to take my choice of all that remains. But there
were obstacles—linguistic, legal, and economic—of which most
of my readers are, perhaps, unaware. Language remains a
barrier so long as we do not have a profession of thoroughly
competent translators, and that we certainly do not have. I
don't know whether any dramatist will prove untranslatable

ultimately, but many have proved untranslatable up to this moment. That explains the absence from my anthologies of, for example, Grillparzer, Hebbel, and Hauptmann. It partially explains the absence of Claudel, but with him we come to the second kind of obstacle: the legal one. Anthologists are blithely criticized in the press for excluding authors whom they would have included except for legal barriers erected by authors, agents, publishers, and (above all, I would say) deceased authors' estates. (When such an estate is *run* by a publisher, all is lost.) To mention many names under this head would perhaps amount to provocation; but I should like readers to know that Hofmannsthal's *The Tower* would certainly be in the present anthology but for the legal barrier. Lastly, economic obstacles. Some authors place themselves or are placed by their representatives beyond the reach of the anthologist's budget. Luckily, however, most of these are authors I myself wouldn't wish to include.

It was still possible to achieve the original aim of at least suggesting the wealth and variety of the modern repertoire. Although this could hardly, under the circumstances, be done systematically, and I was not intending, in any case, to cover a precise tract of territory, the range of the modern dramatic genius is unmistakably indicated by placing side by side, say, O'Casey and Ghelderode, or Beerbohm and Brecht, or Conrad and Labiche, or Saroyan and Giraudoux—pairs of names that clash like cymbals.

Some reviewers have said that I favor the avant-garde. The statement would scarcely explain the inclusion of Frank Loesser or Clyde Fitch, and I think of the accomplished M. Anouilh as anything but a pathbreaker. Some of the plays—such as *Gamblers* and *Italian Straw Hat*—would have to be classified as antiques if they were not classic and therefore permanent. Such plays are familiar items on their native soil, and the only amazing thing is that they have not been familiar in America. I did take it as the function of my volumes to bring these items before our public. To that extent, my scheme was conservative, though admittedly this is not the same as conventional, for a conventional person might well read Aeschylus and Aristophanes and exclaim: how experimental!

The avant-garde label was not wholly inept. Although

nothing of current drama is found in my collections—nothing
of Beckett, say, or Ionesco—the past has been rifled not only
for what is past but for what is most modern. Then again,
certain authors remain avant-garde forever, just as others become the fathers of their country even before they die. Among
the latter are Goethe and Hauptmann, among the former
Büchner and Ghelderode. Or take *Spring's Awakening*. In
1891, when it was first published, it was avant-garde in a
familiar sense: both the style and the point of view were ahead
of the public. By 1959 the play has ceased to be advanced as
far as some of the subject matter is concerned, and we see
the style, now, as the first link in a chain to which a good many
links have subsequently been added. Yet—and this is the important thing—Wedekind's audacity still makes itself felt today. Compared to plays about children of a mere decade ago,
Spring's Awakening is fresh in both the strict and the slang
sense: it has spontaneity and it has a certain insolence, an
unerhörte Frechheit.

The Modern Theatre is avant-garde to the extent that the
choice of plays is in itself a calculated aggression against con-
ventionality. It is clear that Carl Sternheim has a place here
and that Maxwell Anderson has not. Was there a kind of edi-
torial favoritism in all this? Yes. Authors who committed aggression against the established theatre—the "theatre as we
know it"—were given preferential treatment.

The modern drama, one can surely argue, does not begin
with *The Second Mrs. Tanqueray*, nor yet with *A Doll's
House*, but with *Lorenzaccio* and *Danton's Death*. And it has
been brought to an end—doubtless before some new departure
—by the generation, born in the 1890s, of Brecht and Ghelderode. The six volumes of *The Modern Theatre* trace—with
some clarity, I think—the whole curve of that development.
Can the same be said for the contents of the "standard" anthologies or for the play lists of "standard" college courses in
modern drama?

Lorenzaccio, in its entirety, is too long for an anthology,
but, otherwise, this play and *Danton's Death* can stand as
examples *par excellence* of the kind of play I have enjoyed
bringing out. The two plays (written within two years of each
other, incidentally, by men only three years apart in age, both

in their early twenties) are alike "monstrous" and, if you insist, "grotesque" outpourings of the spirit—the kind of work to
which professional drama critics will inevitably apply their
celebrated formula: NOT A PLAY. Though both have become classics of the stage in the twentieth century, neither
was performed in its author's lifetime or for two generations
thereafter. Neither is an example of perfection, for in neither
case has the rich confusion of youthful genius been brought
to order. But both are examples of greatness, of the quintessentially dramatic—and of relevance.

Of their subject, it is not enough to say that it is political
disillusionment (though the age of Arthur Koestler will certainly find an analogy between the French and Russian revolutions and the tyrannies and disenchantments that followed
both) unless we go on to remark that the critique of social
idealism is one of the great dedications of modern writers—in
other words, that these two plays belong not only with *Darkness at Noon* and *Witness* but also with *The Possessed, Under
Western Eyes,* and Pirandello's *The Old and the Young.* It
is curious how little reference has been made to these two
plays in the standing discussion of whether tragedy and modernity are incompatible. There can be no tragedy, some have
said, because we have lost all belief in Fate. Yet Napoleon
said that politics had now become Fate, and these plays of
Musset and Büchner could be regarded as tragedies of a political Fate. Which is not to say that these authors, like later
social dramatists, left out of account the inner life of man. The
tale of tyrannicide which both of them tell is also a tale of
parricide. It is clear, too, that both playwrights had *Hamlet*
in mind. Lorenzo and Danton are our modern Hamlets. . . .

My project of 1947–59 closes with the present volume because my point has been made, insofar as a bundle of plays
can make it. I think that drama publishing in its next phase
should chiefly continue the tradition of the old Mermaid
Series: one volume, one author. Possibly some of the authors
I brought back into circulation, such as Büchner, could now
have a paperback volume to themselves. There should certainly be paperback editions available, if adequate translations
can be made, and rights can be cleared, of Hofmannsthal,
Claudel, Georg Kaiser, and a number of others.

A word about this last volume of *The Modern Theatre*. It
is the only one of the six, so far as I myself am aware, that has
a theme. That theme is: the Individual versus the Collectivity.
Being, perhaps, the characteristic theme of modern drama, it
helps to make a concluding volume really conclusive.

True, our five playwrights do not all arrive at similar conclusions. But they do start from a similar premise, namely,
that, in Emerson's words, "Society everywhere is in conspiracy
against the manhood of every one of its members"; though the
Brecht of *The Measures Taken* would have added: "Everywhere except the Soviet Union."

Brecht is the most recent of the five playwrights. Both he
and Musset—the least recent—show certain individuals organ-
izing a conspiracy against the conspiracy that is Society. That
is to say: *Lorenzaccio* and *The Measures Taken* are about
revolution. And it is curious that, for all the obvious differences between their authors, differences of period as well as
of temperament and conviction, the two plays make the same
double statement: that the rebellious impulse is apt to begin
as a virtue and end as a menace. In both writers, moreover,
emotion seems to speak for rebellion, and intellect against it;
which surely must mean that the emotion of rebellion has
encountered in both men another emotion, and been overwhelmed by it. The gall of disenchantment is stronger in both
than the spring water of argument.

The Musset and Brecht plays in this volume complement
each other; and so do the plays of Sternheim and Wedekind.
In *The Underpants*, Carl Sternheim shows the total victory
of Society. In his Germany, true human individuality is ex-
tinct, even while a meretricious individualism is rampant. It
is the paradox of this individualism that it threatens, not bourgeois Society, which in fact it upholds, but the individual, if
ever he should irrupt into a milieu so hostile to him. In the
1930s, Sternheim might have said: "This was sometime a paradox but now the time gives it proof." For nothing in literature
shows more clearly than Sternheim's plays the social roots of
Nazism. And the Nazis knew how to combine an attack on
the individual with praise of the individual "superman" (or
crazed individualist).

While the irony of Sternheim is rooted in despair, Wedekind's *Spring's Awakening* is an expression of hopeful radicalism. Society comes within an inch of total victory: Moritz has killed himself; Wendla has died from Mother Schmidt's treatments; the suicide of Melchior is a possibility; but under persuasion from the Man in the Mask, Melchior elects to be an individual. The individual knows that Society has to be fought.

As for *A Social Success,* its place here is justified less by its social significance than by its entrancing triviality. Its humor is in the class of Wilde and Labiche. Yet—lest I stray from my theme—it also describes a victorious battle fought by Society against the individual.

Of *The Measures Taken,* it will be noted that it is the third play by Brecht in this anthology. In the interests of variety I have not usually chosen more than one play by one author. The playwrights who are represented by two plays are writers with an unusually prominent place in that revaluation of modern drama which is touched upon above: Musset, Büchner, Gogol, and Giraudoux. If Bertolt Brecht is even more strongly represented here than these, it is partly because his works have been even less available otherwise, and partly because of the editor's close association with him and his work. After all, my complaint against the "standard" anthologies is that their implied claim to definitiveness is completely phony. No such claim is implied here. My choices can be given some general justification—as I have just tried to demonstrate. But they remain the choices of one person. My hope is that this fact makes my anthology, not less, but more interesting to other persons.

E. B.

Summer 1959

LORENZACCIO

by

ALFRED DE MUSSET

English version by
Renaud C. Bruce

Chantons la Liberté, qui refleurit plus âpre,
Sous des soleils plus mûrs et des cieux plus vermeils!

On the night of the 5th January 1537 came the end of Alessandro's vicious life at the age of twenty six, and in the way in which it was bound to come sooner or later. He was assassinated by his young relative and boon companion Lorenzino, of the younger branch of the Medici family, then aged twenty two, assisted by a hired assassin, Scoronconcolo, in a room in Lorenzino's house adjoining the Medici Palace; to which house Alessandro had gone late at night imagining that he would meet there a lady of whom he was enamoured, and who was none other than Lorenzino's own sister . . . Lorenzino, however, was merely deluding him and, instead of his sister, brought in the assassin . . . Lorenzino was a strange youth. He . . . had decided ability and character, while it is specially recorded of him that he had much culture and literary talent. But he is said to have acted at times as though seized with temporary madness . . . He was seventeen when Alessandro was made Duke of Florence, and from that time he became the latter's constant associate and companion in all his vicious courses . . . Leaving Alessandro's body where it lay, Lorenzino forthwith took horse and fled . . . to Venice where was then living Filippo Strozzi, who was at this time the leading man among the *fuorusciti*. When . . . Lorenzino burst into Strozzi's room and related what he had done, Strozzi embraced him, calling him the deliverer of his country and "the Florentine Brutus" . . . Lorenzino's act has been the subject of much controversy . . . There are only three possible motives for his act, personal ambition, the liberation of his country, and the protection of his family from insult. None have considered that he was moved by the first of these motives . . . In the detailed defence of his act which he drew up, he stated that his whole course of action had been a deliberate plan in order to free his country from a monstrous tyranny which had become insupportable; and this account of the matter is believed by historians to be the true one . . .

—*The Medici*, by G. F. Young

Characters

ALESSANDRO DE' MEDICI
Duke of Florence

LORENZO DE' MEDICI (LORENZACCIO*)

COSIMO DE' MEDICI

} *his cousins*

MARIA SODERINI
Lorenzo's mother

CATERINA GINORI
his aunt

CARDINAL CIBO

COUNT LORENZO CIBO
his brother

COUNTESS RICCIARDA CIBO
his wife

SIRE MAURIZIO
Chancellor of the Council of Eight

CAPPONI

GUICCIARDINI

ACCIAIUOLI

CANIGIANI

VETTORI

NICCOLINI

noblemen belonging to the Council of Eight (the other two seem to be Ruccellai and Maurizio.—R.C.B.)

FILIPPO STROZZI

PIETRO STROZZI

TOMASO STROZZI

LEONE STROZZI, PRIOR OF CAPUA

} *his sons*

LUISA STROZZI
Filippo's daughter

CARDINAL BACCIO VALORI
Apostolic Commissioner

---

* The Italian suffix —*accio* implies monstrosity. Lorenzaccio is Lorenzo seen as a monster of iniquity.

ROBERTO CORSINI
Governor of the Fortress

GIULIANO SALVIATI

BINDO ALTOVITI
Lorenzo's uncle

BAPTISTA VENTURI
a merchant

TEBALDEO FRECCIA
a painter

GIOMO THE HUNGARIAN
the Duke's equerry

CORSI
a spokesman for Cardinal Cibo

FIRST STUDENT

SECOND STUDENT

MAFFIO
citizen

PALLA RUCCELLAI

ALAMANNO SALVIATI } *republican noblemen*

FRANCESCO PAZZI

A SILK MERCHANT

PAPA MONDELLA
a goldsmith

SCORONCONCOLO
Lorenzo's hired assassin

AGNOLO
a page in Count Cibo's household

PIPPO

GIACOMO } *Filippo's servants in Venice*

Cavaliers, courtiers, German officers, pages, students, servants, soldiers, monks, novices, exiles, citizens, maskers, etc.

THE TIME: 1536–37
THE PLACE: *Florence*

ACT ONE

SCENE 1

A garden. Moonlight. A pavilion in the background, another in the foreground. Enter the DUKE *and* LORENZO, *wrapped in their cloaks;* GIOMO *carrying a lantern.*

THE DUKE. If she keeps us waiting another quarter of an hour, I'm going. It's cold as the devil.

LORENZO. Patience, Highness, patience.

THE DUKE. She was to leave her mother's at midnight; it's midnight now; and she still hasn't come.

LORENZO. If she doesn't appear, you can call me a fool and her old mother an honest woman.

THE DUKE. Bowels of the Pope! And on top of this I've been robbed of a thousand ducats!

LORENZO. We advanced only half of it. I'll answer for the girl. Two great melting eyes like hers couldn't have deceived me. And what is more exciting for the connoisseur than to snatch a mistress from her mother's breast, to see in a child of fifteen the wanton she is to become; to study, to sew, to weave paternally the mysterious thread of vice into a friendly counsel, a caress on the cheek, to say everything and to say nothing, according to the parents' attitudes, to gently accustom the developing imagination, to give form to its dreams, to touch what frightens it, to scorn what protects it? You can accomplish this more quickly than you'd think; the important thing is to time your actions. And what a treasure this one is! She has what it takes to give Your Highness a delicious night—a pussycat that would like some jam but doesn't want to soil its paw. Neat as a Flemish maid. Middle-class mediocrity personified: no deep principles, just a superficial polish. But beneath that fragile film of ice, which cracks at every step, surges a great river of passion.

THE DUKE. Confound it! I don't see the signal. I must be going to Nasi's ball. It's today he marries off his daughter.

GIOMO. Let's go to the pavilion, my lord. Since it's only a question of carrying off a girl who's half paid for, we can surely tap at the window.

THE DUKE. Come this way! The Hungarian is right.

They withdraw. Enter MAFFIO.

MAFFIO. I dreamt I saw my sister crossing our garden—a masked lantern in her hand—and covered with brilliants. I awoke with a start. God knows it was nothing but a dream, but real enough to drive away sleep. Thanks to Heaven, the windows of the pavilion where she sleeps are closed as usual. I can see the light from her room shining dimly through the leaves of our old fig tree. Now my foolish fears are gone and the wild beatings of my heart give way to a sweet tranquillity. Wait! What do I hear? Who moves there between the branches? Am I awake? It is my sister's ghost! It holds a masked lantern, and a necklace sparkles on its breast in the moonlight. Gabriela! Gabriela, where are you going?

Re-enter GIOMO *and the* DUKE.

GIOMO. That must be the half-wit brother, walking in his sleep. Lorenzo will take your pretty one to the palace through the little door. As for us, what do we have to fear?

MAFFIO. Who are you? Stop!

He draws his sword.

GIOMO. We are your friends, bumpkin.

MAFFIO. Where is my sister? What are you looking for?

GIOMO. Your sister has flown the nest. Open the garden gate for us.

MAFFIO. Draw your sword and defend yourself, assassin!

GIOMO *springs on him and disarms him.*

GIOMO. Not so fast, stupid fool.

MAFFIO. Oh, shame! This is more misery than I can bear! If there are laws in Florence, if justice is still alive on the earth, by all that's true and sacred in the world, I'll throw myself at the Duke's feet and he'll have you both hanged.

GIOMO. At the Duke's feet?

MAFFIO. Yes, yes. I know that scoundrels like you slaughter families with impunity. But if I die—do you hear—I shall not die silent as so many have done. If the Duke doesn't know that his city is a forest full of bandits, poisoners, and dishonored women, here is one who will tell him. Murder! Blood and steel! I'll have you brought to justice!

GIOMO, *sword in hand.* Should I strike, Highness?

THE DUKE. Nonsense! Strike that poor man? Go to bed, my friend. We'll send you some ducats tomorrow.

Exit DUKE.

MAFFIO. It is Alessandro de' Medici!

GIOMO. In person, my good fool! Don't boast of his visit if you value your ears.

Exit GIOMO.

SCENE 2

A street. Daybreak. Several MASKERS *coming out of a lighted mansion. A* SILK MERCHANT *and a* GOLDSMITH *opening their shops.*

THE MERCHANT. It's a pretty windy day.

He spreads out his pieces of silk.

THE GOLDSMITH, *yawning.* It's been enough to give me a headache. The devil take their wedding celebrations. I didn't shut my eyes all night.

THE MERCHANT. Neither did my wife, neighbor. The dear soul turned over and over like an eel. After all, when you're young, you don't fall asleep to the music of violins.

THE GOLDSMITH. Young! Young! It pleases you to say that! You're not young with a beard like this. God only knows how their damned music makes me want to dance!

TWO STUDENTS *pass.*

FIRST STUDENT. There's nothing that's more fun! You push your way through the guards to the gates of the palace and you see them come down with their motley costumes. Look, there's the Nasi house!

He blows into his hands.

My portfolio is freezing my fingers.

SECOND STUDENT. Do you think they'll let us get near?

FIRST STUDENT. By what right could they prevent us? We're citizens of Florence! Look at all the people around the entrance. I can name all the important ones. You study their costumes carefully and at night in your studio you say, "I'm terribly sleepy. I spent the night dancing at Prince Aldobrandini's, at Count Salviati's. The prince was dressed thus and so, the princess thus and so"—and you aren't lying. Come. Hold onto my cape.

They go over against the door of the house.

THE GOLDSMITH. Did you hear those little idlers? I'd like to see one of my apprentices try such tricks.

THE MERCHANT. There now, Papa Mondella. Where pleasures are free, youth has nothing to lose. Those wide-eyed scamps warm my heart. That's the way I was. It seems that the Nasi girl is a good-looking wench and Martelli's a lucky boy. There's a good Florentine family. What a fine impression these great lords make! I get a kick out of these entertainments, I must admit. There you are, lying quietly in your own bed, with a corner of the curtains drawn back, and you look from time to time at the lights coming and going in the palace. You hear bits of a little dance tune without paying for it and you say to yourself: "Heh, heh, those are my silks dancing! My beautiful silks dancing on the dear bodies of all those brave and loyal noblemen!"

THE GOLDSMITH. And many that are dancing there haven't yet been paid for, neighbor. Those are the ones that they spill wine over and rub against the walls with the least regret. Oh, it's all right for the great lords to amuse themselves, they were born for it. But there are pleasures and pleasures, if you know what I mean?

THE MERCHANT. Of course. Dancing, horseback riding, games, and many other things. Or do you mean more than these, Papa Mondella?

THE GOLDSMITH. That's enough. I know what I mean. The walls of all those palaces never showed their strength more than now. They needed less of it to defend themselves against the waters of Heaven than they do against their sons who have drunk too much wine.

THE MERCHANT. You'll have to admit that this carnival has been unruly. Their giant balloon spoiled about fifty florins' worth of my merchandise as they dragged it by. Thank God the Strozzi paid for my loss.

THE GOLDSMITH. The Strozzi! May Heaven confound those who dared to raise their hands against the Strozzi nephew. Filippo Strozzi is the bravest man in Florence.

THE MERCHANT. By the way, Papa Mondella, will we meet at Monte Oliveto?

THE GOLDSMITH. It's not my policy to follow the fairs. However, I will go to Monte Oliveto for piety's sake. It's a holy pilgrimage, neighbor, and one that remits all sins.

THE MERCHANT. And a profitable pilgrimage, neighbor, that brings more money to the merchants than all the other days of the year. It's a pleasure to see all those good ladies coming out from Mass and examining the merchandise. God save His Highness! The court is a beautiful thing.

THE GOLDSMITH. The court! I tell you, the people carry it on their backs. Florence was once—not so very long ago—a good house well built. All the great palaces, which are the homes of our leading families, were its columns. And not one of them was greater than the next. Together they held up our safe world. But there were two bad architects in the world, the Pope and Emperor Charles, who determined to spoil everything. They decided to take one of those columns, that of the Medici, and make it a tower. During a single night that tower grew like a mushroom of misery over us. And then, when it weakened, they replaced it with a lump of misshapen dough made of spit and water which they called the Citadel. Their Germans have made themselves at home in it like rats in a cheese, and, while they are gambling and drinking their sour wine, they keep an eye on us. It does no good for the Florentine families to cry out, or for the people and the merchants to protest: the Medici govern by means of their garrison. They are devouring us as a poisonous growth devours a diseased stomach. It's only be-

cause of those German lances that patrol the ramparts that
a bastard, half a Medici, a boor that heaven created for a
butcher boy or a farm hand, corrupts our daughters, drinks
our wine, smashes our windows. Still, the people pay him
for it.

THE MERCHANT. My, my, how you go on! You seem to know it
all by heart, but it wouldn't be safe to say those things
in every ear, Papa Mondella.

THE GOLDSMITH. What if they banish me like so many others?
You live as well in Rome as here. The devil take the wedding and everyone there!

He goes in. The MERCHANT *mingles with the bystanders. A*
CITIZEN *passes with his* WIFE.

THE WIFE. Martelli is a handsome man and rich. Nicola Nasi
is lucky to have him for a son-in-law.—Why, the ball is still
going on! Look at all those lights!

THE CITIZEN. What about us? When are we going to marry off
our daughter?

THE WIFE. Ah, the lovely lights! Imagine, still dancing at this
hour! What a beautiful party! They say the Duke's there.

THE CITIZEN. By making day of night and night of day, they
manage to avoid seeing any decent people. Placing halberds
at the door of a wedding is a fine thing! May God protect
the city! All those German curs! Every day, more of them
come out of their damned fortress into the city.

THE WIFE. Look at the pretty masks! Ah! what a beautiful
dress! See, there!

They leave.

A SOLDIER, *to the* GOLDSMITH. Look out, dog! Let the horses
pass!

THE GOLDSMITH. Dog yourself, German devil!

The SOLDIER *strikes him with his lance.*

THE GOLDSMITH, *leaving.* These are the fruits of capitulation—
these scoundrels abusing the citizens!

He goes into his shop.

THE STUDENT. See, there! The one taking off his mask is Palla

Ruccellai. He's a gay blade. The little one beside him is Tomaso Strozzi. Masaccio, they call him.

A PAGE, *calling*. The Duke's horse!

SECOND STUDENT. Let's go. There comes the Duke.

FIRST STUDENT. Do you think he'll eat you?

The crowd gathers at the door. The DUKE *comes out costumed as a nun, with* GIULIANO SALVIATI *dressed the same, both masked.*

THE DUKE, *mounting his horse*. Are you coming, Giuliano?

SALVIATI. No, Highness, not yet.

He whispers in his ear.

FIRST STUDENT. That one is Niccolini; and that one the governor.

THE DUKE. Good, good. Agreed!

SALVIATI. She's as beautiful as a devil. Leave everything to me. If I can only get rid of my wife . . .

He returns to the ball.

THE DUKE. You're drunk, Salviati. The devil, you're staggering!

He goes off with his retinue.

FIRST STUDENT. Now that the Duke has left, it'll soon be over.

The MASKERS *go off in all directions.*

SECOND STUDENT. Pink, green, blue . . . my eyes are dazzled, my head is spinning.

FIRST STUDENT. The feasting has been going on a long time. There are two who can hardly stand.

The GOVERNOR *mounts his horse. A broken bottle falls on his shoulder.*

THE GOVERNOR. What the deuce! Who did that?

A MASKER. Don't you see him, Lord Corsini? There! Look at that window. It is Lorenzo dressed as a nun.

THE GOVERNOR. Lorenzaccio, the devil take you! You've hurt my horse.

The window is closed.

Plague take that drunkard and his sly pranks. A scoundrel who hasn't smiled three times in his life! Who spends his time fooling around like a schoolboy on vacation!

Exit.

LUISA STROZZI *comes out of the mansion, accompanied by* GIULIANO SALVIATI; *he holds her stirrup. She mounts her horse; a groom and a governess follow her.*

SALVIATI. What a pretty leg, dear girl! You are a ray of sunlight that burns the marrow of my bones.

LUISA. That is not the language of a gentleman, my lord.

SALVIATI. What beautiful eyes you have, dear heart! What a beautiful shoulder, so soft and fresh! What can I offer you to let me be your chambermaid tonight? What a pretty foot to caress!

LUISA. Let go of my foot, Salviati!

SALVIATI. No, by Bacchus! Not until you've told me when we can sleep together!

LUISA *strikes her horse and goes off at a gallop.*

A MASKER, *to* SALVIATI. The little Strozzi rides away, red as fire. You have offended her, Salviati.

SALVIATI. Bah! A young girl's anger and a morning shower . . .

Exit SALVIATI.

SCENE 3

COUNT CIBO'S *house. The* COUNTESS *and* CARDINAL CIBO. *The* COUNTESS *is waving good-by.*

THE CARDINAL. Countess, are all those tears called for? You'd think my brother was leaving for the Holy Land. I don't believe he's in great danger on his own estate.

THE COUNTESS. Brother, don't mock these tears.

THE CARDINAL. I only wish that virtue would not have to look so sad.

THE COUNTESS. Can't virtue shed tears, sir Cardinal? Or do they all belong to repentance and fear? Good-by, Lorenzo. Come back soon.

THE CARDINAL. It will only take him a week. Then, with the first flower he sees, he'll put aside the cares of the estate and bring you there to enjoy the solitude of your peaceful gardens.

THE COUNTESS. The first flowers of our beautiful lawn are always precious to me. Winter is so long. It always seems to me that the poor little things will never bloom again.

THE CARDINAL. Didn't you ask me to hear your confession today, Countess?

THE COUNTESS. Let it be tonight if Your Eminence is free, or tomorrow, as you wish. At this moment I am not myself.

THE CARDINAL. If regrets were permitted to a faithful servant of God, I would envy my brother's place. Happy is the man still so beloved after seven years of marriage. It is seven years, isn't it, Countess?

THE COUNTESS. Yes, Cardinal. My son is six years old.

THE CARDINAL. Were you at the Nasi wedding yesterday?

THE COUNTESS. Yes, I was there.

THE CARDINAL. Did the Duke attend disguised as a nun? I was told that he had, but I may have been mistaken.

THE COUNTESS. Yes, as a matter of fact, he wore that costume. Ah, Malaspina, these are sorry times for all sacred things!

THE CARDINAL. It's possible to respect sacred things and, on a festival day, take the habit of certain orders without intent to offend the Holy Catholic Church.

THE COUNTESS. The example is what is dangerous, not the intention. I don't agree with you; that revolted me. It's true that I don't know very well what is possible and what is not possible, according to your mysterious rules. Only God knows where they lead. Those that put words on their anvils, and twist them at will with a hammer and file, don't always remember that words represent thoughts—and thoughts actions.

THE CARDINAL. Enough, enough! The Duke is young, Countess, and I wager that bewitching nun's habit was very becoming to him.

THE COUNTESS. Nothing could have been better, I'm sure. It lacked only a few drops of the blood of his cousin, Ippolito de' Medici.

THE CARDINAL. And the red cap of Liberty. Isn't that so, little sister? What hatred you bear the poor Duke!

THE COUNTESS. And you, his right hand, are you indifferent to the fact that the Duke of Florence is the prefect of Charles V, the civil commissioner of the Pope? Don't you care, you who are a brother of my Lorenzo, that our Florentine sun casts German shadows on the walls of the Citadel? That Caesar[1] speaks here through every mouth? That debauchery panders to slavery and makes its gay music over the sobs of the people? Ah! I know that if the German eagle were to fall asleep on our poor roofs the clergy themselves would ring their bells to awaken him.

Exit COUNTESS.

THE CARDINAL, *alone, raises the portière and calls in a low voice.* Agnolo!

Enter a PAGE.

Do you have anything to show me today?

AGNOLO. This letter, my lord.

THE CARDINAL. Give it to me.

AGNOLO. Alas, Eminence, it is a sin.

THE CARDINAL. Nothing is a sin when one obeys a priest of the Roman Church.

AGNOLO *hands him the letter.*

How amusing to listen to the outbursts of that poor Countess, and then to see her running to a rendezvous with the dear tyrant, all bathed in republican tears!

He opens the letter and reads.

"You will be mine or you will cause my misfortune, your own, and that of our two houses." The Duke's style is laconic, but not lacking in energy. Whether the Countess will be convinced or not is difficult to say. Two months of almost constant courtship is a lot for Alessandro; it ought to be enough for Ricciarda Cibo.

He returns the letter to the page.

---

[1] Throughout the play, references to a contemporary Caesar are to the Emperor Charles V. (Translator's note.)

Take that to your mistress. You are always silent, aren't you?

AGNOLO. Trust me.

The CARDINAL *gives him his hand to kiss and goes off.*

SCENE 4

A courtyard of the DUKE'S *palace.* DUKE ALESSANDRO *on a terrace; pages exercising horses in the courtyard. Enter* CARDINAL VALORI *and* SIRE MAURIZIO.

THE DUKE. Has Your Eminence received any news this morning from the court of Rome?

VALORI. Paul III sends a thousand benedictions to Your Highness and his ardent wishes for your prosperity.

THE DUKE. Only wishes, Valori?

VALORI. His Holiness fears that the Duke is creating new dangers for himself by too many indulgences. The people are not accustomed to absolute government, and Caesar, on his last trip, said as much, I believe, to Your Highness.

THE DUKE. There's a beautiful horse, Sire Maurizio. What a devil of a rump he has.

SIRE MAURIZIO. Superb, Highness.

THE DUKE. So, my dear Apostolic Commissioner, there are still a few rotten branches to be chopped off. Caesar and the Pope have made me a king; but, by Bacchus, they put in my hand the kind of scepter that is more a hatchet than the symbol of a ruler. Well, Valori, what do you have to say?

VALORI. I am a priest, Highness. If the words which my duty compels me to report to you faithfully must be interpreted so severely, my heart forbids me to add to them.

THE DUKE. Yes, yes, I know you for a good man. You are, by Heaven, the only priest I've ever seen in my life who was an honest man.

VALORI. My lord, honesty is neither lost nor gained through the wearing of a particular dress; and among men there are more good than evil ones.

THE DUKE. Then you will give me no explanations?

SIRE MAURIZIO. Do you want me to speak, my lord? Everything is easily explained.

THE DUKE. Well?

SIRE MAURIZIO. The licentiousness of the court irritates the Pope.

THE DUKE. What are you saying?

SIRE MAURIZIO. I said, the licentiousness of the court, Highness. The Duke is the only judge of his own actions. It is Lorenzo de' Medici that the Pope claims as a fugitive from his justice.

THE DUKE. From his justice? To my knowledge, Lorenzo has never offended a pope, except Clement VII, my late cousin, who is, at this moment, in hell.

SIRE MAURIZIO. Clement VII allowed the libertine Lorenzo to leave the Papal States even though he had decapitated the statues of the Arch of Constantine in a day of drunkenness.[2] But Paul III cannot forgive Lorenzo, who has since become a model of Florentine debauchery.

THE DUKE. Bah! Alessandro Farnese is a ridiculous fellow! If debauchery shocks him, what the devil is he doing with his bastard, the dear Pietro Farnese? That decapitation episode is always being raked up against poor Renzo. As for me, I find it very funny to have cut off the heads of all those stone men. I protect the arts as well as another, and I have at my court the best artists in Italy, but I cannot understand the regard the Pope has for statues he'd excommunicate tomorrow if they were flesh and blood!

SIRE MAURIZIO. Lorenzo is an atheist; he mocks everything. If the government of Your Highness is not surrounded by the deepest respect, it cannot be strong. The people call Lorenzo "Lorenzaccio." They know that he arranges your pleasures; and that is enough.

THE DUKE. Peace! You forget that Lorenzo de' Medici is cousin to Alessandro.

---

[2] "On one occasion, Lorenzo in a sudden freak knocked off the heads of several fine statues of the Emperor Hadrian; at which act Pope Clement was furious, threatened to hang him, and banished him from Rome." G. F. Young.

Enter CARDINAL CIBO.

Cardinal, listen to these gentlemen! They say the Pope is
scandalized by poor Renzo's licentiousness! They contend
that it weakens my government!

THE CARDINAL. Francesco Nolza has just delivered an harangue
in Latin at the Roman Academy against the mutilation of
the Arch of Constantine.

THE DUKE. Come! You make me lose my temper. Renzo, a
man to fear! The most arrant coward! An effeminate! The
shadow of a nerveless ruffian! A dreamer who never carries
a sword because he's afraid of seeing its shadow at his side!
In addition, a philosopher, a scribbler, a bad poet who
doesn't even know how to compose a sonnet. No, no, I'm
not afraid of shadows. And, by Bacchus! what do I care
about Latin discourses and the jokes of my rabble! I love
Lorenzo, and, by God, he'll stay here.

THE CARDINAL. If I feared that man, it would not be for your
court, nor for Florence, but for yourself, Duke.

THE DUKE. Are you joking, Cardinal, and do you want me to
tell you the truth?

He lowers his voice.

Everything I know about those damned exiles, about those
stubborn republicans who are plotting around me, I know
through Lorenzo. He is as slippery as an eel; he insinuates
himself everywhere; and he tells me everything. Didn't he
find a way to establish contact with all those damned
Strozzi? Yes, indeed, he is my intermediary; his offices, if
they hurt anyone, will not hurt me.

LORENZO *appears at the back of a low gallery.*

Look at that small, skinny body—the walking aftermath of
an orgy. Look at those lifeless eyes, those frail hands, hardly
strong enough to hold a fan, that dull face which sometimes
smiles, but lacks the strength to laugh! Is that a man to
fear? Come, come! you're making fun of him.—Ah! Renzo!
Come over here. Sire Maurizio seeks a quarrel with you.

LORENZO, *climbing the stairs to the terrace.* Good day, gentlemen friends of my cousin!

THE DUKE. Lorenzo, listen here! We've been talking about you for an hour. Can you guess the latest? My friend, you are excommunicated in Latin. Sire Maurizio calls you a dangerous man, and so does the Cardinal. As for the good Valori, he is too virtuous even to pronounce your name.

LORENZO. Dangerous for whom, Eminence, for the trollops or for the saints of Paradise?

THE CARDINAL. Court dogs can be seized with rabies like other dogs.

LORENZO. A priest's insult should be delivered in Latin.

SIRE MAURIZIO. Some are delivered in Tuscan, and those you can answer.

LORENZO. Sire Maurizio, I didn't see you. Excuse me, I had the sun in my eyes. But you look well, and your coat seems brand-new.

SIRE MAURIZIO. Like your wit. I had it made out of my grandfather's old doublet.

LORENZO. Cousin, when you have had enough of one of your country conquests, do send her to Sire Maurizio. It's unhealthy for a man with his short neck and hairy hands to live without a woman.

SIRE MAURIZIO. Anyone who thinks he has the right to joke like that should know how to defend himself. In your place, I'd draw my sword.

LORENZO. If you've been told I was a soldier, it was an error. I am a poor lover of science.

SIRE MAURIZIO. Your wit is a sharp sword, but flexible, I see. It is a vile weapon. Yet each man uses his own.

He draws his sword.

VALORI. A naked sword in front of the Duke!

THE DUKE, *laughing.* Let them be, let them be. Come, Renzo, I want to serve as your second. Somebody give him a sword!

LORENZO. My lord, what are you saying?

THE DUKE. Ah! Does your gaiety vanish so quickly? You tremble, cousin? For shame! You bring dishonor on the name of Medici. I'm only a bastard, and I would bear it better than you who are legitimate. A sword, a sword! A

Medici does not let himself be provoked in this way. Pages, come up here! The whole court shall see this, and I wish all of Florence were here, too.

LORENZO. His Highness is laughing at me!

THE DUKE. I laughed a moment ago, but now I redden with shame. A sword!

He takes a sword from a page and presents it to LORENZO.

VALORI. My lord, this is carrying things too far. A sword drawn in the presence of Your Highness is a crime against the state.

THE DUKE. Who speaks here when I speak?

VALORI. Your Highness could have had no other intention than that of amusing yourself for an instant. And Sire Maurizio, I'm sure, had no other thought in mind.

THE DUKE. Don't you see that I am *still* joking? Who the devil is taking it seriously! Look at Renzo, if you please! His knees shake; he would have turned pale if that were possible. What a sight, dear God! I think he's going to fall.

LORENZO *totters; he leans on the railing and suddenly slides to the ground.*

THE DUKE, *laughing aloud.* Didn't I tell you! No one knows it better than I. The very sight of a sword makes him ill. Come, dear Lorenzetta, have them take you to your mother!

The pages help LORENZO *up.*

SIRE MAURIZIO. Coward!

THE DUKE. Silence, Sire Maurizio! Weigh your words. I am talking now. None of that in front of me!

Exit SIRE MAURIZIO.

VALORI. Poor young man!

Exit.

THE CARDINAL, *alone with the* DUKE. Do you believe it was genuine, my lord?

THE DUKE. How could I help but believe it?

THE CARDINAL. Hmmm! It seemed exaggerated.

THE DUKE. It's exactly because it seemed exaggerated that I accept it. Do you imagine that a Medici would publicly

dishonor himself for the fun of it? Furthermore, it's not the
first time this has happened to him. He has never been able
to bear the sight of a sword.

THE CARDINAL. It's hard to believe! It's hard to believe!

SCENE 5

In front of the Church of San Miniato at Monte Oliveto.[3]
People coming out of the Church.

A WOMAN, *to her neighbor.* Are you going back to Florence
tonight?

THE NEIGHBOR. I never stay here more than an hour, and I
just come one Friday a month. I'm not rich enough to stop
at the fair. For me it's only a matter of religion, and if that's
enough for my salvation, I'm satisfied.

The SILK MERCHANT *and the* GOLDSMITH *in front of their*
shops, with a few CAVALIERS.

THE GOLDSMITH. The Citadel! There's something the people
will never stand for. To see a new Tower of Babel suddenly
rising over Florence, full of the most cursed gibberish. The
Germans will never take root in Florence, and a strong band
would be needed to graft them on here.

A CAVALIER. You have the old Florentine blood in your veins,
Papa Mondella. The hatred of tyranny still makes your
hands tremble over your precious work.

THE GOLDSMITH. That's true, Excellency. If I were a great
artist I would love princes, because they alone can commission great works. Great artists have no country. As for me,
I only make holy chalices and sword handles.

ANOTHER CAVALIER. Speaking of artists, don't you see that big
fellow over there in that small wineshop? He's making wild
gestures in front of some idlers and hitting his glass on the
table. If I'm not mist ' 't's that loudmouth, Benvenuto
Cellini.

[3] The people went to Monte Oliveto every Friday of certain
months. It was to Florence what Longchamp used to be to Paris.
The merchants found conditions suitable for a fair, and would
bring merchandise there for sale. (Author's note.)

THE FIRST CAVALIER. Let's go over. He's amusing when he has a few glasses of wine under his belt, and he may be telling some good story.

Exeunt. Two CITIZENS *enter and sit down.*

FIRST CITIZEN. Has there been a riot in Florence?

SECOND CITIZEN. It was nothing. A few young men were killed in the Old Market Place.

FIRST CITIZEN. Their poor families!

SECOND CITIZEN. That kind of unhappiness is inevitable. What can young people do under a government such as ours? A trumpet fanfare announces that Caesar is at Bologna, and the idle crowd repeats with a knowing air: "Caesar is at Bologna," without once asking what he is doing there. The next day they are even happier to hear and repeat: "The Pope is in Bologna with Caesar." What happens? A public celebration. They don't see any further. And then, one fine morning, they wake up dizzy from the fumes of the imperial wine and they see a sinister figure at the great window of the Pazzi Palace. They ask who that person is and they're told he is their King. The Pope and the Emperor have been delivered of a bastard who couldn't even name his mother but has the right of life and death over our children.

THE GOLDSMITH, *approaching.* You talk like a patriot, my friend. I warn you to be careful of that good-for-nothing.

A GERMAN OFFICER *passes by.*

THE OFFICER. Get up, gentlemen. These ladies want to sit down.

Two ladies of the Court enter and sit down.

FIRST LADY. Is that from Venice?

THE MERCHANT. Yes, your ladyship. Shall I measure out a few yards?

FIRST LADY. Please. And let me have some silk stockings, too.

SECOND LADY. I thought I saw Giuliano Salviati pass.

THE OFFICER. He's walking back and forth in front of the church. He's a real gallant.

FIRST LADY. He's insolent.

SECOND LADY, *to the officer*. As long as you've seen Giuliano, go tell him that I have to speak to him.

THE OFFICER. I'm going and I'll bring him back.

They withdraw. Enter the PRIOR OF CAPUA, LEONE STROZZI.

THE PRIOR. Give me a glass of lemonade, my good man.

He sits down.

THE GOLDSMITH. Here's the Prior of Capua. That is a patriot for you!

THE PRIOR. Do you come from church, gentlemen? What did you think of the sermon?

THE MERCHANT. It was beautiful, sir Prior.

A BOURGEOIS, *to the* GOLDSMITH. The noble Strozzi are dear to the people because they are not proud. Isn't it pleasant to see a great lord address himself freely to his neighbors in a friendly manner?

THE GOLDSMITH. That's more important than you think.

Enter SALVIATI.

SALVIATI. I was told that there were women here looking for me, but I see no other dress than yours, Prior. Am I mistaken?

THE MERCHANT. Excellency, you were not misinformed. The ladies have stepped away, but I think they'll return. I have ten yards of cloth and four pairs of silk stockings for them.

SALVIATI, *sitting down*. Isn't that Luisa Strozzi passing on the green?

THE MERCHANT. It is, your lordship. Few of the ladies of our nobility are unknown to me. And, if I'm not mistaken, she is holding her youngest sister by the hand.

SALVIATI. I met that Luisa last night at the Nasi ball. Truly, she has a pretty leg. We're going to sleep together—as soon as possible.

THE PRIOR, *turning*. What do you mean by that remark?

SALVIATI. It's very simple. That's what she told me. I was holding her stirrup, without an evil thought in my head, when, I don't quite know what happened, I found myself caressing her leg. And that's how it all came about.

THE PRIOR. Giuliano, I don't know if you are aware that you're speaking of my sister.

SALVIATI. I know it very well. Women are made to sleep with men, and your sister can perfectly well sleep with me.

THE PRIOR, *rising.* Do I owe you something, my good man? *He throws a coin on the table and goes out.*

SALVIATI. I'm very fond of that good Prior: an insult to his sister can make him forget his change. It's enough to make one believe that all the virtue of Florence has taken refuge in the Strozzi. See, there! He's looking back. Stare all you want, you won't scare me.

Exit.

SCENE 6

On the bank of the Arno. MARIA SODERINI, CATERINA.

CATERINA. The sun is setting. You can see wide bands of purple through the foliage. How strange it is when all the harmonies of evening mingle with the faraway sounds of the city!

MARIA. It's time to go in. Tie your veil around your neck.

CATERINA. You have been anxious since morning.

MARIA. Not anxious, but distressed. You've heard that dreadful story about Lorenzo, haven't you? He is the laughing-stock of Florence.

CATERINA. Oh, Maria! Cowardice is not a crime; courage is not a virtue. Why is weakness to be condemned?

MARIA. Would you love a man who is afraid? You blush, Caterina. Lorenzo is your nephew, but imagine he were called by any other name. What would you think of him? What woman would lean on his arm to mount her horse? What man would shake his hand?

CATERINA. What you say is sad. But that is not why I pity him. His heart may not be the heart of a Medici, but, alas, it is still less the heart of an honest man.

MARIA. My Renzo will never be a warrior, I said to myself, seeing him come home from school, all bathed in perspiration, with his heavy books under his arm and a holy love of truth shining on his lips and in his black eyes. He worried about everybody, always saying: "This one is poor, this one is ruined . . . What can we do?" Ah! Caterina, he is no longer even handsome. The defilement of his heart, like a poisonous vapor, has mounted to his face.

CATERINA. He is still handsome sometimes—in his strange melancholy.

MARIA. Didn't his birth entitle him to a throne? And couldn't he one day have ascended it with the learning of a scholar and the most beautiful youthfulness in the world, and crowned with a golden diadem all my cherished dreams? Shouldn't I have expected this to happen? Ah! Cattina, if we want to sleep peacefully, we must never have certain dreams. It is too cruel to have lived in a fairy palace where angels sang and to have been rocked to sleep by your son, and then to have awakened in a blood-filled hovel, filled with the debris of orgies and human remains, and held in the arms of a hideous specter who destroys you while still calling you mother.

CATERINA. Those silent shadows are beginning to move across the road. Let's go in, Maria. These exiles frighten me.

MARIA. Ah! Can I no longer see anything that does not pierce me to the heart? Must I never open my eyes again? Alas, my Cattina, this is also the work of Lorenzo. All those poor people had confidence in him. There is not one among those fathers driven from their homes who has not been betrayed by my son. Their letters, signed with their names, are shown to the Duke.

She strikes the ground.

When shall I be there?

CATERINA. My poor sister. Your tears are mine.

They leave. The sun has set. A group of EXILES *in the middle of the field.*

AN EXILE. Where are you going?

ANOTHER EXILE. To Pisa. And you?

THE FIRST EXILE. To Rome.

ANOTHER EXILE. And I to Venice. These two go to Ferrara. What's to become of us, so far apart from each other?

A FOURTH EXILE. Good-by, neighbor, until better times.

He starts off.

Good-by, you and I can go together as far as the Cross of the Virgin.

Exit with another. MAFFIO *enters.*

FIRST EXILE. Is that you, Maffio? How do you happen to be here?

MAFFIO. I am one of you. You must know that the Duke has carried off my sister. I drew my sword, but some sort of tiger with muscles of steel threw himself on my neck and disarmed me. After that I received a purse full of ducats and an order to leave the city.

SECOND EXILE. Is your sister still in Florence?

MAFFIO. She was pointed out to me this evening, leaving the theatre in a dress fit for an empress. May God forgive her! An old woman accompanied her, and I had the greatest pleasure of my life in knocking out three of her teeth.

THIRD EXILE. Let them all croak in their own filth and we'll die happy!

FOURTH EXILE. Filippo Strozzi will write to us in Venice. Some-day we'll all be surprised to find an army at our command.

THIRD EXILE. Long live Filippo! As long as there is a hair on his head the cause of Liberty in Italy is not dead.

The group divides; all the EXILES *embrace.*

A VOICE. Until better times!

ANOTHER VOICE. Until better times!

Two EXILES *mount a platform from which the city can be seen.*

FIRST EXILE. Farewell, Florence, plague of Italy! Farewell, sterile mother who no longer has milk for her children!

SECOND EXILE. Farewell, Florence, the bastard, hideous spec-ter of old Florence! Farewell, scum without name!

ALL. Farewell, Florence! Cursed be the breasts of your women! Cursed be your sobbing! Cursed be the prayers of your churches, the bread of your harvests, the air of your streets! Damned be the last drop of your corrupt blood!

ACT TWO

SCENE 1

The Strozzi Palace.

FILIPPO, *in his study.* Ten citizens banished from this neighborhood alone! Old Galeazzo and young Maffio exiled! His sister corrupted in a single night! Is corruption, then, a law of nature? Poor humanity! Do you bear the name of your birth or of your baptism? And what original stain have all of us old dreamers washed from the human face during the four or five thousand years that we have been yellowing among our books? It is painful to believe that man's happiness is only a dream, but I will never believe that evil is irrevocable, eternal, impossible to change! Why does the philosopher who labors for mankind look about him? That is his mistake. The smallest insect passing in front of his eyes hides the sun. Let us proceed more boldly. "Republic"—we must keep that word. It is only a word, but it means much to the people, and they will rise when they hear it.—Ah, good morning, Leone!

Enter the PRIOR OF CAPUA.

THE PRIOR. I have just come from the fair at Monte Oliveto.

Enter PIETRO.

FILIPPO. How was it? Here is Pietro, too. Sit down, I want to talk to you.

THE PRIOR. The fair was pleasant, and I had rather a good time, except for an unpleasant incident.

PIETRO. What was it?

THE PRIOR. I had gone into a shop for a glass of lemonade—— But no, what's the use?

FILIPPO. You seem disturbed.

THE PRIOR. It's nothing, a rude remark, nothing more.

PIETRO. A remark? About whom? About you?

THE PRIOR. No, no. I wouldn't be concerned if it had been that.

PIETRO. About whom, then? Speak!

THE PRIOR. No. When a man knows the difference between a gentleman and a Salviati he doesn't remember such things.

PIETRO. Salviati? What did that scoundrel say?

THE PRIOR. You're right. He is a scoundrel, and it doesn't matter what he said.

PIETRO. Speak, Leone! Whom did he slander? Us? Our father? Blood of Christ! I don't waste any love on that Salviati. I must know what he said, do you understand?

THE PRIOR. Since you insist: While speaking to me he insulted our sister.

PIETRO. Oh, my God! How?

THE PRIOR. He spoke of her in the grossest terms.

PIETRO. Priest that you are! You can see I'm beside myself with impatience, and you're weighing your words! We're not talking about God now!

FILIPPO. Pietro, Pietro, you're not showing respect for your brother.

THE PRIOR. He said he was going to sleep with her—those are his words—because she had promised to.

PIETRO. She had prom—— Ah, death of death, a thousand deaths! What time is it?

FILIPPO. Where are you going? Don't! You are too hotheaded. What do you need that sword for? You have one at your side!

PIETRO. I'm not going to do anything with it.

    Exit.

SCENE 2

In front of a church. Enter LORENZO *and* VALORI.

VALORI. How satisfying is the magnificent pomp of the Roman Church to a Christian! What man could remain insensitive to it? Doesn't the artist find his heart's desire there?

Don't the warrior, the priest, and the merchant find everything they love there? The harmonies of the organ, the
splendid velvet hangings and tapestries, the paintings by
great masters, the warm and subtle perfumes rising from
the censers, and the delightful music of silvery voices! Nothing is more beautiful to my mind than a religion which appeals to the heart in so many ways. Why should priests
want to serve a jealous God? Religion is not a bird of prey:
it is a compassionate dove, soaring peacefully over all
dreams and all loves.

LORENZO. Of course, what you say is perfectly true, and perfectly false, like everything in the world.

TEBALDEO FRECCIA, *approaching* VALORI. Ah, Eminence, to
hear from the lips of a good man the sentiments in one's
own heart—that is the greatest happiness.

VALORI. Aren't you young Freccia?

TEBALDEO. My works have small merit. I know how to love
art better than I know how to practice it. My entire youth
has been spent in the churches. I can't seem to admire
Raphael and our divine Buonarroti anywhere else. I spend
whole days before their works, in unspeakable ecstasy.

VALORI. You have the true heart of an artist. Come to my
palace, and bring your palette and brushes with you when
you come. I'd like you to do some work for me.

TEBALDEO. Your Eminence honors me too much. I am but a
humble servant of the holy religion of painting.

LORENZO. Why do you put off our offers of patronage? It
seems to me you have a frame in your hands.

TEBALDEO. It's true, but I don't dare show it to such critical
judges. It's a poor sketch of a magnificent dream.

LORENZO. You paint pictures of your dreams? I'll have some of
mine pose for you.

TEBALDEO. The life of the artist is a realization of dreams. Unfortunately, the dreams of mediocre artists are not easy
plants to nourish, even when watered with bitter tears.

He shows his picture.

VALORI. Without flattery, that is beautiful. Not of the first rank,
it's true, but then you are still a young man.

LORENZO. Is it a landscape, or a portrait? Should it be viewed lengthwise, or crosswise?

TEBALDEO. Your lordship is laughing at me. It's a view of the Campo Santo.

LORENZO. How far is it from here to immortality?

VALORI. It is wrong of you to tease the child. See how his great eyes get sad at each of your jests!

TEBALDEO. Immortality is faith. Those to whom God has given wings arrive there joyously.

VALORI. You talk like a pupil of Raphael.

TEBALDEO. Eminence, he was my master. What I have learned I owe to him.

LORENZO. Come to my house. I'll have you paint La Mazzafirra in the nude.

TEBALDEO. I do not respect my brush, but I respect my art. I couldn't paint the portrait of a courtesan.

LORENZO. As long as God took the trouble to make her you could take the trouble to paint her. Would you like to paint a picture of Florence for me?

TEBALDEO. Yes, my lord.

LORENZO. How will you do it?

TEBALDEO. From the eastern side of the city, the left bank of the Arno. From that point the perspective is broadest and most pleasing.

LORENZO. You'd paint Florence, the squares, the buildings, and the streets?

TEBALDEO. Yes, my lord.

LORENZO. Now, since you can paint an evil city, why can't you paint a courtesan?

TEBALDEO. I haven't yet been taught to talk about my mother that way.

LORENZO. Whom do you call your mother?

TEBALDEO. Florence, my lord.

LORENZO. Then you're a bastard, for your mother's a whore.

TEBALDEO. The divine flower of art sometimes needs a fertilizer to enrich its soil.

LORENZO. What do you mean by that?

TEBALDEO. Peaceful and happy nations have sometimes burned with a clear but feeble light. Enthusiasm goes hand in hand with suffering.

LORENZO. Do you mean that an unhappy people brings forth great artists? I'd like to be the alchemist of your alembic—in which the tears of the people become pearls. By Satan, you please me. Families mourn, nations die in misery, all to excite your imagination, sir! You are an admirable poet! But how do you reconcile all this with your piety?

TEBALDEO. I pity unhappy people; but I believe that they bring forth great artists. The corpses on the battlefield help the crops to grow. Corrupted soil produces celestial manna.

LORENZO. Your doublet is worn. Would you like one of my livery?

TEBALDEO. I belong to no one. When thought wishes to be free, the body must be free, too.

LORENZO. I think I'll tell my footman to give you a good beating.

TEBALDEO. Why, my lord?

LORENZO. The idea amuses me. Were you crippled at birth or by an accident?

TEBALDEO. I am not crippled. What do you mean by that?

LORENZO. Either you are crippled or you are a fool.

TEBALDEO. Why, my lord? You're making fun of me.

LORENZO. If you're neither crippled nor a fool why do you stay in a city where a Medici valet could have you killed without anyone objecting?

TEBALDEO. I love my mother Florence, so I stay with her. I know that a citizen can be assassinated in broad daylight on the street if it pleases the whims of those who govern her. That's the reason I carry this stiletto at my belt.

LORENZO. If it amused the Duke to commit another of his playful murders, and he attacked *you*, would you stab him?

TEBALDEO. I would kill him.

LORENZO. You say that to me!

TEBALDEO. Why would anyone have anything against me? I

hurt nobody. I spend my days at the studio. On Sunday I go to one of the churches. Those are the only times when I appear in public. In the evening I visit my mistress, and when the night is beautiful I spend it on her balcony. No one knows me, and I know no one. To whom would my life or my death be of use?

LORENZO. Are you a republican? Do you love princes?

TEBALDEO. I am an artist. I love my mother and my mistress.

LORENZO. Come to my palace tomorrow. I'd like to order an important painting from you for my wedding day.

Exit.

SCENE 3

COUNT CIBO's *house.*

THE CARDINAL, *alone.* Yes, I will obey your orders, Farnese![4] You knew the man I was when you placed me near Alessandro without title or any power over him. He will obey me unwittingly while remaining suspicious of another. Let him use up his strength against the shadows of men swollen with the shadow of power! I will be the invisible link in the iron chain binding him hand and foot to Rome and Caesar. Alessandro is in love with my sister-in-law. Who knows how far the influence of an exalted woman might go, even with that coarse man, that living suit of armor? Such a little sin for such a good cause. It's tempting, isn't it, Ricciarda? To speak, in tears, of the unhappiness of your country, while the adored tyrant passes his rough hands through your flowing hair, to strike the divine spark from a rock—surely all that is worth the small sacrifice of matrimonial honor and of a few other trifles. Florence would gain so much by it—these good husbands lose nothing! You shouldn't have taken me for your confessor. Here she comes now, her prayer book in her hand. Today all will be made clear. Simply whisper your secret in the ear of the priest: the courtier will know how to profit thereby, though, in all conscience, he'll say nothing about it.

4 Pope Paul III. (Author's note.)

Enter the COUNTESS CIBO.

THE CARDINAL, *seating himself.* I am ready.

The COUNTESS *kneels beside him upon her prie-dieu.*

THE COUNTESS. Bless me, Father, for I have sinned.

THE CARDINAL. Have you said your *Confiteor?* We can begin, Countess.

THE COUNTESS. I confess I have given way to fits of anger and that I have had irreligious and harmful thoughts about our Holy Father, the Pope.

THE CARDINAL. Continue.

THE COUNTESS. I said yesterday, in public, that the Holy Catholic Church was a place of debauchery.

THE CARDINAL. Continue.

THE COUNTESS. I have listened to words which urged me to break my marriage vows.

THE CARDINAL. Who talked to you in this way?

THE COUNTESS. I have read a letter with the same thought in it.

THE CARDINAL. Who wrote you this letter?

THE COUNTESS. I am confessing what *I* have done, not what others have done.

THE CARDINAL. My daughter, you must answer me if you wish me to give you full absolution. In the first place, tell me if you answered the letter.

THE COUNTESS. I answered it by word of mouth, but not in writing.

THE CARDINAL. What did you reply?

THE COUNTESS. I granted the person who wrote it permission to see me as he requested.

THE CARDINAL. What took place at that meeting?

THE COUNTESS. I have already confessed to listening to talk against my honor.

THE CARDINAL. How did you answer it?

THE COUNTESS. As a self-respecting woman would.

THE CARDINAL. Didn't you let it be seen that you might be easily persuaded?

THE COUNTESS. No, Father.

THE CARDINAL. Did you tell this person of your resolution not to listen to such talk in the future?

THE COUNTESS. Yes, Father.

THE CARDINAL. Does this person please you?

THE COUNTESS. I hope that my heart is not involved.

THE CARDINAL. Have you informed your husband?

THE COUNTESS. No, Father. A virtuous woman should not disturb her marriage with this sort of story.

THE CARDINAL. Are you hiding anything from me? Do you hesitate to confide in me what may have happened between you and the person in question?

THE COUNTESS. There was nothing, Father.

THE CARDINAL. No tender look, no stolen kiss?

THE COUNTESS. No, Father.

THE CARDINAL. Are you sure, my daughter?

THE COUNTESS. Brother-in-law, I am not in the habit of lying before God.

THE CARDINAL. You refused to tell me the name I asked you for a moment ago. I cannot give you absolution without knowing it.

THE COUNTESS. Why? It may be a sin to read a letter, but not a signature. What does the name matter?

THE CARDINAL. It matters more than you think.

THE COUNTESS. Malaspina, you want to know too much. You can refuse me absolution if you want. I will take the next priest who will give it to me as my confessor.
She rises.

THE CARDINAL. What violence, Countess! Don't I know it's the Duke you're talking about?

THE COUNTESS. The Duke! Very well, if you know it, why do you want to make me say it?

THE CARDINAL. Why do you refuse to say it? That's what surprises me.

THE COUNTESS. And what do you want to do with it, my confessor? Repeat it to my husband? Yes, that's it. One is wrong to have a relative for a confessor. Heaven is my wit-

ness that in kneeling before you I forget that I am your
sister-in-law, but you take pains to remind me of it. Beware, Cibo. Look to your eternal salvation, Cardinal though
you are.

THE CARDINAL. Come back here, Countess. It's not as serious
as you make it seem.

THE COUNTESS. What do you mean?

THE CARDINAL. I mean that a confessor must know everything,
but that a brother-in-law must, under certain conditions, say
nothing.

THE COUNTESS. What conditions?

THE CARDINAL. I made a mistake. That wasn't the word I
meant to use. I meant that the Duke is powerful and that
a rupture with him could injure the richest families, but
that a secret of importance in experienced hands might become a source of abundant benefits.

THE COUNTESS. A source of benefits! Experienced hands! I am
confused! What are you hatching, priest, under these am-
biguous words?

THE CARDINAL. Come back! Sit down, Ricciarda. I have not
yet given you absolution.

THE COUNTESS. Talk all you wish, I'm not so sure that I want it.

THE CARDINAL, *rising*. You had better be careful, Countess.
Who defies me should have a solid and a flawless armor! I
don't want to threaten you. But I have this to say to you:
take another confessor.

Exit.

THE COUNTESS, *alone*. It's incredible! To go away with clenched
fists and eyes blazing with anger! He talked of experienced
hands, of the direction which could be given to certain
things! What is it all about? I can readily understand his
wanting to learn my secret in order to tell my husband, but
if that's not his aim, what does he wish to do with me?
Make me the Duke's mistress? Did he say: to know everything and to manage everything?—That's impossible.—There
is some darker and more inexplicable mystery at the bottom
of it. Cibo would never do a thing like that. I'm sure of it;
I know him too well. He must have had some secret mean-

ing, greater and deeper than that. Ah, how suddenly men reveal themselves after ten years of silence! It is frightening! Now, what shall I do? Do I love Alessandro? No, surely I do not love him; I said so in my confession; and I told the truth. Why is Lorenzo at Massa? Why does the Duke urge me? Why did I say that I did not wish to see him again? Why? Ah, why am I so strongly attracted?

She opens her window.

How beautiful you are, Florence, but how sad! There is more than one house down there that Alessandro has secretly entered at night. He is a libertine, I know. And why are you now in my thoughts, Florence? Whom do I love? Is it you, or him?

AGNOLO, *entering.* Madam, His Highness has entered the courtyard.

THE COUNTESS. How strange! Malaspina has left me trembling.

SCENE 4

The Soderini Palace. MARIA SODERINI, CATERINA, LORENZO, *seated.*

CATERINA, *a book in her hand.* What story shall I read you?

MARIA. My Cattina is making fun of her poor old sister. What do I know about your Latin books?

CATERINA. This is not a Latin book, but a translation. It's the history of Rome.

LORENZO. I'm very good at Roman history. Once upon a time there was a young nobleman named Tarquin.

CATERINA. Ah, that is a bloody story.

LORENZO. Not at all: it's a fairy story. Brutus was nothing but a fool,[5] a monomaniac. Tarquin was a duke, and full of wisdom. He'd wander about in his slippered feet, and watch little girls sleep.

[5] A trap for the modern reader who thinks of the Brutus who helped to kill Julius Caesar. *Lorenzaccio* is full of references to the earlier (or legendary) Brutus who drove the Tarquins from Rome. However, it would seem that Musset confused the two Brutuses. See Act Three, Scene 3. (Translator's note.)

CATERINA. Do you also criticize Lucretia?

LORENZO. She gave herself the pleasure of sin, and the glory of death. She allowed herself to be taken alive like a lark in a snare, and then she very gracefully plunged a little dagger into her belly.

MARIA. Though you despise women, why do you try to degrade them in the eyes of your mother and your aunt?

LORENZO. I esteem you both, but—the world horrifies me.

MARIA. Do you know the dream I had last night, my child?

LORENZO. What dream?

MARIA. It was not really a dream, for I was not asleep. I was alone in this great room, the lamp was far from me, on that table by the window. I was thinking of the days when I was happy, of the days of your childhood, my Lorenzino. I observed the dark night, and I said to myself: He who used to spend his nights in study does not return now until morning. My eyes filled with tears, and I shook my head as I felt them flowing. Suddenly I heard footsteps in the gallery. I turned around. A man clad in black, with a book under his arm, was coming toward me. It was you, Renzo. "You are back early!" I exclaimed. But the ghost seated itself beside the lamp without a word. It opened the book, and I recognized my Lorenzino of the past.

LORENZO. You saw it?

MARIA. As plainly as I see you.

LORENZO. When did it go away?

MARIA. When you rang the bell this morning coming in.

LORENZO. My ghost! And it left when I returned?

MARIA. It arose with a melancholy air, and vanished like morning mist.

LORENZO. Caterina, Caterina, read me the story of Brutus.

CATERINA. What is the matter with you? You're trembling from head to foot.

LORENZO. Mother, sit this evening where you were last night, and if my ghost returns, tell it that it will soon see something astonishing.

Somebody knocks.

CATERINA. It's Uncle Bindo and Baptista Venturi.

BINDO *and* VENTURI *enter.*

BINDO, *in a low voice to* MARIA. I'm coming to try one last time.

MARIA. We'll leave you. God grant that you may succeed!

Exit with CATERINA.

BINDO. Lorenzo, why don't you deny the scandalous story that people are spreading about you?

LORENZO. What story?

BINDO. They say you fainted at the sight of a sword.

LORENZO. Do you believe them, uncle?

BINDO. I saw you fence at Rome, but it wouldn't surprise me if you had become a vile coward, practicing the profession that you have here.

LORENZO. The story is true. I did faint. Good morning, Venturi. How are prices? How is business?

VENTURI. My lord, I am the head of a silk factory, but it is an insult to call me a merchant.

LORENZO. True, I only meant to say that, while at school, you had formed the innocent habit of selling silk.

BINDO. I have confided to Signor Venturi the plans which are occupying so many families in Florence at this time. He is a worthy friend of Liberty, and I insist, Lorenzo, that you shall treat him as such. The time to joke is past. You once told us that the Duke's great confidence in you had been created by you as a deliberate snare. Is that true or false? Are you on our side, or are you not? We must know. All the great families see clearly that the despotism of the Medici is neither just nor tolerable. By what right should we allow that proud house to rise to unmolested power over the ruins of our privileges? The terms of the capitulation have been violated. The might of Germany makes itself felt more absolutely from day to day. Now is the time to put an end to it, and assemble the patriots. Will you respond to such an appeal?

LORENZO. What have you to say, Venturi? Speak, speak. See,

my uncle is getting his second wind. Seize this opportunity, if you love your country.

VENTURI. My lord, I feel exactly the same way. I don't have a word to add.

LORENZO. Not a word? Not one pretty, little, sonorous word? You're a master of true eloquence, because you're able to turn a great sentence around one pretty little word that is neither too short nor too long and as round as a top. You throw back your left arm to give a dignity tempered by grace to the folds of your mantle. Then you let loose your sentence—which unwinds like a humming string, and the little top is off with a delicious murmur. You could almost hold it in the palm of your hand.

BINDO. You're an insolent fellow! Answer our questions.

LORENZO. I am one with you, uncle. Don't you see, by the way I wear my hair, that I'm a republican at heart? Look how my beard is trimmed. Don't doubt for a moment that patriotism doesn't burn brightly throughout my being.

The doorbell rings; the courtyard fills with horses and pages.

A PAGE, *entering.* The Duke.

Enter ALESSANDRO.

LORENZO. What a great honor, Prince. You deign to visit this poor servant!

THE DUKE. Who are these men? I want to talk to you.

LORENZO. I have the honor of presenting to your lordship my uncle, Signor Bindo Altoviti, who regrets that a long stay in Naples has prevented him from paying his respects to you before. This other gentleman is the illustrious Signor Baptista Venturi, who manufactures silk, it's true, but who doesn't sell it. Don't let the unexpected presence of so great a prince in this humble house disturb you, my dear uncle, nor you either, my worthy Venturi. Whatever you ask for will be granted, or you'll have the right to say that my supplications carry no weight with my gracious Sovereign.

THE DUKE. What do you want, Bindo?

BINDO. My lord, I am very sorry that my nephew——

LORENZO. The title of Ambassador to Rome belongs to no one at the moment. My uncle hoped to obtain it through your kindness. In all Florence there's no one who's his equal when it is a question of devotion to the Medici.

THE DUKE. Indeed, Renzino? Very well, my dear Bindo, that's settled. Come to the palace tomorrow morning.

BINDO. My lord, I am overwhelmed! How can I repay you . . . ?

LORENZO. Signor Venturi, although he doesn't sell silk, asks a privilege for his factories.

THE DUKE. What privilege?

LORENZO. Your arms on the door, with the patent. Grant it to him, my lord, if you love those that love you.

THE DUKE. All right. Is that all? Go, gentlemen, and peace go with you!

VENTURI. My lord, you overwhelm me with your . . . I can't express . . .

THE DUKE, *to his guards.* Allow these two gentlemen to pass.

BINDO, *aside to* VENTURI *as they leave.* That was a vicious trick.

VENTURI, *aside.* What are you going to do about it?

BINDO, *aside.* What the deuce can I do? I'm appointed.

VENTURI, *aside.* It's terrible!

Exit.

THE DUKE. The Countess is mine.

LORENZO. I'm sorry.

THE DUKE. Why?

LORENZO. Because that will deprive the other ladies.

THE DUKE. Hardly. She already bores me. Tell me, my pet, who is that pretty woman tending her flowers at the window? For several weeks now, everytime I pass by, I've seen her.

LORENZO. Where?

THE DUKE. In the palace across the street.

LORENZO. Oh! that's nothing.

THE DUKE. Nothing? Do you call those arms nothing? Bowels of Satan, what a Venus!

LORENZO. She's a neighbor of mine.

THE DUKE. I want to speak to that neighbor. Ah! It's Caterina Ginori, if I'm not mistaken.

LORENZO. No.

THE DUKE. Now I recognize her very well. She's your aunt. Damn! I'd forgotten that. Bring her to supper!

LORENZO. That's easier said than done. She's a virtuous woman.

THE DUKE. Come, come! Is there such a thing—as far as we're concerned?

LORENZO. I'll ask her, if you want, but I warn you she's very pedantic: she speaks Latin.

THE DUKE. So? She doesn't make love in Latin. Come this way. We can see her better from the gallery.

LORENZO. Some other time, my pet. Just now I must go to the Strozzi's.

THE DUKE. What! Visit that old fool?

LORENZO. Yes, that old scoundrel. It seems he can't cure himself of a strange obsession. He opens his purse to all those foul exiles and they, like beggars, meet every day at his house. My plan now is to dine with that old gallows-bait and reassure him of my cordial friendship. Tonight I'll have some good story to tell you, and then we'll play a charming little prank and rout a few of those rascals early tomorrow morning.

THE DUKE. How fortunate I am to have you, my pet. But I confess I don't know why they still receive you.

LORENZO. Nonsense! If you only knew how easy it is to lie to a fool's face. It must be you've never tried it. By the way, didn't you tell me you wanted to give your portrait to—I forget to whom? And I have a painter to bring you, a protégé of mine.

THE DUKE. Very well, but don't forget your aunt. It was on her account I came to see you. Devil take me! I can't forget that aunt of yours!

LORENZO. And the Countess?

THE DUKE. Talk to me about your aunt!
Exit.

A *room at the Strozzi Palace.* FILIPPO STROZZI, *the* PRIOR, LUISA *doing some needlework;* LORENZO, *lying on a sofa.*

FILIPPO. Ah, Leone, Leone! What difference would it have made to Luisa and to me if you had said nothing? Can't the virtue of a Strozzi forget the idle word of a Salviati? Should the inhabitant of a marble palace know the obscenities that the rabble write on his walls? What does the speech of a Giuliano matter? Will my daughter be less able to find a worthy husband because of it? Will her children respect her less? Shall I remember it ·as I kiss her good night? What are we coming to, if the insolence of a nobody unsheathes swords like ours? Now all is lost. Pietro has gone off to the Pazzi's. God knows what will happen! If he should meet Salviati, blood will be spilled. My blood upon the stones of Florence! Ah, why am I a father?

THE PRIOR. If anyone had made remarks about my sister, whatever they were, I'd have turned my back, and that would have ended it. But this remark was addressed to me and was so coarse I imagined the boor didn't know whom he was speaking of. But he knew very well.

FILIPPO. Yes, they know, base wretches! They know very well where they strike. The trunk of an old tree is too strong; they will not touch that. But they know its heart's delicate fiber trembles when they attack its weakest branch. My Luisa!

THE PRIOR. Pietro is too violent.

FILIPPO. Poor Pietro! how the blood rushed to his face! How he trembled, hearing the insult to his sister! I was a fool for allowing you to tell it! Yet it was wonderful to see his righteous anger mounting to his blameless brow! I thought, "O my country! there is one, and he my first-born." Ah, Leone, it is no use, I am a Strozzi.

THE PRIOR. Perhaps there's not as much danger as you think. There's not much chance that he'll meet Salviati tonight. Tomorrow we'll all see things more calmly.

FILIPPO. No, it will not happen like that. Pietro will either kill him or die in the attempt.

He opens the window.

Where are they now? The city is wrapped in darkness, and those somber streets inspire me with horror. Blood is flowing somewhere, I am sure of it.

THE PRIOR. Calm yourself, Father. Close that window.

FILIPPO. Now, Florence, let your pavements learn the color of my noble blood! It flows in the veins of forty of your sons. And more than once, as the head of this great family, I'll lean my gray head from these high windows in paternal anguish. More than once that blood which you are perhaps drinking at this very hour will dry in the sunshine of your indifferent squares! But do not laugh tonight at poor old Strozzi who fears for his child! Take his family sparingly, for there will come a time when you will depend upon it, when you will place yourself with him at the window, and your heart will also beat when you hear the sound of our swords!

LUISA. Father! Father! you frighten me!

FILIPPO. Poor city! where fathers must await fearfully the return of their children! Poor country! Poor country! The speech of some drunken wretch fills us with rage and scatters our sons and our friends into the dark streets! But public misfortunes do not disturb the dust on our firearms. Many think Filippo Strozzi an honest man because he does right without preventing wrong. I would give anything to get my son back and have the insult to my daughter legally punished. But why should people protect *me* from wrong, when I, who had the power, did nothing to protect *them?* I spent years reading my books and dreaming that my country would have what I most admired in antiquity. The very walls around me cried out for vengeance, and I stopped up my ears to bury myself in meditations. Tyranny has had to slap me in the face to make me say, "Let us act now!" And my vengeance comes late.

Enter PIETRO, TOMASO, *and* FRANCESCO PAZZI.

PIETRO. It is done. Salviati is dead.

He kisses his sister.

LUISA. How horrible! You are covered with blood!

PIETRO. We waited for him at the corner of Archers' Street. Francesco stopped his horse. Tomaso stabbed him in the leg, and I——

LUISA. Stop! stop! You terrify me! Your hands are hideous, you tremble, and are pale as death.

LORENZO, *rising*. You are beautiful, Pietro! You are great as vengeance!

PIETRO. Who said that? What are you doing in this house, Lorenzaccio?

He goes over to his father.

When will you close your door to that scoundrel! Don't you know what he is, to say nothing about the story of his duel with Maurizio?

FILIPPO. If Lorenzo is here, it is because I have my reasons for receiving him. We will discuss that at a suitable time.

PIETRO, *between his teeth*. Hm! reasons for receiving that scoundrel? I could easily find a good one for throwing him out the window one of these fine days. Say what you want, it suffocates me to see such a leper in this room, lounging on our chairs!

FILIPPO. Peace! You are a hothead! And God grant that what you did this evening may not bring evil consequences to all of us! To begin with, you must hide.

PIETRO. Hide? In the name of all the saints, why should I hide?

LORENZO, *to* TOMASO. So you hit him on the shoulder? . . . Tell me a little more . . .

He leads him into the recess of a window; the two converse in a low voice.

PIETRO. No, Father, I won't hide. The insult was public. He gave it to us in a public place. I struck him down in the middle of the street, and tomorrow morning I want to tell the whole city about it. Since when does a man hide after avenging his honor? I would be willing to walk openly about with my sword drawn and still covered with his blood.

FILIPPO. Come this way. I must talk to you. You are not wounded, my child? You escaped without any injury?

Exeunt.

SCENE 6

The DUKE'S *palace. The* DUKE *with his shirt open,* TEBALDEO *painting his portrait;* GIOMO *playing the guitar.*

GIOMO, *singing.*

When I die, good squire, alas!
Take my heart to my mistress fair.
Let her weep no final prayer;
To the devil with priests and Mass.

Tears are water, that is clear.
Tell her to serve wine all around;
Let friends sing a chorus over my bier,
I'll answer from beneath the ground.

THE DUKE. I knew there was something I wanted to ask you. Tell me, Hungarian, what had the young man I saw you thrashing done to you?

GIOMO. I couldn't say, and neither can he.

THE DUKE. Why, is he dead?

GIOMO. He was a boy from a house in the neighborhood. Just now, in passing, I thought I saw them burying him.

THE DUKE. When my Giomo strikes, he strikes hard.

GIOMO. If you like. But I've seen you kill a man with a single blow more than once.

THE DUKE. Do you think so? I must have been drunk. When I'm drunk, my lightest blows are deadly. What's the matter with you, my boy? Is your hand shaking? You're making a strange face.

TEBALDEO. It's nothing, my lord, may it please Your Highness.

Enter LORENZO.

LORENZO. How is it going? Are you pleased with my protégé? *He takes the* DUKE'S *coat of mail from the sofa.*

This is a fine coat of mail, my pet! But it must be very warm.

THE DUKE. Of course not. I wouldn't wear it if it were uncomfortable. It's made of steel wire. The sharpest blade couldn't cut a link of it, and at the same time it's as light as silk. There isn't another like it, perhaps, in all Europe. I hardly ever take it off. Never, to be more exact.

LORENZO. It is very light but very strong. Do you think it would protect you against a stiletto?

THE DUKE. Certainly.

LORENZO. Oh yes, I remember now. You always wear it under your doublet. The other day, during the hunt, as I was riding behind you on your horse and holding onto you, I felt it distinctly. It's a prudent habit.

THE DUKE. It isn't that I mistrust anybody. It's just that, as you say, it's a habit—the habit of a soldier.

LORENZO. Your costume is magnificent! How nice these gloves smell! Why do you pose half naked? This coat of mail would have produced a striking effect in your portrait. You were wrong to take it off.

THE DUKE. The painter wanted it this way. And, anyway, it's always better to pose this way. Look at the men of antiquity.

LORENZO. Where the deuce is my guitar? I must accompany Giomo.

Exit.

TEBALDEO. I will paint no more today, my lord.

GIOMO, *at the window.* What is Lorenzo doing? Looking down into the well in the middle of the garden? It doesn't seem to me that he should be looking there for his guitar.

THE DUKE. Give me my clothes. Where is my coat of mail?

GIOMO. I don't find it; I've looked everywhere. It must have flown away.

THE DUKE. Lorenzo was holding it not five minutes ago. With his lazy habits he must have thrown it into some corner when he left.

GIOMO. This is incredible. There's no trace of it.

THE DUKE. That's impossible. It must be somewhere.

GIOMO. See for yourself, my lord. The room is not so large.

THE DUKE. Renzo was holding it there, on the sofa.

Re-enter LORENZO.

What have you done with my coat of mail? We can't find it anywhere.

LORENZO. I put it back where it was. Wait! No, I put it on that chair; no, it was on the bed. I don't remember what I did with it, but I have found my guitar.

He sings to his own accompaniment.

Good morning, Madam Abbess . . .

GIOMO. At the bottom of the well, apparently. Just now you were bending over it, greatly absorbed.

LORENZO. Spitting into a well to make circles in the water is my greatest pleasure. Aside from drinking and sleeping, I have no other occupation.

He continues to play.

Good morning, good morning,
Abbess of my heart.

THE DUKE. It's not possible that that coat of mail has been lost. I don't think I've taken it off twice in my life, except when I went to bed.

LORENZO. Now, don't make a valet of a Pope's son. Your servants will find it.

THE DUKE. The devil take you! You mislaid it.

LORENZO. If I were Duke of Florence, I'd worry about other things besides coats of mail. By the way, I spoke of you to my dear aunt. Everything is arranged. Come and sit over here and let me whisper in your ear.

GIOMO, *low to the* DUKE. It is strange, to say the least. The coat of mail has been carried off.

THE DUKE. Somebody will find it.

He sits down beside LORENZO.

GIOMO, *aside.* It isn't natural to leave good company to go and spit in a well. I'd like to find that coat of mail, and get rid of an old idea which bothers me from time to time. Bah! Lorenzaccio! The coat must be under some chair.

SCENE 7

In front of the DUKE's *palace. Enter* SALVIATI *covered with blood, and limping; two men help him.*

SALVIATI, *shouting.* Alessandro de' Medici! Open your window and see how your servants are treated!

THE DUKE, *at the window.* Who is there in the mud? Who crawls to my palace walls with such frightful cries?

SALVIATI. The Strozzi have assassinated me; I am dying at your door.

THE DUKE. Which of the Strozzi, and why?

SALVIATI. Because I said their sister was in love with you, my noble Duke. The Strozzi thought their sister insulted because I said that she liked you. Three of them assassinated me. I recognized Pietro and Tomaso. I didn't know the third.

THE DUKE. Have them bring you up here. By Hercules, the murderers will spend the night in jail, and be hanged in the morning!

SALVIATI *enters the palace.*

ACT THREE

SCENE 1

LORENZO's *bedroom*. LORENZO, SCORONCONCOLO, *fencing*.

SCORONCONCOLO. Have you played enough, sir?

LORENZO. No! Cry louder! There, parry that! there, die! Take that, wretch!

SCORONCONCOLO. Ah, the assassin! He's killing me! He's cutting my throat!

LORENZO. Die! die! die! Stamp your foot.

SCORONCONCOLO. Help, archers! help! He's killing me, this demon of a Lorenzo.

LORENZO. Die, base wretch! I'll stick you, pig . . . I'll stick you! To the heart . . . to the heart! He is ripped open! Shout then . . . strike! Kill! Open his bowels! Let's cut him in pieces . . . and let's eat him . . . eat him! I am up to my elbow! Get into his throat, roll him . . . roll him! Let's bite him . . . bite him and eat!

He sinks exhausted.

SCORONCONCOLO. You have invented a rough game, master, and you go at it like a real tiger. You roar like a cave full of lions and panthers.

LORENZO. Oh, day of blood! Oh, my wedding day! Oh, sun, sun, you have been dry long enough, you are dying of thirst, sun! His blood will intoxicate you. Oh, my vengeance! How long your nails have been a-sprouting! Oh, teeth of Ugolino, you must have the skull . . . the skull!

SCORONCONCOLO. Are you delirious?

LORENZO. Coward! coward! ruffian! The poor little ones, the fathers, the daughters, farewells, endless farewells . . . the banks of the Arno full of farewells! The urchins write them on the walls. Laugh, old man! Laugh under your white cap! Don't you see that my claws are sprouting? Ah, the skull . . . the skull!

He faints.

SCORONCONCOLO, *dashing water into his face.* Come, master, there's no need to make yourself so angry. Master, if you have an enemy, say so. I will get rid of him for you, and no one will be the wiser.

LORENZO. It's nothing. I tell you my only pleasure is to frighten my neighbors.

SCORONCONCOLO. We've been making such a racket in this room, turning everything upside down, they ought to be accustomed to it by now. I think you could cut off the heads of thirty men in the corridor, and roll them over your floor, without anybody in the house noticing anything unusual. If you want to frighten your neighbors, you go about it the wrong way. They were scared the first time, it's true, but now they just get angry and don't even take the trouble of getting up or opening their windows.

LORENZO. You think so?

SCORONCONCOLO. You have an enemy, master. Haven't I seen you stamp your foot and curse the day you were born? Haven't I got ears? And in the midst of your rages, haven't I distinctly heard the clear sound of one little word—revenge? You are growing thin; you do not joke as you used to. Believe me, there is nothing so bad for the digestion as a bitter hatred. When two men stand in the sunlight, isn't there always one whose shadow disturbs the other? Your physician is here in my scabbard, let me cure you.

He draws his sword.

LORENZO. Has that physician ever cured you?

SCORONCONCOLO. Four or five times. In Padua there was once a young lady who said to me——

LORENZO. Show me that sword. Ah, it is a fine blade!

SCORONCONCOLO. Try it, and you will see.

LORENZO. You have guessed my sickness. I have an enemy. But for him I won't use a sword that has been used for others. The one that kills him will have only one baptism—that man's name.

SCORONCONCOLO. Who is he?

LORENZO. What does it matter? Are you devoted to me?

SCORONCONCOLO. I would nail Christ back on the cross for you.

LORENZO. I tell you in confidence—I shall do the deed in this chamber. Listen closely and make no mistake. If he is helpless from my first blow, do not dare lay a hand on him. But I am no bigger than a flea, and he is a wild boar. If he defends himself, I count on you to hold his hands. Nothing else—do you hear? He belongs to me. I'll tell you more at the proper time.

SCORONCONCOLO. Amen!

SCENE 2

The Strozzi Palace.

PIETRO. I could cut off my right hand when I think about it. To have missed that scoundrel! A blow so well aimed, and yet it missed! And what a service it would have been to everyone if I could have said: "One less Salviati in the streets." But the knave drew in his hooked legs like a spider as he fell, and played dead for fear of being finished off.

FILIPPO. What do you care if he lives? They say he has been wounded so badly that he'll remember it all his life. Isn't your revenge even more complete?

PIETRO. Yes, I know very well that's the way you look at things. Father, you are a good patriot and a still better father of a family, but do not meddle in all this.

FILIPPO. What are you planning? Where are you going?

PIETRO. Why do you want to know? I am going to the Pazzi.

FILIPPO. Wait for me, then. I'm going there, too.

PIETRO. Not now, Father. It isn't a good time for you to be there.

FILIPPO. Speak frankly to me, Pietro.

PIETRO. In confidence, then, there are some fifty of us, the Ruccellai and others, who have no love for the bastard.

FILIPPO. And then?

PIETRO. And then an avalanche is sometimes started by a pebble no larger than the end of your finger.

FILIPPO. But have you formed any resolutions, made any plans? Have you taken any steps? Oh, children, children, to play with life and death! Questions that have shaken the earth to its foundations, ideas that have whitened thousands of heads and have caused them to roll like grains of sand at the feet of the executioner, projects which Providence itself regards with fear and trembling and leaves in man's hands without daring to interfere, you discuss these things while fencing, or in drinking a glass of wine, as though they were questions of a horse or a masquerade! Do you know the meaning of the word Republic? Do you know the meaning of the artisan at his workbench, the laborer in the field, the citizen in the streets, the whole life of a realm? The welfare of men, God of justice! And what have those Pazzi done to God? They invite their friends to come and conspire as they would invite them to come play dice. And their friends—entering their courtyard—slip in the blood of their grandfathers. For what are their swords thirsting? What do you want? What do you want?

PIETRO. Why are you taking this attitude? Haven't I heard you say a hundred times what we are saying now? Don't we know what you're doing when the servants see your windows still lighted in the morning?

FILIPPO. What are you driving at? Tell me.

PIETRO. The Medici are a pestilence. The man who is bitten by a serpent has no need of a physician. He has only to cauterize the wound.

FILIPPO. And when you have overthrown what exists now, what will you put in its place?

PIETRO. We are always sure of finding nothing worse.

FILIPPO. I'm telling you: be careful.

PIETRO. It's easy to count the heads of a hydra.

FILIPPO. You intend to act? That's decided?

PIETRO. We intend to destroy the murderers of Florence.

FILIPPO. Nothing can change your mind?

PIETRO. Good-by, Father. Let me go alone.

FILIPPO. Since when does the old eagle stay in the nest when his eaglets seek their quarry? Oh, my children, my brave and beautiful young! You who have the strength that I have lost, you who are what young Filippo used to be, allow him to grow old for you! Take me along, my son. I'll not preach you a long sermon. Just a few words. There ought to be a little wisdom in this gray head: two words and I am finished. I won't be a burden to you. Wait till I get my cloak.

PIETRO. Come, noble father. Liberty is ripe. Come, old gardener of Florence, and see the plant you love sprouting from the earth!

SCENE 3

A street. A GERMAN OFFICER *and soldiers.* TOMASO STROZZI *in their midst.*

THE OFFICER. If you don't find him at home, we'll find him at the Pazzi's.

TOMASO. Go chase yourselves. You know what'll happen to you for this.

THE OFFICER. No threats. I am carrying out the Duke's orders. I don't have to take anything from anybody.

TOMASO. Imbecile! Who arrests a Strozzi on the word of a Medici?

A group gathers around them.

A CITIZEN. Why do you arrest this gentleman? We know him well. He's Filippo's son.

ANOTHER CITIZEN. Let him go. We'll be responsible for him.

FIRST CITIZEN. Yes, yes. We'll answer for the Strozzi. Let him go, or look out for your ears!

THE OFFICER. Clear out! Let the Duke's justice pass, if you don't want this halberd in your belly!

PIETRO *and* FILIPPO *arrive.*

PIETRO. What's the matter? What's all the shouting about? What are you doing there, Tomaso?

THE CITIZENS. Stop him, Filippo, he wants to take your son to jail!

FILIPPO. To jail? On whose orders?

PIETRO. To jail? Do you know whom you're dealing with?

THE OFFICER. Arrest that man!

The soldiers arrest Pietro.

PIETRO. Let go of me, wretches, or I'll stick you like pigs!

FILIPPO. By what authority do you act, sir?

THE OFFICER, *showing the* DUKE's *order*. There is my warrant. I have an order to arrest Pietro and Tomaso Strozzi.

The soldiers press back the people, who throw stones at them.

PIETRO. What are we accused of? What have we done? Help me, my friends; let's thrash this rabble.

He draws his sword. Another detachment of soldiers arrives.

THE OFFICER. Come here. Help me!

PIETRO *is disarmed.*

March! The first one who comes too close gets a halberd in his belly!

PIETRO. No one has the right to arrest me without an order from the Council of Eight. I don't care about Alessandro's orders. Where is the order of the Eight?

THE OFFICER. We're taking you before the Eight.

PIETRO. If that's where I'm going, I have no objection. What am I accused of?

A VOICE IN THE CROWD. Filippo! Will you allow your children to be taken before the Eight?

PIETRO. Answer me! What am I accused of?

THE OFFICER. That's no business of mine.

The soldiers go off with PIETRO *and* TOMASO.

PIETRO, *leaving*. Don't be anxious, Father. The Council of Eight will send me back home for supper, and the bastard will have to pay the costs of his justice.

FILIPPO, *alone, seating himself on a bench*. What are we coming to, if a vengeance as just as Heaven is punished as a crime! What! the two oldest sons of a family as old as the city, imprisoned like highway robbers! O Christ! Has justice become a pander? The honor of the Strozzi is affronted in a public place and the tribunal sides with a ruffian's insults! A Salviati throws down his gauntlet, stained with wine and blood, to the noblest family of Florence, and when chastised uses the executioner's ax in his defense! Merciful heavens! Only a few minutes ago I spoke against rebellion, and this is the bread I'm given to eat, with the words of peace still on my lips. Come! old body, bent by age and study: prepare for action!

Enter LORENZO.

LORENZO. Are you asking for alms, Filippo, sitting like this at the street corner?

FILIPPO. I'm begging for man's justice. My honor is in rags and I'm a beggar, hungry for justice!

LORENZO. What's happening in the world if the marks of anger have fallen over the august and peaceful face of old Filippo? What are these lamentations, father? For whom do you scatter on the earth the most precious jewels under the sun, the tears of a man without fear and without reproach?

FILIPPO. We must rid ourselves of the Medici, Lorenzo. You are a Medici yourself, but only in name. I have understood you, I have been a grieving spectator to the hideous comedy you play. But now let the man replace the actor. If you ever had any honesty in you, show it today. Pietro and Tomaso are in prison.

LORENZO. Yes, yes, I know.

FILIPPO. Is that your reply? Is that your attitude?

LORENZO. Tell me what you want, and you'll have my reply.

FILIPPO. To act! How? I don't know what means to employ, what device to put beneath that Citadel of death, to push it into the river. What should we do, what should we decide, what men should we look for? I don't yet know. But to act, to act, to act! O Lorenzo! The time has come. Aren't you everywhere defamed, treated like a dog and a heartless wretch? But, in spite of everything, I have kept my door open to you, my heart and hand open to you. Speak, and let me see if I have been mistaken. Didn't you speak once of another Lorenzo, hiding behind the Lorenzo we see? Doesn't *that* man love his country? Isn't he devoted to his friends? You spoke, and I believed you.

LORENZO. If I am not the person you wish me to be, let me be struck down!

FILIPPO. Friend, it is wrong to laugh at a desperate old man. If you speak the truth, then let us act! I have received promises from you which would be binding on God himself, and it was on their account that I received you. When the very stones cried out at your passing, when your every step left pools of blood behind it, I called you by the sacred name of friend. In order to believe you, I made myself deaf; in order to love you, I made myself blind. I permitted the shadow of your reputation to darken my honor, and my children distrusted me because I shook your hand. Be sincere with me as I have been with you! Act! For you are young, and I am old. O Lorenzo! Lorenzo! You are a man of decision: talk to me. I have meditated too long; I have been too self-centered; I am no longer fit for battle. Tell me what you think I should do: I will do it.

LORENZO. Return to your home, my dear sir.

FILIPPO. I must go to the Pazzi's. Fifty determined young men are there, sworn to act. I will speak to them nobly, as a Strozzi and as a father, and they will listen. For this is not the end. Let the Medici look out for themselves! Farewell, I'm on my way to the Pazzi's.

LORENZO. There are many devils, Filippo, and the one tempting you now is not the least dangerous.

FILIPPO. What do you mean?

LORENZO. Beware of it. It is a demon more beautiful than Gabriel. Liberty, Patriotism, Human Happiness—these words vibrate like harp strings at its approach.

FILIPPO. I don't follow you.

LORENZO. Have you only this thought in your head: to deliver your sons? Look into your conscience. Does not another thought, more vast, more terrible, drive you into the midst of those young men?

FILIPPO. Yes! I wish the injustice done to my family to be the rallying point of Liberty.

LORENZO. Beware of yourself, Filippo: you have thought of the welfare of humanity.

FILIPPO. What do you mean? Are you infected and foul inside as well as out, you who spoke to me of the precious liquid you carry within you? Is this what it's like?

LORENZO. I am indeed precious to you—because I will kill Alessandro.

FILIPPO. You?

LORENZO. I. Tomorrow or the day after. Return home. Try to deliver your sons. If you cannot, let them submit to a.light punishment. I know they face no other dangers. In a few days there will no more be an Alessandro de' Medici in Florence than there is a sun at midnight.

FILIPPO. If this is true, why am I wrong to think of Liberty? Won't it come when you have killed Alessandro—if you do?

LORENZO. Filippo, Filippo, beware of yourself! Your sixty years of virtue are too valuable to risk on a throw of the dice.

FILIPPO. If you're hiding something under those somber words that I should hear, speak!

LORENZO. No matter how I seem to you now, Filippo, I once was virtuous. I believed in virtue, in human greatness, as a martyr believes in his God. I have shed more tears over poor Italy than Niobe over her daughters.

FILIPPO. Well, Lorenzo?

LORENZO. My youth was as pure as gold. But in twenty years of silence, a thunderbolt was forming in my breast. Truly, I must have been the spark for that thunderbolt, for suddenly, one night, seated in the ruins of the Colosseum, I rose, stretched my young arms toward heaven, and swore that I would kill one of my country's tyrants. At that time I was a quiet student, occupied only with art and science. How can I explain the strange vow I made? Perhaps it is what a man feels when he falls in love.

FILIPPO. I have always had confidence in you, and yet, to listen to you, I think I'm dreaming.

LORENZO. And so do I. I was happy then. My heart and hands

were at peace. I was entitled to the throne, and I had but to let the sun rise and set, to see all human hopes flower around me. Men had influenced me neither toward good nor evil, but I was good, and, to my everlasting sorrow, I wanted to be great. But I must confess that if Providence led me to the decision to kill a tyrant, whoever he might be, pride led me to it also. What more can I say to you? All the Caesars of the world spoke to me of Brutus.

FILIPPO. Pride in virtue is a noble pride. Why do you apologize for it?

LORENZO. You will never know, unless you are mad, the fevered exaltation that possessed me. Perhaps a statue coming down from a pedestal to walk among men would be what I felt like on the day I began to live with this idea! I must be a Brutus.

FILIPPO. You astonish me more and more.

LORENZO. At first I wanted to kill Clement VII. I was banished from Rome before I could. I started over again with Alessandro. I wanted to act alone, without any man's aid. I was acting for the sake of humanity. But my pride lay in wait among my philanthropic dreams. I did not want to arouse the masses, nor to gain the talkative glory of a paralytic Cicero. I wanted to get to the man himself, to struggle hand to hand with living tyranny, to kill it, and afterward carry my bloody sword to the rostrum, and let the stench of Alessandro's blood revive the sluggish brains of the speechmakers!

FILIPPO. What a will of iron you have, my friend!

LORENZO. My task was difficult with Alessandro. Then, as it is now, Florence was drowned in wine and blood. Caesar and the Pope had made a duke of a butcher's boy. To please my cousin, to become his friend and gain his confidence I had to be willing to wipe all the remains of his orgies from his thick lips. I was as pure as a lily, and yet I did not recoil from that task. Let us not speak of what I have become as a result. I became vicious, cowardly, an object of shame. But what does it matter? That is not the question.

FILIPPO. You lower your head. There are tears in your eyes.

LORENZO. I'm not blushing. Plaster masks that serve dishonor are not able to blush. I have done what I have done. All you will need to know is that I've succeeded in my enterprise. Alessandro will soon come to a certain place; he won't leave it alive. I'm at the end of my ordeal, and you can be sure, Filippo, that the wild buffalo, when the herdsman strikes him to the ground, is not surrounded with more snares than I have woven around my bastard. That heart, which an army could not have gotten to in a year, is now bared beneath my hand. I have only to let my stiletto fall to penetrate it. All will be done. Now, do you know what has happened to me, and do you understand my warning?

FILIPPO. If you are telling the truth you are indeed our Brutus.

LORENZO. I believe I *am* a Brutus, my poor Filippo. Ah! you have lived alone, Filippo. Like a bright beacon you have remained motionless beside the ocean of men, and you have seen in the waters a reflection of your own light. From the depths of your solitude you found the ocean magnificent under its splendid skies, but you did not count each wave, you did not sound the depths. You were full of confidence in God's handiwork. But I, during this time, plunged into the rough sea of life. I have explored all its depths, and while you admired the surface I saw the shipwrecks, the bones, and the leviathans.

FILIPPO. Your sadness breaks my heart.

LORENZO. It is because I see you on the point of doing what I have done that I speak to you like this. I do not despise men. The fault of books and of historians is that they show them different from what they are. Life is like a city: one may stay in it for fifty or sixty years without seeing anything but parks and palaces; but then you must take care not to enter the gambling dens, nor stop in the vile neighborhoods on your way home. This is my advice, Filippo. If it is a question of saving your children, I tell you to keep quiet. It is the best means of having them restored to you after a slight reprimand. If it is a question of attempting something for humanity, I advise you not to—for it won't be long before you discover you stand alone.

FILIPPO. I can see how the role you are playing would have given you these ideas. If I understand you, you have taken

a vile road to arrive at a sublime end, and you believe all
life must resemble what you have seen.

LORENZO. I have awakened from my dreams, that's all. And I
am telling you of the dangers of dreaming. I know life and it
is an ugly thing, believe me. If you have respect for anything, do not meddle with it.

FILIPPO. Stop! Don't destroy the staff of my old age. I believe
in all those things you call dreams. I believe in Virtue, Modesty, and Liberty.

LORENZO. Haven't you seen me, Lorenzaccio, in the streets? The
children do not throw mud at me. The beds of young girls
are still warm from my sweat, and their fathers do not attack me as I pass. The air you breathe, Filippo, I breathe
too. My silk mantle trails lazily over the fine sand of the
shaded walks; not one drop of poison falls into my cup. O
Filippo! The mothers of the poor shamefully lift their daughters' veils when I pause upon their thresholds. They let me
look upon their beauty with a smile viler than the kiss of
Judas, while I, pinching the maiden's cheek, clench my fists
in rage, as I rattle four or five paltry gold pieces in my
pocket.

FILIPPO. Let not the tempter despise the weak. Why tempt, if
there is any doubt?

LORENZO. Am I Satan? Light of Heaven, I would have wept
for the first girl that I seduced, if she hadn't begun to laugh.
When I began to play my role of the modern Brutus, I
marched in my new habit of the vast brotherhood of vice,
as a child of ten marches in the armor of a fairy-tale giant.
I thought that corruption was a stigma and that only mon-
sters bore it on their foreheads. I had started to shout loudly
that my twenty years of virtue were a suffocating mask—
O Filippo, I was just entering into life, and I saw, on my
approach, that everyone was doing what I was doing. All the
masks fell before me. Humanity lifted its dress and showed
itself to me in all its monstrous nudity as if I were a skillful
pupil worthy of her. I saw men as they are, and I asked
myself: "What am I striving for?" When I wandered about
the streets of Florence, with my ghost by my side, I looked
at a passer-by and said to myself: "When I've done my

deed, will that one profit by it?" I saw the republicans
in their studies, I went into the stores, I listened to the talk
of the people and I saw tyranny's effect on them, I swal-
lowed between two kisses the most virtuous tears, I was always waiting for humanity to show me an honest face. I
watched as closely as a lover watches his fiancée while
waiting for the wedding day.

FILIPPO. If you have only observed evil, I pity you; but I cannot believe you. Evil exists, but not without good; as shadow
exists, but not without light.

LORENZO. If you only see in me a despiser of men, you do me
an injustice. I know perfectly well that there are good ones;
but what cause are they serving, what are they doing, how
are they acting? What use is it that conscience is alive, if
the arm is dead? From certain points of view, everything
becomes good. A dog is a faithful friend. You can discover
in him the most loyal servant, just as you can also see him
turn over cadavers, and learn that the tongue that licks his
master smells of carrion a league away. All I can see is that I
am lost and that men will not profit by my action any more
than they will understand me.

FILIPPO. Poor child, this is heart-breaking. But, if you were
virtuous, when you have delivered your country you will become so again. To think that you are virtuous, Lorenzo,
this is what makes my old heart rejoice. Then you will be
able to throw away your hideous disguise, and you will once
again become as pure a metal as the bronze statues of
Harmodius and Aristogiton.[6]

LORENZO. Filippo, Filippo, I have been virtuous. The hand
which has once raised the veil of truth can never let it fall
again; it rests unmoving until the end, always holding that
horrible veil and lifting it higher and higher above the head
of the man until the angel of death seals his eyes.

FILIPPO. All diseases can be cured, and vice also is a disease.

LORENZO. It is too late. I have become used to my calling. Vice
used to be a garment for me, but now it is part of me. I am
really a scoundrel, and when I joke with my equals, I feel

[6] Murderers of the tyrant, Hipparchus. (Translator's note.)

as serious as Death in the midst of my gaiety. Brutus pretended to be mad in order to kill Tarquin, and what astonishes me about him is that he did not really lose his mind. Profit by my example, Filippo, that is what I have to say to you. Do not work for your country.

FILIPPO. It may be true that you have taken a dangerous road. But why shouldn't I take another, which would lead me to the same point? My intention is to appeal to the people and to act openly.

LORENZO. Take what road you will, you always have to deal with men.

FILIPPO. I believe in the honesty of republicans.

LORENZO. I'll make a wager with you. I am going to kill Alessandro. Once my deed is accomplished, if the republicans act as they should, it will be easy for them to establish a republic, the finest that ever flourished on this earth. Let's say they may even have the people with them. I wager that neither they nor the people will do anything. Let me do what I have to do. You have clean hands; I have nothing to lose. Come, go home to your palace, and try and deliver your children.

FILIPPO. But why will you kill the Duke if you have such ideas?

LORENZO. Why? You ask that?

FILIPPO. If you believe this murder useless to your country, why do you commit it?

LORENZO. You ask me that to my face? Just look at me. I used to be handsome, happy, and virtuous.

FILIPPO. What an abyss—what an abyss you open to me!

LORENZO. You ask why I'm going to kill Alessandro? Do you want me to poison myself or jump into the Arno? If I am the shadow of myself, do you want me to break the only thread which today joins my heart to a few fibers of the heart I had in the past? Do you realize that this murder is all that's left to me of my virtue? Do you realize that for two years I've been sliding down a steep wall and that *that* was the only thing I had to hold onto? Do you think I have no more pride because I have no more shame? And would

you let the enigma of my life die in silence? This much is
certain. If I could become virtuous again, if my knowledge
of vice could be blotted out, perhaps I would spare the
Duke. But I love wine, women, and amusements, do you
understand that? If you honor anything in me, it is this murder which you honor—perhaps only because you would not
commit it yourself! I'm tired of the sound of men's idle talk.
The world must know who I am and who he is. Thank God!
Tomorrow—or in two days at the most—I'll kill Alessandro.
Whether men understand me or not, whether they act or
not, I'll have said all I have to say. Let them call me what
they will, Brutus or Herostratus,[7] I don't want them to forget me. My entire life is at the end of my dagger, and
whether Providence favors me or not, in two days men will
appear before the tribunal of my will.

FILIPPO. All this astonishes me. But Pietro and Tomaso are in
prison, and I could not trust anyone but myself to help them.
You may be right in all you say, but I must do something.
I shall assemble the members of my family.

LORENZO. As you wish. But beware of yourself!

SCENE 4

The Soderini Palace. Enter CATERINA.

CATERINA, *reading a note.* "Lorenzo must have spoken to you
about me, but whose words could do justice to a love like
mine? Let my pen tell you what my lips cannot say and
what my heart would like to sign with its blood. Alessandro
de' Medici." If this were not addressed to me, I would think
that the messenger had made a mistake. What I read makes
me doubt my eyes.

Enter MARIA.

Oh, my dear sister, look at this letter. Explain it to me, if
you can.

MARIA. Unfortunate girl! He loves you? Where has he seen
you? Where have you spoken to him?

[7] He set fire to the Temple of Artemis to immortalize himself.
(Translator's note.)

CATERINA. Nowhere. A messenger gave this to me as I was leaving church.

MARIA. Lorenzo, he says, must have spoken to you? Ah, Caterina, to have such a son! Yes, to make his mother's sister the Duke's mistress—not even mistress. What do they call such creatures? This is Lorenzo's final shame. Come, I want to show him this letter, and hear, before God, what he's going to say.

CATERINA. I thought that the Duke was in love . . . pardon, sister, but I thought the Duke was in love with the Countess Cibo. Someone had told me that.

MARIA. That's true. He loved her, if he's capable of love.

CATERINA. He no longer loves her? How could he so shamelessly offer me such a heart? Come, sister, come and see Lorenzo.

MARIA. Give me your arm. I don't know what's been the matter with me the last few days. I've had a fever every night. Indeed, it hasn't left me for the past three months. I have suffered too much, my poor Caterina. Why did you read me that letter? I can bear no more. I am no longer young, and all that I see draws me toward the grave. Come, help me, my poor child! I shall not trouble you for long.

Exit.

SCENE 5

COUNTESS CIBO's *boudoir. The* COUNTESS; *the* DUKE.

THE COUNTESS. To be a king! Do you know what that means? To have a hundred thousand men at your command! To be the ray of sunlight which dries men's tears! To be both joy and sorrow! Ah, how exciting that is! How that old man in the Vatican would tremble if you were to spread your wings, my eaglet! Caesar is so far away! The garrison is loyal to you! Oh, for the day when you have rallied the whole nation to you, when you shall be the leader of a free people! Ah! do you know what it is to have a nation take its benefactor to its arms?

THE DUKE. As long as they pay me the taxes, what do I care about the people?

THE COUNTESS. But somebody will assassinate you finally. The very stones of the earth will rise up to crush you. It is easy to be a great king when one is king. Declare Florence independent, demand compliance to the treaty that was made with the empire, draw your sword and show it. They will tell you to return it to its scabbard, that it dazzles their eyes. Think how young you are! Nothing has yet been decided for you. The hearts of the people are very indulgent to princes, and public favor forgets past faults. You have had poor advice; you have been deceived. But there is still time. You have only to speak. As long as you are alive, the page has not been turned in the book of history. And are you sure that your last sleep will be a peaceful one? You who never go to Mass, and care only for taxes, are you sure that eternity is deaf and that there is no echo of life in the hideous house of the dead? Do you know where the tears of the people go when the wind carries them away?

THE DUKE. You have a pretty leg.

THE COUNTESS. Listen to me. You are thoughtless, I know, but you are not wicked. No, above all things you are not that—you could not be. Come, rouse yourself. Think a moment, only a moment, what I'm saying to you. Doesn't it mean anything at all?

THE DUKE. I understand everything you say, but what do I do that is so bad? I'm as good as my neighbors. I am as good as —no—better than the Pope. You remind me of the Strozzi with all your talk, and you know how I detest them. You want me to revolt against Caesar; Caesar is my stepfather, my dear friend. You imagine that the Florentines don't love me. I'm sure they do. Confound it! Even if you were right, who should I be afraid of?

THE COUNTESS. You are not afraid of your people, you are afraid of Caesar. You have slain or dishonored hundreds of citizens, and you think you have taken every precaution because you wear a coat of mail under your doublet.

THE DUKE. Peace! No more of this!

THE COUNTESS. Oh, I lose my temper, and I say things I don't

want to say. My dear, who doesn't know you are brave? You
are as brave as you are handsome. Whatever wrong you
have done is due to your youth, your temperament. It's the
hot blood that runs in your veins; it's the suffocating sun
which weighs upon us. But tell me, have you nothing there?
Nothing, nothing there?

She touches his heart.

THE DUKE. What a demon! Sit down there, my darling.

THE COUNTESS. All right. I'll confess that I am ambitious—not
for myself, but for you—you and my dear Florence! O God!
You are a witness to what I suffer.

THE DUKE. You suffer? What's the matter with you?

THE COUNTESS. No, I don't suffer. Listen! Listen! I see you are
getting bored with me. You count the minutes, you turn
your head. Don't go yet. It may be the last time I'll see you.
Listen! I tell you that Florence calls you her new pestilence.
You must know that. If I am mad, if you should hate me
tomorrow, what does it matter to me?

THE DUKE. Woe to you, if you play with my anger!

THE COUNTESS. Yes, woe to me! Woe to me!

THE DUKE. Another time—tomorrow morning, if you wish—we'll
see each other again and talk about that. Don't be angry if
I leave now. I'm going to the hunt.

THE COUNTESS. Yes, woe to me! Woe to me!

THE DUKE. Why? You are as solemn as hell itself. Why the
devil do you meddle in politics? There, there! Your little role
as a virtuous woman is so becoming to you! You are too
devout, but that will take care of itself. Won't you help me
put on my coat?

THE COUNTESS. Good-by, Alessandro.

The DUKE *kisses her. Enter* CARDINAL CIBO.

THE CARDINAL. Oh! Excuse me, Highness, I thought my sister-
in-law was alone. I beg you to excuse me.

THE DUKE. What do you mean by this? Now you're behaving
like a priest. Should you watch such things? Come! What
the devil does it matter to you?

Exeunt together.

SCENE 6

The Strozzi Palace. The forty STROZZI *in the banquet hall.*

FILIPPO. My children, be seated.

THE GUESTS. Why are there two empty seats?

FILIPPO. Pietro and Tomaso are in prison.

THE GUESTS. Why?

FILIPPO. Because Salviati publicly insulted my daughter Luisa,
whom you see, at the fair at Monte Oliveto, and in front of
her brother Leone. Pietro and Tomaso have killed Salviati,
and Alessandro de' Medici has had them arrested to avenge
the death of his ruffian.[8]

THE GUESTS. Death to the Medici!

FILIPPO. I have gathered my family together to tell them my
sorrows and to beg them to help me. Let us eat our supper,
and then go out, sword in hand, to free my sons.

THE GUESTS. We will! We will!

FILIPPO. It's time for it to end. They would kill our sons and
dishonor our daughters. It's time for Florence to teach these
bastards what the right over life and death means. The
Eight have no right to condemn my sons, and I would not
survive their death!

THE GUESTS. Have no fear, Filippo. We are here.

FILIPPO. I am the head of the family: how could I dismiss an
insult? Why should the Medici have the power to destroy
our children rather than we theirs? Are we men? Shall it be
said that the noble families of Florence can be uprooted at
a single stroke? They have begun with us; we must stand
firm. Our first cry of alarm will call together in the Florentine
sky a whole army of eagles that have been driven from the
nest. They are not far away: they are circling about the city,
their eyes fixed on its towers. We will plant the black ban-
ner of pestilence on them; and they will flock together at
that signal of death. These are the colors of divine anger.

---

[8] So Musset's text. Yet, above, Salviati was said to be only
wounded. (Translator's note.)

Tonight let us go and deliver our sons; tomorrow we will go together, with drawn swords, to the doors of all the great families. There are more than eighty palaces in Florence, and from each of them a band like ours will issue forth when Liberty knocks at the door.

THE GUESTS. Long live Liberty!

FILIPPO. God is my witness that violence has forced me to draw my sword; that for sixty years I have been a good and peaceful citizen; that I have never injured anyone in the world; and that half my fortune has been used to help the unfortunate.

THE GUESTS. That is true, Filippo.

FILIPPO. It is a just vengeance that drives me to revolt, and I am becoming a rebel because God made me a father. I have no motives of ambition, interest, or pride. My cause is loyal, honorable, and sacred. Fill your glasses and rise! Our vengeance is holy and we can share it with God. I drink to the death of the Medici!

THE GUESTS, *rising and drinking.* To the death of the Medici!

LUISA, *putting down her glass.* Oh! I am dying!

FILIPPO. What is the matter, my daughter, my beloved child? What's the matter? My God, what has happened? My God, my God, how pale you are! Speak— What is the matter with you? Speak to your father. Help! Help! A doctor! Quick! Quick! There's no time to lose!

LUISA. I am dying! I am dying!

She dies.

FILIPPO. She is dying, my friends! She is dying! A doctor! My daughter is poisoned!

He falls on his knees beside LUISA.

A GUEST. Have her drink warm water. If it is poison, warm water is what she needs.

The servants run in.

ANOTHER GUEST. Slap her hands! Open the windows and slap her hands!

ANOTHER GUEST. Perhaps it is only a dizzy spell.

ANOTHER GUEST. Poor child! How calm her features are! She cannot be dead as suddenly as that!

FILIPPO. My child, are you dead? Are you dead, Luisa, my beloved daughter?

THE FIRST GUEST. Here comes the doctor.

A doctor enters.

THE SECOND GUEST. Hurry, sir, tell us if it's poison!

FILIPPO. It's a dizziness, isn't it?

THE DOCTOR. Poor girl! She's dead.

A profound silence in the room; FILIPPO *continues kneeling beside* LUISA, *holding her hands.*

A GUEST. It is the poison of the Medici.

ANOTHER GUEST. I'm sure I'm right. There was a servant waiting on table who used to be employed by Salviati.

ANOTHER GUEST. He did it, without any doubt. We must seize him.

Exit.

FIRST GUEST. Filippo doesn't reply to anything that's said to him. He's overwhelmed.

ANOTHER GUEST. It's horrible! An unbelievable murder!

ANOTHER GUEST. It cries for vengeance to high Heaven. Let's go and cut Alessandro's throat!

ANOTHER GUEST. Death to Alessandro! He's the one who ordered it done. Fools that we are! He has long hated us. We are acting too late.

ANOTHER GUEST. Salviati did not want that poor Luisa for himself, he was acting for the Duke. Come, let's go, even if they kill us to the last man!

FILIPPO, *arising.* My friends, you will bury my poor daughter, will you not,

He puts on his cloak,

in my garden, behind the fig trees? Farewell, my dear friends, farewell!

A GUEST. Where are you going, Filippo?

FILIPPO. I have borne enough. My two sons are in prison, and now my daughter is dead. I can bear no more. I am going away.

A GUEST. Going away without revenge?

FILIPPO. Yes, yes. Farewell, my friends! Go home!

A GUEST. Do not let him go. He has lost his mind.

FILIPPO. Don't force me. Don't make me stay in the same room with my daughter's dead body. Let me go.

A GUEST. Avenge yourself, Filippo! Let us avenge you! Let your Luisa be our Lucretia!

ANOTHER GUEST. Think of your country, Filippo! Don't go back on what you have said!

FILIPPO. Liberty, revenge. What do they mean? I have two sons in prison, and here is my daughter dead. If I stay, all around me will die. Farewell, my friends. If I'm no longer here, they will do nothing to you. I am going to Venice. Don't bury my poor child. My old monks will come tomorrow and take her away. God of justice, God of justice, what have I done to you?

He runs off.

ACT FOUR

SCENE 1

The DUKE's *palace. Enter the* DUKE *and* LORENZO.

THE DUKE. I wish I'd been there to see all those angry faces. But I can't imagine who poisoned Luisa.

LORENZO. Nor can I—unless it was you.

THE DUKE. Filippo must be furious. They say that he's gone to Venice. Thank God, I'm rid of that insufferable old man! As for the dear family, I hope they'll be good enough to keep quiet. Do you know they almost started a little revolution in the neighborhood? Two of my Germans were killed.

LORENZO. What annoys me most is that the good Salviati had to have his leg amputated. Have you found your coat of mail yet?

THE DUKE. No, and that irks me more than I can say.

LORENZO. Beware of Giomo. He's the one: he stole it from you. What do you wear in its place?

THE DUKE. Nothing. I can't bear any others. None of them are as light.

LORENZO. That's unfortunate for you.

THE DUKE. You haven't told me a thing about your aunt.

LORENZO. Only because I forgot. She adores you. She can't even sleep since the star of your love has risen in her poor heart. I pray you, my lord, have pity on her; tell me when you want to receive her and at what hour she'll be permitted to sacrifice to you the little virtue she has.

THE DUKE. Are you serious?

LORENZO. Serious as Death itself. I'd certainly like to see an aunt of mine refuse to sleep with you!

THE DUKE. Where can I see her?

LORENZO. In my room, my lord. I'll put white curtains around my bed and flowers on the table. And so you won't forget it after supper, I'll write in your notebook that my aunt will be ready for you at twelve o'clock sharp.

THE DUKE. I won't forget it. Plague! Caterina is a morsel fit for a king, but tell me, my smart boy, how are you sure she'll come? How did you manage it?

LORENZO. I'll tell you later.

THE DUKE. I'm going to look at a horse I just bought. Good-by till tonight. Come for me after supper, and we'll go to your house together. As for the Countess, I'm bored to death with her. Yesterday, again, I had her on my neck—all during the hunt! Good-by, my pet.

Exit.

LORENZO, *alone.* So it's settled. Tonight I'll take him home with me, and tomorrow the republicans will see what they have to do; for the Duke of Florence will be dead. I must alert Scoronconcolo. Hurry, sun, if you're curious about the news this night will bring!

SCENE 2

COUNT CIBO's *house. Enter the* CARDINAL *and the* COUNTESS.

THE CARDINAL. Do you want me to counsel you, Ricciarda? Put on your cloak and steal into the Duke's alcove. If he expects you to talk, prove to him that you know when to keep quiet, and see to it that, if he falls asleep on that republican breast, it is not from boredom. It doesn't take a great deal of skill to keep a lover a little longer than three days. Are you a virgin? Isn't there any more wine in Cyprus? Haven't you read Aretino?

THE COUNTESS. O Heavens! Are you so sure the Heavens are empty that you dare shame your purple with such words?

THE CARDINAL. There is nothing so virtuous as the ear of an immoral woman. Pretend to understand me or not, as you choose, but remember: my brother is your husband.

THE COUNTESS. You horrify me! What do you want from me?

THE CARDINAL. Seek a reconciliation with Alessandro, and if I offended you just now by telling you how to do it, there is no need for me to repeat my instructions. Be guided by me. In a year, in two years, you will thank me. I have struggled a long time to become what I am, and I know how far one may go. If I were sure of you, I could tell you things that God himself will never know. The day when, as a woman, you have gained the necessary control, not over the mind of Alessandro, Duke of Florence, but over the heart of Alessandro your lover, I'll tell you the rest, and you will know what I expect.

THE COUNTESS. So then, when I have read Aretino to gain my first experience as a duke's mistress, I will learn what my second is to be in the secret book of your thoughts? Do you want me to tell you what you don't dare tell me? You will serve the Pope until the Emperor discovers that you are a better valet than the Pope himself. You hope that one day Caesar will be truly obligated to you for the complete enslavement of Italy. And on that day, yes, that day, surely the man who is the King of half the world can very easily reward you with the meager heritage of Heaven. A little while ago, in order to govern Florence while governing the Duke, you would have made yourself into a woman, if that were possible. When poor Ricciarda Cibo has helped Alessandro make two or three major political moves, people will be quick to say that Ricciarda Cibo leads the Duke by his nose, but that she herself is led by her brother-in-law. And, as you say, who knows where the tears of the people, grown to an ocean, could carry your ship? Isn't this your plan?

THE CARDINAL. Go to the Duke tonight, or you are lost.

THE COUNTESS. Lost? How?

THE CARDINAL. Your husband will know all.

THE COUNTESS. Tell him, tell him! I will kill myself.

THE CARDINAL. A woman's threat! Listen! Whether you have understood me or not, go to the Duke tonight.

THE COUNTESS. No, no, no!

THE CARDINAL. Body of Christ!

Exit.

SCENE 3

LORENZO'S *room.* LORENZO, *two servants.*

LORENZO. When you've arranged those flowers on the table, and these at the foot of the bed, make a good fire. But make sure that by tonight there are no flames burning, and the hot coals give no light. Then leave me the key and go to bed.

Enter CATERINA.

CATERINA. Your mother is sick. Aren't you coming to see her, Renzo?

LORENZO. Mother is sick?

CATERINA. Alas, I can't hide the truth from you. Yesterday I received a note from the Duke telling me you had spoken to me of his love. This is what has hurt Maria.

LORENZO. I never spoke to you of Alessandro. Couldn't you have told her I had nothing to do with it?

CATERINA. That's what I did tell her. Why is your room so beautifully, so carefully arranged?

LORENZO. The Duke wrote to you? It's strange I knew nothing of it. And what did you think of his letter?

CATERINA. What did I think of it?

LORENZO. Yes, of Alessandro's declaration of love. What did that innocent little heart think of it?

CATERINA. What do you want me to think?

LORENZO. Weren't you flattered? A love that is the envy of so many women! A title so beautiful: mistress of . . . Go, Caterina! Tell my mother I'm coming! Leave me!

Exit CATERINA.

By Heaven! What kind of man of wax am I? Has vice, like the robe of Dejanira, become so much a part of my body that I can't speak with my own tongue? The very air between my lips is vile despite myself. I was going to corrupt Caterina. I think I would corrupt my mother if it occurred to my brain to do so. For only God knows about the bow which the gods have drawn inside my head, and how strong its arrows are! If all men are particles in an immense fire-place, surely the Unknown Being who fashioned me let a burning log drop into this feeble, staggering body, instead of a spark! I can deliberate and choose, but, having chosen, I cannot retrace my steps. Oh, God! Don't the young people, to be fashionable, glory in their wickedness? And don't the children, leaving school, have something more important to do than pervert themselves? What filth mankind is—running through the taverns with lips hungry for debauchery! And yet I, who did not wish to wear a mask that resembled their faces, and who went to the brothels firmly resolved to remain pure beneath my soiled clothes, can neither find myself nor wash my hands clean, even with blood. Oh, Alessandro! I am not devout, but, in all sincerity, I hope you say a prayer before coming here tonight. What tiger was my mother dreaming of when she carried me? When I remember how I loved flowers, and meadows, and the sonnets of Petrarch, the specter of my youth rises, shuddering, before me. Oh, God! Why does that single phrase, "Until tonight!" burn joyfully through me like a hot iron? From what animal womb, from what hairy embrace, did I come? What had this man ever done to me? When I put my hand there, on my heart, and I think about it, who tomorrow will hear me say, "I have killed him!" without answering, "Why did you kill him?" It is very strange. He has hurt others, but to me he's been good, at least after his fashion. If I'd stayed quiet and solitary at Cafaggiuolo, he wouldn't have come to find me. And yet I came to find him in Florence. Why did I pursue him? Was my father's spirit leading me, like an Orestes—toward a new Aegisthus? Then again: did he offend me? It is very strange. And yet, to commit this act, I have abandoned everything. The single thought of this murder has crumbled to dust all the dreams of my life. I have been nothing but an empty shell ever since this murder, like a terrifying raven, alighted on my path and called to me. What does it all mean? On the square, a little while ago, I heard two men talking of a comet. Could I say that I feel the rhythm of a human heart within my chest? Ah! why has this idea come to me so often lately? Am I the hand of God? Is there a halo above

my head? When I enter this room and want to draw my
sword, I am in fear of drawing the flaming sword of the
Archangel, and falling in ashes on my prey.

SCENE 4

A convent in the background. Enter FILIPPO STROZZI *and
two monks; some novices carrying the coffin of* LUISA; *they
place it in a tomb.*

FILIPPO. Let me kiss her before you place her in her last bed.
I used to bend over her like this to kiss her good night.

They close the tomb.

From this bed you will never rise again. O, Luisa! Only
God has known what you meant to me. And I, I, I!

PIETRO, *entering.* A hundred men at Sestino have arrived from
Piedmont. Come, Filippo, the time for tears is past!

FILIPPO. Child, do you know what the time for tears *is?*

PIETRO. The exiles have assembled at Sestino. It is time to
think of vengeance. Let us march boldly upon Florence
with our little army. If we can surprise the citadel guards
during the night, it will all be over. By heaven, I'll raise
another monument than that to my sister!

FILIPPO. Not I. Go without me, my friends.

PIETRO. We cannot go without you. You know our confeder-
ates count on your name. Francis I himself is expecting a
move from you in the cause of Liberty. He writes to you as
to the leader of all Florentine republicans. Here is his letter.

FILIPPO, *opening the letter.* Tell the King of France: the day
when Filippo takes up arms against his country he will
have become a madman.

PIETRO. What is this new attitude?

FILIPPO. The one that suits me.

PIETRO. Will you ruin the cause of all the exiles for the pleasure of striking an attitude? Beware, Father, this isn't a passage from Pliny! Think well before you say no!

FILIPPO. I have known for sixty years what my reply should be
to the King of France's letter.

PIETRO. This is unbelievable! You will force me to say things I don't want to say. Come with us, Father, I beg of you! When I was going to the Pazzi's, didn't you ask me to take you with me? And was the situation any different then?

FILIPPO. Very different. An offended father who goes out, sword in hand, along with his friends, to demand justice, is very different from a rebel who bears arms against his country, openly, and in contempt of the law.

PIETRO. It wasn't a question of demanding justice. It was a question of killing Alessandro! And how is it any different now? You do not love your country, or you would take advantage of an occasion like this!

FILIPPO. An occasion! My God! This, an occasion!

He strikes the tomb.

PIETRO. Let me try to persuade you.

FILIPPO. My sorrow is not ambitious. Leave me alone. I have said enough.

PIETRO. Obstinate old man, you will be our ruin!

FILIPPO. Stop! You are an insolent boy! Get out of here!

PIETRO. Go where you please. We'll act without you this time. Death of God! It won't be said all was lost through the fault of a translator of Latin.

Exit.

FILIPPO. Your day has come, Filippo. Everything points to the end.

SCENE 5

A bank of the Arno; a quay. In the distance a long line of palaces. Enter LORENZO.

LORENZO. The sun is setting. I have no time to lose, and yet I'm sure I'm wasting my time here.

He knocks at a door.

Hallo, Signor Alamanno! Hallo!

ALAMANNO, *upon his terrace.* Who is there? What do you want?

LORENZO. I've come to tell you the Duke will be killed to-night! If you love Liberty, you and your friends, prepare for tomorrow!

ALAMANNO. By whom is Alessandro to be killed?

LORENZO. By Lorenzo de' Medici.

ALAMANNO. Is that you, Lorenzaccio? Come in and have supper with some good fellows who are visiting me!

LORENZO. I have no time. Prepare to act tomorrow!

ALAMANNO. You intend to kill the Duke yourself? Go on! Wine has gone to your head.

Exit.

LORENZO, *alone.* Perhaps I'm wrong to tell them it is I who'll kill Alessandro: no one believes me.

He knocks at another door.

Hallo, Signor Pazzi! Hallo!

PAZZI, *upon his terrace.* Who is calling me?

LORENZO. I've come to tell you that the Duke will be killed tonight. Plan to act for the Liberty of Florence tomorrow!

PAZZI. Who is going to kill the Duke?

LORENZO. No matter. You and your friends take action! I cannot tell you the man's name.

PAZZI. You are mad, imbecile! Go to the devil!

Exit.

LORENZO, *alone.* Obviously, if I don't say I'm going to do it, they'll believe me still less.

He knocks at a door.

Hallo, Signor Corsini!

THE GOVERNOR, *on his terrace.* What is it?

LORENZO. Duke Alessandro will be killed tonight.

THE GOVERNOR. Indeed, Lorenzo! If you're drunk, take your jokes elsewhere! Your prank at Nasi's ball injured my horse!

Exit.

LORENZO. Poor Florence! Poor Florence!

Exit.

SCENE 6

A public square; it is night. Enter LORENZO.

LORENZO. I will tell him that, for modesty's sake, I am taking
the light away. It happens every day. A bride, for instance,
will insist on darkness when her husband enters the nuptial
chamber; and Caterina is supposed to be very virtuous.—
Poor girl, who under the sun is more virtuous than she?—
My mother may die; that is what might happen.

But all is ready. Patience! One hour is as good as another;
the clock has just struck. If you want, however . . . And
why not? Take the candelabra away, if you want; it's natural when a woman gives herself for the first time. Come
in, warm yourself. Oh, my, yes! merely the caprice of a
young girl. And what reason do they have to believe in this
murder? It will astonish everyone, even Filippo.

The moon appears.

There you are, with your livid face!

What a revolution there'd be in the city tomorrow, if the
republicans were men! But Pietro is too ambitious, and the
Ruccellai are the only ones that are good for anything. Ah,
words, words, everlasting words! If there *is* Someone up
there, He might very well laugh at us all. It's really very
funny, it really is.—O chatter of humankind! O killer of
dead bodies, breaker-in of open doors, O men without arms!

No, no! I will not take away the light. I will go straight to
the heart. He will see himself killed . . . Blood of Christ!
People will rush to their windows tomorrow.

Let's hope he hasn't invented some new armor. Cursed in-
vention! I'll go in after him. He'll put his sword down there
—or there, yes, on the sofa. And it will be easy to wind the
crossbelt around its guard. If he should take it into his head
to lie down, that would give me the best opportunity. Lying,
sitting, or standing? Preferably sitting. I'll begin by leaving.
Scoronconcolo is in the study. Then we come in. I wouldn't
like to have him turn his back, though. I'll go straight up
to him. Well, peace! peace! the hour has arrived. I must

go to some wineshop. I'd empty a flagon of wine now. No, I don't want to drink. Where the devil shall I go, anyway? The wineshops are closed.

How many days I have spent sitting under the trees! What peace! What a view at Cafaggiuolo! And Giannina, the caretaker's young daughter, how pretty she was drying her clothes! How she chased the goats that came walking over her linen when it was stretched out on the grass! And the white goat with the long slender feet would always come back.

A clock strikes.

I must go down there. Good evening, my pet! Eh, drink with Giomo!—Good wine! It would be very amusing if he should ask me, "Is your room private? Can your neighbors hear what goes on here?" Amusing!

Well, what now? I have the strangest desire to dance. I think that, if I let myself go, I'd hop like a sparrow over the old pavement. Ah, my pet! my pet! Put on your new gloves and your best clothes. Tra-la-la! Make yourself handsome, the bride is beautiful! But let me whisper this in your ear, look out for her little knife.

Exit, running.

SCENE 7

The DUKE's *palace. The* DUKE, *at supper;* GIOMO. *Enter* CARDINAL CIBO.

THE CARDINAL. Beware of Lorenzo, Highness!

THE DUKE. There you are, Cardinal! Sit down and have a glass of wine.

THE CARDINAL. Beware of Lorenzo, Duke! This evening he went to the Bishop of Marzi for post horses—for tonight.

THE DUKE. That can't be so.

THE CARDINAL. The bishop told me himself.

THE DUKE. Nonsense! I have good reason to know it can't be true.

THE CARDINAL. Perhaps it's impossible to make you believe me; but I'm doing my duty in warning you.

THE DUKE. If it should be true, what's so frightening about it? Perhaps he is going to Cafaggiuolo.

THE CARDINAL. This is what's frightening, my lord. In crossing the square, on my way here, with my own two eyes I saw him jumping on the pavement like a madman! I called to him. And the look in his eyes frightened me. You can be sure that he is plotting something for tonight.

THE DUKE. And why should his plans be dangerous to me?

THE CARDINAL. Should one tell everything when one talks of a favorite? Then you must know that he told two people of my acquaintance, publicly, on their terraces, that he would kill you—tonight.

THE DUKE. Drink a glass of wine, Cardinal. Don't you know that Renzo is usually drunk by sundown?

Enter SIRE MAURIZIO.

SIRE MAURIZIO. Your Highness, beware of Lorenzo! He told three of my friends he intended to kill you—tonight.

THE DUKE. You too, good Maurizio, you believe in fairy tales? I thought you more of a man than that.

SIRE MAURIZIO. Your Highness knows that I do not get frightened without cause. What I say, I can prove.

THE DUKE. Sit down, and take a drink with the Cardinal. I hope you won't be offended if I go about my affairs. Well, my pet, is it time?

Enter LORENZO.

LORENZO. It's just twelve o'clock.

THE DUKE. Give me my sable doublet.

LORENZO. Let's hurry. Your lady is perhaps already at the rendezvous.

THE DUKE. What gloves should I take, those of a warrior, or those of a lover?

LORENZO. Those of a lover, Your Highness.

THE DUKE. Good, because tonight I want to be a brilliant lover.
Exit.

SIRE MAURIZIO. What do you think of this, Cardinal?

THE CARDINAL. That the will of God is done in spite of men.
Exeunt.

SCENE 8

LORENZO's *room. Enter the* DUKE *and* LORENZO.

THE DUKE. I'm frozen. It's really cold.
He takes off his sword.
Well, my pet, what are you doing?

LORENZO. I'm winding your crossbelt around your sword. I'll put it under your pillow. It's always well to have a weapon at hand.
He winds the crossbelt in such a way as to prevent the sword from coming out of the scabbard.

THE DUKE. You know I hate talkative women, and I seem to remember that Caterina is supposed to be quite a talker. To avoid conversation, I'm going to get into bed. By the way, why did you ask the Bishop of Marzi for post horses?

LORENZO. To go and see my brother who wrote me that he's very ill.

THE DUKE. Go fetch your aunt.

LORENZO. One moment.
Exit.

THE DUKE, *alone.* To continue to pay court to a woman who— when she is asked yes or no—answers yes, has always appeared to me very foolish, and altogether worthy of a Frenchman. Especially tonight, when I've eaten as much as three monks, I'd be unable to even say, "My heart!" or "Dearest belovèd!" to the Spanish Infanta. I'll pretend to be asleep. It's not very gallant, but it will be convenient.
He gets into bed. LORENZO *returns, sword in hand.*

LORENZO. Are you asleep, my lord?
He stabs him.

THE DUKE. Is it you, Renzo?

LORENZO. My lord, have no doubt of it.

He stabs him again. Enter SCORONCONCOLO.

SCORONCONCOLO. Is it done?

LORENZO. Look, he has bitten my finger. I'll treasure this bloody ring until I die.

SCORONCONCOLO. Oh, my God! It's the Duke of Florence!

LORENZO, *seating himself at the window.* What a beautiful night! How pure the air is! Breathe, breathe, O heart filled with joy!

SCORONCONCOLO. Come, master, we have done too much. Let's get away!

LORENZO. How soft and fragrant are the evening winds! How wonderfully the flowers of the fields are budding! O magnificent nature! O eternal tranquillity!

SCORONCONCOLO. The wind will freeze the sweat that's trickling down your face. Come, my lord!

LORENZO. Ah, God of kindness, what a moment!

ACT FIVE

SCENE 1

The DUKE's *palace.* VALORI, SIRE MAURIZIO *and* GUICCIAR-
DINI. *A crowd of courtiers circulate about the salon and
grounds of the palace. Enter* GIOMO.

SIRE MAURIZIO. Well, what did you find out?

GIOMO. Nothing at all.

Exit.

GUICCIARDINI. He doesn't want to answer. Cardinal Cibo is
closeted in the Duke's study, and the news comes only to
him.

Enter another MESSENGER.

Well, has the Duke been found? Does anyone know what
has become of him?

THE MESSENGER. I do not know.

He goes into the study.

VALORI. This disappearance is a dreadful thing, gentlemen.
No news of the Duke yet? Didn't you say, Sire Maurizio,
that you saw him last evening? Did he appear to be ill?

Re-enter GIOMO.

GIOMO *to* SIRE MAURIZIO. I must whisper it to you: the Duke
has been assassinated.

SIRE MAURIZIO. Assassinated! By whom? Where did you find
him?

GIOMO. Where you told us: in Lorenzo's room.

SIRE MAURIZIO. Blood of the devil! Does the Cardinal know?

GIOMO. Yes, my lord.

SIRE MAURIZIO. What has he decided? What is to be done
about it? Crowds of people are already coming toward the
palace. We're dead men when the Duke's murder is confirmed. They'll massacre us!

Valets carrying casks of wine and baskets of food pass in the background.

GUICCIARDINI. What does this mean? Are they going to give them out to the people?

Enter COURTIERS.

SIRE MAURIZIO, *to* GIOMO. Has he been buried?

GIOMO. Yes, indeed, in the sacristy. There was nothing else we could do. If the people were to learn of this death it would be the cause of many more. In due time he'll be given a public funeral. Meanwhile, we took him away in a rug.

VALORI. What will become of us?

SEVERAL COURTIERS, *drawing near.* Will we soon be permitted to pay our respects to His Highness? What do you think about it, gentlemen?

CARDINAL CIBO, *entering.* Yes, gentlemen, you may go in in an hour or two. The Duke spent the night at a masquerade party, and he is resting just now.

The valets hang dominoes at the casements.

THE COURTIERS. Let us withdraw. The Duke is still in bed. He spent the night at a ball.

Exeunt COURTIERS. *Enter the rest of the* EIGHT.

NICCOLINI. Well, Cardinal, what has been decided?

THE CARDINAL.
"The first golden bough torn down is replaced by another,
And as quickly there grows a similar branch of a similar metal."[9]

Exit.

NICCOLINI. All very fine, but what has that to do with it? The Duke is dead; another must be chosen; and as soon as possible. If we don't have a duke by this evening, or tomorrow, it's the end of us. The people are in a ferment.

VETTORI. I propose Ottavio de' Medici.

CAPPONI. Why? He's not first in line.

ACCIAIUOLI. We might take the Cardinal.

---

[9] *Primo avulso, non deficit alter/ Aureus, et simili frondescit virga metallo.* Virgil, *The Aeneid,* Book 6, ll. 143–44.

SIRE MAURIZIO. Are you joking?

RUCCELLAI. Why, indeed, shouldn't you take the Cardinal, since you have allowed him to declare himself sole judge in this affair, contrary to all law?

VETTORI. He is a man who directs things well.

CANIGIANI, *approaching*. Gentlemen, if you will take my advice, this is what we should do: we shall elect his natural son, Giuliano, Duke of Florence.

RUCCELLAI. Bravo! A child of five! Isn't he five, Canigiani?

GUICCIARDINI, *low*. Don't you see the point? It was the Cardinal who put that foolish thought in his head. Cibo would be regent, and the child would eat sweets.

RUCCELLAI. This is shameful! If you go on talking in this manner, I'll leave the room.

Enter CORSI.

CORSI. Gentlemen, the Cardinal has just written to Cosimo de' Medici.

THE EIGHT. Without consulting us?

CORSI. The Cardinal has likewise written to Pisa, to Arezzo, and to Pistoia, to the military commanders. Giacomo de' Medici will be here tomorrow, with as large a force as he can muster. Alessandro Vitelli is already in the fortress with the entire garrison. As for Lorenzo, he has dispatched three messengers to overtake him.

RUCCELLAI. Your Cardinal had better proclaim himself duke at once, and have done with it.

CORSI. Under the provisional title of Governor of the Florentine Republic, he ordered me to beg you to put the election of Cosimo de' Medici to a vote.

SIRE MAURIZIO. Come, gentlemen, to the voting. Here are your ballots.

VETTORI. Cosimo is indeed the first by right after Alessandro. He is his nearest relative.

ACCIAIUOLI. What kind of a man is he? I know him very slightly.

CORSI. He is the best prince in the world.

GUICCIARDINI. Ha, ha, not altogether that. If you were to say the most vague and polite of princes, it would be nearer the truth.

SIRE MAURIZIO. Your votes, gentlemen!

RUCCELLAI. I formally object to this vote, for myself, and in the name of all the citizens.

VETTORI. Why?

RUCCELLAI. The republic no longer needs either princes or dukes or lords. Here is my vote!

He shows a blank ballot.

VETTORI. Your vote is only one vote. We can do without you.

RUCCELLAI. Farewell then! I wash my hands of it.

Exit.

NICCOLINI. Your votes, gentlemen!

He unfolds the ballots thrown into a hat.

It is unanimous. Has the messenger left for Trebbio?

CORSI. Yes, my lord. Cosimo will be here tomorrow morning—unless he declines.

VETTORI. Why should he decline?

NICCOLINI. Ah! my God! If he should decline, what would become of us? Fifteen leagues from here to Trebbio to find Cosimo, and as many to return, will mean a whole day lost. We ought to have chosen someone who was nearer.

VETTORI. It can't be helped! Our vote is cast.

Exit.

SCENE 2

Venice. FILIPPO STROZZI *in his study.*

FILIPPO. I was sure of it. Pietro is corresponding with the King of France. And I'm told he's at the head of a motley army, and ready to put the city to fire and the sword. This, then, is what the poor name of Strozzi, so long respected, will have produced—a rebel and two or three massacres. O my Luisa, you alone are at peace.

Someone knocks at the door.

Come in!

Enter LORENZO.

LORENZO. Filippo! I bring you the most beautiful jewel of your crown.

FILIPPO. What is it you have thrown down—a key?

LORENZO. That key opens the door of my room, and in my room is Alessandro de' Medici, dead by this hand!

FILIPPO. Really! Really! It's hard to believe.

LORENZO. Believe it, if you wish. You will hear it from others.

FILIPPO, *taking the key*. Alessandro is dead! Is it possible?

LORENZO. What would you say if the republicans were to offer you the title of Duke in his place?

FILIPPO. I should refuse it, my friend.

LORENZO. Really! Really! It's hard to believe.

FILIPPO. Why? It's very easy for me.

LORENZO. As it was for me to kill Alessandro. Why don't you want to believe me?

FILIPPO. Oh, our new Brutus! I believe you, and I embrace you. Then Liberty is saved! Yes, I believe you. You are what you told me you were. Give me your hand. The Duke is dead! There is no hate in my joy. There is only the purest, most holy love for my country. As God is my witness!

LORENZO. Calm yourself. Nothing is saved but me, and I have had my back broken by the Bishop of Marzi's horses.

FILIPPO. Didn't you notify our friends? Aren't they in arms by this time?

LORENZO. I notified them. I knocked at every republican door. I told them to polish their swords, for when they awakened Alessandro would be dead. I think that by this time they have awakened, more than once, and gone back to sleep.

FILIPPO. Did you notify the Pazzi? Did you tell it to Corsini?

LORENZO. To everybody. I might as well have said it to the moon.

FILIPPO. What do you mean by that?

LORENZO. I mean that they shrugged and returned to their dinners, their games, and their women.

FILIPPO. Didn't you explain to them what was happening?

LORENZO. What the devil would you have me explain? Did you think I had an hour to lose with each one of them? I said to them, "Prepare yourselves"; and I did my deed.

FILIPPO. And you believe that the Pazzi are doing nothing? What do you know about it? You have had no news since you left, and you were several days in coming here.

LORENZO. I believe that the Pazzi are doing something. I believe they are fencing in their antechamber, and drinking wine from time to time, whenever their throats are dry.

FILIPPO. You seem to have won your wager, but wait! I am still hopeful.

LORENZO. I am more than hopeful, I am certain.

FILIPPO. Why didn't you carry the Duke's head through the streets? The people would have followed you as their savior!

LORENZO. I left the stag to the hounds. Let them eat up the quarry.

FILIPPO. You would have deified men—if you didn't despise them.

LORENZO. I don't despise them: I know them. I am certain that there are very few who are very evil, many cowards, and a great many who are indifferent.

FILIPPO. I am filled with joy and hope. My heart beats high in spite of me.

LORENZO. So much the better for you.

FILIPPO. Since you know nothing about it, why do you speak as you do? To be sure, not all men are capable of great acts, but all are responsive to great acts: do you deny the history of the whole world? Doubtless a spark is needed to set fire to a forest, but a spark can come from a stone, and then that forest is in flames. And thus the flash of a single sword may light up an entire century.

LORENZO. I don't deny history; but I was not there.

FILIPPO. Let me call you Brutus. If I am a dreamer, leave me that dream. Oh, my friends, my compatriots! You can make a fine deathbed for the old Strozzi if you wish to!

LORENZO. Why are you opening the window?

FILIPPO. Don't you see that a messenger is coming? My Brutus, my great Lorenzo, Liberty is in the air. I feel it, I breathe it.

LORENZO. Filippo, Filippo, no more of that. Close your window. Those words sicken me.

FILIPPO. There seems to be a crowd gathering in the street and a town crier about to read a proclamation. Hallo, Giovanni, go and buy that crier's proclamation.

LORENZO. O God! O God!

FILIPPO. You're pale as death! What's the matter with you?

LORENZO. Didn't you hear?

Enter a servant bearing the proclamation.

FILIPPO. No, but read.

LORENZO, *reading.* "To any man, noble or commoner, who will kill Lorenzo de' Medici, a traitor to his country and the assassin of his master, in whatever place and by whatever means, in any part of Italy, the Council of Eight at Florence promise the following reward: 1. Four thousand gold florins net; 2. An annuity of one hundred gold florins, to be given to him during his life, and to his direct descendants after his death. 3. A perpetual pardon for all his transgressions past and future, ordinary or extraordinary. Signed: the Hand of the Eight."

Well, Filippo! Just a moment ago you wouldn't believe that I had killed Alessandro. You see now that I did.

FILIPPO. Ssssh! Somebody's coming up the stairs. Hide in that room.

Exeunt.

SCENE 3

A square. Florence. The GOLDSMITH *and the* SILK MERCHANT.

THE GOLDSMITH. Cosimo arrives today. That's the only thing that has come of all this. Death in life! Isn't it a shame? When they saw the Eight pass in the street, all my workmen, neighbor, struck their tools on their tables and called out, "If you don't know how to act—or can't act—call on us —*we* will."

THE SILK MERCHANT. Your workmen were not the only ones

who shouted. There is a clamor in the city like never before.

THE GOLDSMITH. Some are running after the soldiers, others after the wine that is being given away. They fill their mouths and brains with it, so they lose what little common sense and decent speech they might have had.

THE SILK MERCHANT. There are some who would like to re-establish the Council, and freely elect a *Gonfaloniere*, as in days of old.

THE GOLDSMITH. There are some who would like to, as you say, but there are none who have taken any steps. Old as I am, I went to the market place, and received a halberd in my leg. Not a soul tried to help me. Only the students showed themselves.

THE SILK MERCHANT. I can easily believe that. Do you know what they say, neighbor? They say that the governor, Roberto Corsini, went last night to a meeting of the republicans.

THE GOLDSMITH. Nothing is truer than that. He offered to turn over the fortress to the friends of Liberty, with the supplies, keys, and all the rest.

THE SILK MERCHANT. Did he really, neighbor? That would be high treason!

THE GOLDSMITH. Yes, indeed! They brawled, drank sweet wine, smashed windowpanes, but the brave man's proposal was not even listened to. Because they didn't dare do what he wanted, they said that they distrusted him and suspected him of treachery. How mad it makes me! Look—the messengers from Trebbio! Cosimo isn't far away. Good night, neighbor, I must find out what is going on. I'm going to the palace.

Exit.

THE SILK MERCHANT. Wait for me, neighbor, I'll go with you.

Exit.

SCENE 4

Venice. STROZZI's *study. Enter* FILIPPO *and* LORENZO, *holding a letter.*

LORENZO. Here is a letter which tells me that my mother is dead. Take a little walk with me, Filippo.

FILIPPO. I beg of you, my friend, don't tempt fate. You come and go as if that death sentence did not exist.

LORENZO. When I was going to kill Clement VII, a price was put on my head in Rome. Now that I've killed Alessandro, naturally there's a price on my head all over Italy. If I were to leave Italy, I'd be hunted all over Europe; and at my death the Good God wouldn't fail to post my eternal condemnation at every crossroads of the universe.

FILIPPO. Your gaiety is as sad as death: you have not changed, Lorenzo.

LORENZO. No, indeed. I wear the same clothes, I walk upon my legs, and I yawn with my mouth. Only misery has changed within me. That is, I am hollower than a tin statue.

FILIPPO. Let's go away together. Become a man again. You have been guilty of many things, but you are still young!

LORENZO. I'm older than Methuselah. I beg you, take a walk with me.

FILIPPO. Your mind tortures itself with inactivity. That is your misfortune. You have faults, my friend.

LORENZO. I admit it. It's a great fault of mine that the republicans have done nothing in Florence; that a hundred brave students have been butchered in vain; that Cosimo, a mere clodhopper, has been unanimously elected—oh! I confess, these are unpardonable faults of mine.

FILIPPO. Let's not argue over what isn't yet finished. The most important thing for you is to get out of Italy. Your life isn't over yet.

LORENZO. I was an instrument of murder, but of one murder only.

FILIPPO. Didn't you ever enjoy happiness before this murder? Even if you should only live as an honest man from now on, why should you wish to die?

LORENZO. I can only repeat my own words to you: I used to be virtuous. Perhaps I might become so again—were it not for the boredom which seizes me. I still love women and wine. That is enough, it is true, to make me a rake; but it is not enough to make me want to be one. Let's go out, I beg of you!

FILIPPO. You will get yourself killed on one of these walks.

LORENZO. It amuses me to see them. The reward is so large it almost makes people courageous. Yesterday, a tall fellow with bare legs followed me along the edge of the water for a quarter of an hour without being able to decide to kill me. The poor man carried some kind of a knife as long as a sword. He looked at it with such a sheepish air, I pitied him. Perhaps he was the father of a family dying of hunger.

FILIPPO. Lorenzo, Lorenzo, your heart is sick! He may have been an honest man who had respect for an unfortunate!

LORENZO. Credit him with whatever motive you want. I'll take a turn on the Rialto.

Exit.

FILIPPO. I must have some of my people follow him. Hallo, Giovanni! Pippo! Hallo!

Enter a servant.

Take a sword, you and one of your comrades, and follow Signor Lorenzo at a suitable distance—so you can help him if he's attacked.

GIOVANNI. Yes, my lord.

Enter PIPPO.

PIPPO. My lord, Lorenzo is dead! A man was hiding behind the door. He stabbed him in the back as he left the building.

FILIPPO. Let's hurry! Perhaps he's only wounded.

PIPPO. Don't you see that mob out there? The people have thrown themselves upon him. Merciful God, they are throwing the body into the lagoon!

FILIPPO. How horrible! How horrible! What, not even a tomb?

Exit.

SCENE 5

Florence. The great square. The public galleries are filled with people.

THE CROWD, *running from all sides.* Long live Cosimo de' Medici! He is Duke! He is Duke! Duke!

THE SOLDIERS. Keep back, you dogs!

CARDINAL CIBO, *upon a stage, to* COSIMO DE' MEDICI. My lord, you are Duke of Florence. Before receiving from my hands the crown which the Pope and Caesar have charged me to confer upon you, it is my duty to ask you to swear to four things.

COSIMO. What are they, Cardinal?

THE CARDINAL. To administer justice without restriction; to attempt nothing against the authority of Charles V; to avenge the death of Alessandro; and to be kind to Signor Giuliano and Signorina Giulia, his natural children.

COSIMO. How must I take this oath?

THE CARDINAL. Upon the Bible.

He gives him a Bible.

COSIMO. I swear before God, and before you, Cardinal. Now give me your hand.

They advance toward the people. COSIMO *is heard speaking in the background.*

"Most Noble and Most Powerful Lords, in return for the great benefits which I owe to your most illustrious and gracious lordships, I promise, young as I am, ever to have before my eyes, along with the fear of God, honesty and justice and the intention to injure no man; and, as to the government of Florence, I promise never to deviate from the counsel and judgment of their most prudent and judicious lordships, to whom I offer myself entirely, and commend myself most devoutly."

SPRING'S AWAKENING

A Tragedy of Childhood

by

FRANK WEDEKIND

English version by
Eric Bentley

Dedicated
by the author
to
The Man in the Mask

Characters

MRS. BERGMANN

WENDLA BERGMANN
INA MÜLLER
} *her daughters*

MR. GABOR

MRS. GABOR

MELCHIOR
their son

RENTIER* STIEFEL

MORITZ STIEFEL
his son

OTTO
GEORG
ROBERT
ERNST
LÄMMERMEIER
HÄNSCHEN RILOW
} *schoolboys*

THEA
MARTHA
} *schoolgirls*

ILSE
a model

REKTOR SONNENSTICH (Sunstroke)**
AFFENSCHMALZ (Calflove)
KNÜPPELDICK (Cudgelthick)
HUNGERGURT (Starveling)
ZUNGENSCHLAG (Stickytongue)
KNOCHENBRUCH (Bonebreaker)
FLIEGENTOD (Flykiller)
} *schoolmasters*

* German title for one who lives on a private income (rents and dividends).

** In cases where the German names are in the tradition of Aguecheek and Belch, English equivalents are supplied in paren-

HABEBALD (Catchemquick)
school porter

PASTOR KAHLBAUCH (Skinnybelly)

FRIEND ZIEGENMELKER (Goatmilker)

UNCLE PROBST (Provost)

DIETHELM ⎫
REINHOLD ⎪
RUPRECHT ⎬ *boys in the Reformatory*
HELMUTH ⎪
GASTON ⎭

DR. PROCRUSTES

LOCKSMITH

DR. VON BRAUSEPULVER (Seidlitz powder)

VINTAGERS

A MAN IN A MASK

THE TIME: 1892

THE PLACE: *Germany*

---

thesis. Wedekind's daughter, Mrs. Kadidja W. Biel, tells me she thinks the English equivalents should actually be used in performance. I, on the other hand, think it is essential not to pretend that the action takes place anywhere but Germany. Besides, many other German names *could* be given such literal translation though no one would propose such a line of action. Should Müller be changed to Miller, Bergmann to Hillman? E.B.

A NOTE on the Language: It is a pity the term "period piece" carries overtones that are wholly unfavorable. For a piece like this is still full of life, while belonging unmistakably to an earlier period. While I have not attempted to reproduce the speech of 1891 with exactitude, neither have I tried to give the effect of the mid-twentieth century.

Even as of 1891, Wedekind's language is peculiar. His background was international, and his German has no single regional root. By consequence, it is always a little abstract and more than a little idiosyncratic.

In addition, his children's talk is the talk, very often, of children pretending to be grown-up. The awkwardness of adolescent gestures is a familiar enough fact: Wedekind explored the awkwardness of adolescent speech. Adolescents of Germany, 1891, differ from adolescents of America, 1960, in carrying a much heavier load of Culture. Some of Wedekind's children know more of literature than of life.

By "Germany" in these notes, I mean the German-speaking part of Europe. The school Wedekind went to and based much of his story on was in Aarau, Switzerland.

E. B.

ACT·ONE

SCENE 1

A living room. WENDLA BERGMANN *and her mother.*

WENDLA. Why have you made my dress so long, Mother?

MRS. BERGMANN. You're fourteen today.

WENDLA. If I'd known you were going to make my dress as long as that I'd rather have stayed thirteen.

MRS. BERGMANN. The dress isn't too long, Wendla. What do you expect? I can't help it if my daughter is an inch taller every spring. A big girl like you can't go around in a little-girl dress.

WENDLA. The little-girl dress suits me better than that old sack. —Let me wear it a little longer, Mother! Just for the summer! This penitential robe will keep.—Hold it till my next birthday. I'd only trip on the hem now.

MRS. BERGMANN. I don't know what to say. I'd like to keep you exactly as you are, child. Other girls are gawky and gangling at your age. You're just the opposite.—Who knows what you'll be like when the others are fully developed?

WENDLA. Who knows? Maybe I won't be around.

MRS. BERGMANN. Child, child, where do you get such ideas?

WENDLA. Oh, Mother, please don't be sad!

MRS. BERGMANN, *kissing her.* My little precious!

WENDLA. They just come to me in the evening when I can't go to sleep. And I don't feel sad, either. I know I'll sleep all the better.—Is it sinful to think of such things, Mother?

MRS. BERGMANN. Oh, all right, go and hang the penitential robe in the closet and put your little-girl dress on again if you must.—When I have time I'll put a strip of flouncing on it.

WENDLA, *hanging the dress in the cupboard.* Oh, no! In that case I'd rather be twenty right away!

MRS. BERGMANN. I only hope you won't be cold.—That little dress *was* long enough, but . . .

WENDLA. What, now, with summer coming on?—Oh, Mother, a girl doesn't get diphtheria in the back of her knees, how could you be so fainthearted? You don't feel the cold at my age, specially not in the legs. And would it be any better if I was too hot, Mother?—You can think yourself lucky if one fine morning your little precious doesn't cut her sleeves off or come home in the evening without shoes and stockings. —When I wear my penitential robe I shall be dressed like the queen of the fairies underneath . . . Don't scold, Mother darling. No one will ever see it!

SCENE 2

Out of doors. Sunday evening. MELCHIOR, MORITZ, OTTO, GEORG, ROBERT, ERNST.

MELCHIOR. This is boring. I'm going to stop playing.

OTTO. Then the rest of us will have to stop too!—Have you done the homework, Melchior?

MELCHIOR. You don't have to stop.

MORITZ. Where are you going?

MELCHIOR. For a walk.

GEORG. But it's getting dark!

ROBERT. Finished your homework already?

MELCHIOR. Why shouldn't I take a walk in the dark?

ERNST. Central America!—Louis the Fifteenth!—Sixty lines of Homer!—Seven equations!

MELCHIOR. This damned homework!

GEORG. If only that Latin exercise wasn't for tomorrow!

MORITZ. One can't think of anything without homework getting in the way.

OTTO. I'm going home.

GEORG. I am too. Homework!

ERNST. I am too.

ROBERT. Good night, Melchior.

MELCHIOR. Good night.

All leave but MORITZ *and* MELCHIOR.

What I'd like to know is: why do we exist?

MORITZ. I'd rather be a cab horse than have to go to school! —Why *do* we go?—We go to school to take exams!—And why do they examine us?—So they can flunk us!—They have to flunk seven—the classroom above only holds sixty.—I've felt so strange since Christmas . . . If it wasn't for Father, damned if I wouldn't pack my bag and leave for Hamburg!

MELCHIOR. Let's talk about something else.

They take a walk.

MORITZ. Did you see that black cat with its tail in the air?

MELCHIOR. You believe in omens?

MORITZ. I'm not sure.—She came over from the other side. Doesn't mean a thing, of course.

MELCHIOR. Pull free of the Scylla of religious delusion and you fall victim to the Charybdis of superstition!——Let's sit under this beech tree. A warm breeze is blowing in from the mountains. How I wish I were a young dryad up there in the forest tossed and cradled all night long in the topmost branches!

MORITZ. Unbutton your vest, Melchior.

MELCHIOR. Ah! How it blows one's clothes around!

MORITZ. Darned if it isn't getting so dark you can't see your hand before your face. Where are you actually?——Don't you agree, Melchior, that the sense of shame is simply a product of a person's upbringing?

MELCHIOR. I was thinking about that the day before yesterday. But I must say it seems to me rooted in human nature. Imagine having to undress—completely—in front of your best friend. You wouldn't unless he was doing.—Then again, it's more or less a question of fashion.

MORITZ. If I have children, I'll have them sleep in the same room from the start. If possible in the same bed. Boys *and* girls. I'll make them help each other dress and undress, and in hot weather boys as well as girls will wear nothing but a short white, woolen tunic with a leather strap.—Brought up like this, they'll be, well, less disturbed than we usually are.

MELCHIOR. I'm sure you're right, Moritz.—The only question is, when the girls have babies, what then?

MORITZ. How do you mean, have babies?

MELCHIOR. Well, if you ask me, I believe there's some kind of instinct at work. For example, if you took two kittens, a he and a she, and shut them up together for life, and never let any other cats in—if in short you left them entirely to their instincts—I believe that, sooner or later, the she-cat would become pregnant—even though neither she nor the tom had had any opportunity to learn it by example.

MORITZ. I suppose you're right. With animals it must come all by itself.

MELCHIOR. With humans too! That's *my* theory. May I ask, Moritz, when your boys sleep in the same bed as the girls, and then suddenly feel . . . the first stirrings of their manhood, well, I bet anything—

MORITZ. You may be right.—Even so . . .

MELCHIOR. And at the corresponding age exactly the same thing would happen to your girls! Not that girls are exactly . . . it's hard to judge precisely . . . anyway we can certainly assume . . . and curiosity can be relied on to play its part!

MORITZ. By the way, I have a question.

MELCHIOR. Well?

MORITZ. Will you answer it?

MELCHIOR. Of course!

MORITZ. Really?

MELCHIOR. Cross my heart!—Well, Moritz?

MORITZ. Have you done the exercise yet?

MELCHIOR. Oh, come on! There's no one to see or hear us!

MORITZ. Naturally, my children will have to work all day either in the garden or at the farm or amuse themselves with games that provide physical exercise. Riding, climbing, gymnastics . . . Above all they mustn't sleep on such soft beds as we do. Those beds have made us soft.—I don't believe you dream if you sleep on a hard bed.

MELCHIOR. From now till after grape harvest I'll be sleeping exclusively in my hammock. I've put my bed behind the stove. It folds up.—Once last winter I dreamt I'd been flogging our dog Lolo so long he couldn't move his legs. That's the most horrible thing I ever dreamt.—Why are you looking at me like that?

MORITZ. Have you felt them yet?

MELCHIOR. What?

MORITZ. What did you call them?

MELCHIOR. The stirrings of manhood?

MORITZ. Uh, huh.

MELCHIOR.—Certainly!

MORITZ. Me too. —

MELCHIOR. I've known for ages.—A year at least!

MORITZ. I felt like I'd been struck by lightning.

MELCHIOR. You'd had a dream?

MORITZ. A short one . . . About legs in sky-blue tights climbing over the lectern. At least I *think* that's what they were trying to do.—I only caught a glimpse of them.

MELCHIOR. Georg Zirschnitz dreamt of his mother.

MORITZ. Did he tell you so?

MELCHIOR. Out on Gallows Lane.

MORITZ. If you only knew what I've been through since that night!

MELCHIOR. The prickings of conscience?

MORITZ. Prickings of conscience? —— The fear of death!

MELCHIOR. Good God!

MORITZ. I thought there was no hope for me. I was sure I must be suffering from some internal complaint.—In the end I calmed down, but only because I began to write my memoirs. Yes, my dear Melchior, the last three weeks have been my Gethsemane.

MELCHIOR. When it happened to me I was more or less prepared for it. I was a bit ashamed.—But that was all.

MORITZ. And yet you're almost a year younger than me!

MELCHIOR. I wouldn't worry about that, Moritz. In my experi-

ence, there's no fixed time for the arrival of these . . .
phantoms. You know the big Lämmermeier boy with the
straw-colored hair and the hook nose? He's three years older
than me. Hänschen Rilow says that he still dreams of nothing but pound cake and apricot jelly.

MORITZ. Now how can Hänschen Rilow know about that?

MELCHIOR. He asked him.

MORITZ. He asked him?—I'd never have dared to *ask* anyone!

MELCHIOR. You asked *me*.

MORITZ. So I did!—It wouldn't surprise me if Hänschen had
even made his will!—A strange game they play with us.
And we're supposed to be grateful. I can't recall ever feeling any longing for excitements of this kind. Why didn't
they let me sleep quietly on till everything had calmed
down again? My dear parents could have had a hundred
better children than me. Yet here I am, I don't know how
I got here, and I'm supposed to answer for not having
stayed away.—Haven't you ever wondered, Melchior, how
we got into this whirlpool actually?

MELCHIOR. You still don't know, Moritz?

MORITZ. How should I know?—I see that hens lay eggs, and
I hear that Mama carried me under her heart. Is that
enough? And I can remember even as a child of five feeling embarrassed if anyone turned up the queen of hearts:
she wore a décolleté. That feeling has gone. On the other
hand, today I can scarcely talk to any girl without thinking something disgusting—though, I swear to you, Melchior,
I don't know what.

MELCHIOR. I'll tell you everything.—I got it partly from books,
partly from pictures, partly from observing nature. You'll
be surprised; it made an atheist of me for the time.—I told
Georg Zirschnitz. Georg Zirschnitz wanted to tell Hänschen Rilow but Hänschen learnt it all from his governess
when he was still a kid.

MORITZ. I've been through Meyer's *Lexicon* from A to Z.
Words! Nothing but words! Not one simple explanation. Oh
this sense of shame!—What's the good of an encyclopedia

that doesn't answer the most pertinent question in the world?

MELCHIOR. Have you, for instance, ever seen two dogs run across the street?

MORITZ. No!—— Don't tell me any more today, Melchior. I still have Central America and Louis the Fifteenth to take care of. And on top of that the sixty verses of Homer, the seven equations, the Latin exercise. I'd only flunk everything again tomorrow. To get anywhere with studying, I'll have to develop a thick hide.

MELCHIOR. Come back to my room. In three quarters of an hour I'll whip through the Homer, the equations, and *two* exercises. I'll slip in a few harmless mistakes for you, and the job's done. Mama will make us some of her lemonade, and we'll have a nice relaxed talk about reproduction.

MORITZ. I can't.—I can't relax on a subject like reproduction! If you want to do me a favor, give me your explanations in writing. Write down what you know. Make it as brief and clear as you can and stick it among my books during gym. I'll take it home without knowing I've got it. I'll come upon it unexpectedly. I'll have no choice but to glance through it . . . with a weary eye . . . and if it's absolutely necessary, you could add a few illustrations in the margin.

MELCHIOR. You're like a girl.—But just as you say. It's quite an interesting assignment.—— One question, Moritz.

MORITZ. Hm?

MELCHIOR.—Have you ever *seen* a girl?

MORITZ. Yes, I have!

MELCHIOR. All of her?

MORITZ *nods.*

Me too.—Then illustrations won't be needed.

MORITZ. During the Shooting Contest. In Leilich's Anatomical Museum. If they'd ever found out about it, they'd have thrown me out of school.—Beautiful as sunlight! And quite natural!

MELCHIOR. Last summer I was with mother in Frankfort and——Do you have to be going, Moritz?

MORITZ. Homework!—Good night.

MELCHIOR. So long.

SCENE 3

THEA, WENDLA, *and* MARTHA *come up the street arm in arm.*

MARTHA. How the water gets into your shoes!

WENDLA. How the wind whistles about your cheeks!

THEA. How your heart beats!

WENDLA. Let's go out to the bridge. Ilse says the river's sweeping plants and trees along. The boys have a raft on the water. They say Melchi Gabor nearly got drowned last night.

THEA. Oh, he can swim.

MARTHA. I should say so!

WENDLA. If he hadn't been able to, he'd have drowned.

THEA. Your braid's coming undone, Martha, your braid's coming undone!

MARTHA. Pooh, let it! It's a nuisance—all day and all night. I'm not allowed to wear my hair short like yours or loose like Wendla's. I can't wear bangs. I have to braid it even at home. All because of my aunts.

WENDLA. I'll bring a pair of scissors to Bible class tomorrow. And while we're reciting "Happy is he that walketh" I'll cut it off.

MARTHA. For heaven's sake, Wendla! Papa would beat me black and blue, and Mama would lock me in the coalhole three nights on end.

WENDLA. What does he beat you with, Martha?

MARTHA. I sometimes think they'd feel something was missing if they didn't have a little mess like me for a daughter.

THEA. But Martha!

MARTHA. Some of you were allowed to thread a blue ribbon through the yoke of your nightdress, weren't you?

THEA. Mine's pink satin! Mama maintains that pink suits me —with my coal-black eyes.

MARTHA. Blue looked so lovely on me!—Mama pulled me out

of bed by my braids. I fell on the floor with my hands out like this.—Mama prays with us every evening . . .

WENDLA. If I were you I'd have run away long ago.

MARTHA. . . . "So that's it, that's what you have in mind!" she says. "Well, I just wanted to see it, I just wanted to see it. At least," says she, "you'll have nothing to reproach your mother with later . . ."

THEA. Oh, won't you?

MARTHA. Can you imagine what mother meant by that, Thea?

THEA. I can't.—Can you, Wendla?

WENDLA. I'd have asked her.

MARTHA. I lay on the floor and shrieked and yelled. Enter papa. Rip! Off comes my nightdress! I head for the door. "So that's it," he shouts, "you'd like to go out like that, wouldn't you?"

WENDLA. Oh, now you're telling stories, Martha!

MARTHA. It was freezing. I went back in. I had to spend the whole night on the floor in a sack.

THEA. I could never sleep in a sack as long as I live.

WENDLA. I'd be glad to sleep in your sack for you.

MARTHA. It's only the beatings . . .

THEA. Oh, it's enough to stifle you to death.

MARTHA. Your head sticks out. You tie the sack under your chin.

THEA. And then they beat you?

MARTHA. No. Only when there's something special.

WENDLA. What do they beat you with, Martha?

MARTHA. Oh, I don't know. Anything.—Does *your* mother think it's indecent to eat a piece of bread in bed?

WENDLA. Oh no!

MARTHA. I suppose they have fun, though they never mention it.—If I ever have children I'll let them grow like the weeds in our flower garden. No one bothers about them, and they're so thick, so tall, while the roses—staked out in those beds—bloom more miserably every summer.

THEA. If I have children I'll dress them all in pink. Pink hats, pink dresses, pink shoes. Only the stockings—the stockings shall be as black as night. And when I take them out I'll make them all walk in front of me.—What about you, Wendla?

WENDLA. You both know if you're going to have some?

THEA. Why shouldn't we have some?

MARTHA. Well, Aunt Euphemia hasn't got any.

THEA. Because she's not *married*, silly!

WENDLA. My Aunt Bauer's been married three times and hasn't got a single one.

MARTHA. If you have some, Wendla, which would you rather have, boys or girls?

WENDLA. Boys! Boys!

THEA. Boys for me too!

MARTHA. Me too! I'd rather have twenty boys than three girls.

THEA. Girls are boring.

MARTHA. If I hadn't been a girl up to now I certainly wouldn't want to become one.

WENDLA. I think that's a matter of taste, Martha! I give thanks every day that I'm a girl. Believe me, I wouldn't change places with a king's son.—I want to *have* sons!

THEA. That's a lot of nonsense, Wendla, just nonsense!

WENDLA. But surely, Thea, it must be a thousand times more inspiring to be loved by a man than by a girl!

THEA. You don't mean to tell me Forestry Commissioner Pfälle loves Melitta more than she loves him?

WENDLA. I certainly do, Thea.—Pfälle's proud. Pfälle is proud of being Forestry Commissioner, he doesn't have money.— Melitta is radiantly happy because she gets ten thousand times more than she gives.

MARTHA. Aren't you proud—of yourself, Wendla?

WENDLA. That would be foolish.

MARTHA. How proud *I'd* be in your shoes!

THEA. Just see how she places her feet, how she looks straight ahead, how she carries herself, Martha!—If that isn't pride!

WENDLA. But what for? I'm so happy to be a girl. If I weren't a girl I'd kill myself—so that the next time . . .

MELCHIOR *passes and greets them.*

THEA. He has a marvelous head.

MARTHA. That's how I picture the young Alexander when he was a pupil of Aristotle's.

THEA. Oh Lord, Greek history! All I can remember is how Socrates lay in the barrel when Alexander sold him the ass's shadow.

WENDLA. He's supposed to be third in his class.

THEA. Professor Knochenbruch says if he wanted to he could be first.

MARTHA. He has a lovely forehead, but his friend has a more spiritual look.

THEA. Moritz Stiefel?—*He'll* never be anybody!

MARTHA. I've always got on with him quite well.

THEA. He embarrasses you when you meet him. At the children's party the Rilows gave he offered me some chocolates. Just imagine, Wendla, they were soft and warm! Isn't that . . . ?—He said he'd had them too long in his trouser pocket!

WENDLA. Just think, Melchi Gabor told me that night he didn't believe in anything: God, an afterlife, or anything at all.

SCENE 4

A park in front of the school.—MELCHIOR, OTTO, GEORG, ROBERT, HÄNSCHEN RILOW, LÄMMERMEIER.

MELCHIOR. Can any of you tell me where Moritz Stiefel's hiding?

GEORG. He's headed for trouble. Oh, he's headed for trouble!

OTTO. He goes on and on till he's in the soup!

LÄMMERMEIER. A little bird tells me I wouldn't care to be in that man's shoes!

ROBERT. What a nerve!—What absolute gall!

MELCHIOR. Wha . . . wha . . . what is it you all know?

GEORG. What do we know?—Well, let's see—

LÄMMERMEIER. I'm not talking.

OTTO. Nor me. Good God!

MELCHIOR. If you don't tell me right now . . .

ROBERT. In short: Moritz Stiefel got into the Faculty Room.

MELCHIOR. The Faculty Room?

OTTO. The Faculty Room. Right after the Latin class.

GEORG. He was the last. He stayed behind on purpose.

LÄMMERMEIER. As I turned the corner I saw him open the door.

MELCHIOR. The devil take it . . . !

LÄMMERMEIER. If only the devil doesn't take *him!*

GEORG. The Rektor must've forgotten to take the key away.

ROBERT. Or else Moritz Stiefel has a skeleton key.

OTTO. I wouldn't put it past him.

LÄMMERMEIER. At best, he'll be kept in on Sunday afternoon.

ROBERT. Also a remark on his report card!

OTTO. Provided he isn't kicked out—with the report *he'll* get.

HÄNSCHEN RILOW. There he is.

MELCHIOR. White as a sheet.

Enter MORITZ, *greatly agitated.*

LÄMMERMEIER. Moritz, Moritz, what you have done!

MORITZ.——Nothing——Nothing——

ROBERT. You're feverish!

MORITZ.—With happiness—bliss—jubilation—

OTTO. Did they catch you?

MORITZ. I've got my promotion!—Melchior, I've got my promotion!—Now the world can come to an end!—I've got my promotion!—Who would have thought I'd get my promotion?—I can't take it in even now!—I've read it twenty times.—I can't believe it—great God, it was still there, it was still there! I'VE GOT MY PROMOTION!
Smiling.
I don't know—I feel so strange—the ground's going up and

down . . . Melchior, Melchior, if you knew what I've been through!

HÄNSCHEN RILOW. Congratulations, Moritz.—Be glad you got away with it.

MORITZ. You've no idea how much was at stake, Hänschen, how could you? For the past three weeks I've been slinking past that door as if it was the jaws of Hell. And then today, there it was, unlocked. I think if someone had offered me a million—no, nothing could have stopped me!—So there I am in the middle of the room, I open the register, turn the pages, find the place—and the whole time . . . it makes me shudder—

MELCHIOR. . . . The whole time what?

MORITZ. The whole time the door was standing wide open behind me. How I got out . . . how I got down the stairs I don't know.

HÄNSCHEN RILOW.—Has Ernst Röbel got his promotion too?

MORITZ. Oh, surely, Hänschen, surely! Ernst Röbel is up too!

ROBERT. That just shows you must have read the thing wrong. Not counting the dunce's bench, with you and Röbel we come to sixty-one, and the classroom upstairs won't hold more than sixty.

MORITZ. I read it right! Ernst Röbel is just as much going up as I am. But for both of us it's only provisional. The first term is supposed to decide which of us must give up his place to the other.—Poor Röbel!—Heaven knows I no longer fear for myself. I've been looking too deep into things for that!

OTTO. I bet you five marks you'll give up the place.

MORITZ. You haven't a penny, and I wouldn't want to rob you. —God, how I'll grind from now on. Now I can tell you all —whether you believe it or not—nothing matters any more— I—I know how true it is: if I didn't get my promotion I was going to shoot myself!

ROBERT. Show-off!

GEORG. Yellow-belly!

OTTO. I'd like to see you shoot *anything!*

LÄMMERMEIER. I bet you a smack in the eye.

MELCHIOR, *gives him one.*——Come on, Moritz. Let's go to the keeper's cottage.

GEORG. You don't mean you believe that stuff?

MELCHIOR. Mind your business.——Let them gab, Moritz. Let's get out! Into the town!

PROFESSORS HUNGERGURT *and* KNOCHENBRUCH *pass by.*

KNOCHENBRUCH. That my best student should feel himself attracted to my worst is quite incomprehensible to me, dear colleague.

HUNGERGURT. To me also, dear colleague.

SCENE 5

A sunny afternoon. MELCHIOR *and* WENDLA *meet in the forest.*

MELCHIOR. Is it really you, Wendla?—What are you doing all alone up here?—I've been roaming all over the forest for the last three hours without meeting a soul and suddenly *you* pop out of the thickest thicket!

WENDLA. Yes, it's me.

MELCHIOR. If I didn't know you were Wendla Bergmann I'd take you for a dryad fallen from the branches!

WENDLA. No, no, I'm Wendla Bergmann.—What are you doing here?

MELCHIOR. Having my own thoughts.

WENDLA. I'm looking for woodruff. Mama wants to make May wine. At first she wanted to come too, but at the last moment my Aunt Bauer paid us a visit, and she doesn't like to walk uphill.—So I came by myself.

MELCHIOR. Did you find your woodruff?

WENDLA. A basketful. Over there under the bushes it's as thick as clover.—As a matter of fact, I'm looking for a way out, I seem to have got lost. Can you tell me what time it is?

MELCHIOR. Just after half past three.—When are they expecting you?

WENDLA. I thought it was later. I lay a long time in the moss by the stream, just dreaming. The time went so fast. I was afraid evening might be coming on.

MELCHIOR. If they're not expecting you yet, let's lie here a bit longer. Under the oak tree there is my favorite spot. If you lean your head back against the trunk and look up at the sky through the branches you're hypnotized. The ground is still warm from the morning sun.—I've been wanting to ask you something for weeks, Wendla.

WENDLA. But I must be home by five.

MELCHIOR. We'll go together. I'll carry the basket, we'll take the path through the gully, and in ten minutes we'll be on the bridge!—When you lie here with your forehead on your hands you have the strangest thoughts . . .

Both lie down under the oak.

WENDLA. What did you want to ask me, Melchior?

MELCHIOR. I heard that you often visit the poor, Wendla. That you take them food and clothes and money. Do you do it of your own accord, or does your mother send you?

WENDLA. Usually mother sends me. They're poor day laborers with a mob of children. Often the man can't find work, and they go cold and hungry. At home we've got all sorts of things in closets and chests, things we don't use, that are just piling up . . . But what made you think of it?

MELCHIOR. When your mother sends you somewhere like that do you like to go or not?

WENDLA. I love to go, of course!—How can you ask?

MELCHIOR. The children are dirty, the women are ill, their houses are full of vermin, the men hate you because you don't work . . .

WENDLA. That's not true, Melchior. And if it was, all the more reason for me to go.

MELCHIOR. What makes you say that, Wendla?

WENDLA.—It would make me even happier to be able to do something for them.

MELCHIOR. So you visit the poor for your own pleasure?

WENDLA. I visit them because they're poor.

MELCHIOR. But would you go if it didn't give you pleasure?

WENDLA. Can I help it if it gives me pleasure?

MELCHIOR. At that you get yourself into heaven by it.—It's true, then, this thought that's been eating at me for the past month.—Can a man help it if he's closefisted and it *doesn't* give him pleasure to visit dirty, sick children?

WENDLA. It would certainly give you a lot of pleasure!

MELCHIOR. He's supposed to die an eternal death because it doesn't.—I shall write a treatise and send it to Pastor Kahlbauch. He's the cause of it all. How he drools about the joys of self-sacrifice!—If he can't answer me I shall stop going to catechism class, I shall refuse to be confirmed.

WENDLA. Why hurt your parents like that? Go through with your confirmation. It won't cost you your head. If it wasn't for our horrid white dresses and your long pants it could even be something to get excited about.

MELCHIOR. There's no such thing as sacrifice! No such thing as unselfishness!—I see the virtuous rejoicing and the wicked trembling and groaning—I see you, Wendla Bergmann, shaking your curls and laughing, and I can't join in because I feel like an outlaw!——What were you dreaming of just now, Wendla, in the grass by the stream?

WENDLA.——Nonsense—foolishness—

MELCHIOR. With your eyes open?

WENDLA. I dreamt I was a poor, poor beggar child. I was sent into the streets at five in the morning. I had to beg all day, in rain and storm, among rough hardhearted people, and if I came home in the evening, shivering with hunger and cold, and didn't bring as much money as my father expected, I'd get beaten—beaten—

MELCHIOR. I know all about that, Wendla. You have those stupid children's stories to thank for it. Believe me, such brutal people don't exist any more.

WENDLA. They do, Melchior, you're wrong.—Martha Bessel is beaten night after night. Next day you can see the welts. What she must have to suffer! It makes your blood boil to hear her talk about it. I pity her so, I often cry into my pillow in the middle of the night. I've been wondering for months how we could help her. I'd gladly take her place for a week or so.

MELCHIOR. Someone should report her father. They'd take the girl away from him.

WENDLA. I've never been beaten in my life, Melchior. Not once. I can hardly imagine what it's like to be beaten. I've tried beating myself to find out how it feels inside.—It must be a shuddery sensation.

MELCHIOR. I don't believe a child is ever the better for it.

WENDLA. Better for what?

MELCHIOR. For being beaten.

WENDLA.—With this switch for instance?—Phew, it's thin and tough!

MELCHIOR. It would draw blood.

WENDLA. Wouldn't you like to hit me with it once?

MELCHIOR. Hit who?

WENDLA. Hit me.

MELCHIOR. What's got into you, Wendla?

WENDLA. I bet there's nothing to it.

MELCHIOR. Oh, don't worry, I *won't* hit you.

WENDLA. Not if I let you?

MELCHIOR. Never, girl.

WENDLA. Not if I ask you to, Melchior?

MELCHIOR. Are you out of your mind?

WENDLA. I've never been beaten in my life.

MELCHIOR. If you can *ask* for a thing like that . . .

WENDLA. Please! Please!

MELCHIOR. I'll teach you to say please!

He beats her.

WENDLA. Oh dear, I don't feel a thing!

MELCHIOR. I believe you. With all those skirts on.

WENDLA. Then hit me on the legs.

MELCHIOR. Wendla!

He hits her harder.

WENDLA. You're just stroking me!—You're stroking me!

MELCHIOR. Just wait, you little witch, I'll beat the hell out of
    you!

*He throws the branch away and pommels her with his fists
till she breaks out in fearful yelling. Not in the least de-
terred, he lets fly at her in a rage, while his tears run down
his cheeks. Suddenly he springs upright, clasps his temples
with both hands, and plunges into the forest sobbing piti-
fully and from the depths of his soul.*

ACT TWO

SCENE 1

Evening in MELCHIOR's *study. The window is open. There is a lighted lamp on the table.—*MELCHIOR *and* MORITZ *on the sofa.*

MORITZ. Now I'm quite cheerful again, only a little excited.— But in the Greek class I slept like the drunken Polyphemus. I'm surprised old Zungenschlag didn't pull my ears.—This morning I was within an inch of being late.—My first thought on waking was of the verbs in *mi.* Christ Almighty, Hell and Damnation—all during breakfast and on the way to school I was conjugating till my head swam.—I must have dropped off just after three. On top of everything, my pen had made a blot on the book. The lamp was smoking when Mathilda woke me. The thrushes were twittering in the lilac bushes below, so glad to be alive, and I started feeling indescribably melancholy again. I put my collar on and drew the brush through my hair.——But you feel so good when you've won a victory over yourself!

MELCHIOR. May I roll you a cigarette?

MORITZ. Thank you, I don't smoke.—If only I can go on like this! I mean to work and work till my eyes pop out of my head.—Ernst Röbel has already failed six times since the vacation, three times in Greek, twice with Knochenbruch, and the last time in Lit. I've only been in that unfortunate situation five times, and from now on it's not going to happen again!—Röbel won't shoot himself. Röbel hasn't got parents who are sacrificing their all for him. He can be a mercenary if he wants to, or a sailor or a cowboy. If *I* don't get through, Papa will have a stroke and Mama will go to the madhouse. That's more than a fellow could bear.—Before the exam I asked God to make me consumptive so that the cup might pass from me. It *has* passed. But even now it kind of glimmers at me from a distance, so I don't dare to raise my eyes, day or night.—Having taken hold of the pole I'll hoist myself up all right. My surety for that is the inescapable fact that I can't fall without breaking my neck.

MELCHIOR. Life's meaner than one could ever have expected. I wouldn't mind hanging myself from a branch.—Where can Mama be with the tea!

MORITZ. Your tea will do me good, Melchior. I'm trembling. I feel so strangely disembodied. Just touch me. I see—I hear —I feel much more clearly—and yet everything's so like a dream—there's such an atmosphere.—The way the park stretches away in the moonlight—so still, so deep, as if into infinity. Dim figures step out from behind bushes, scurry with breathless haste across the clearings, and disappear into the semi-darkness. It seems to me there's a council meeting on under the chestnut tree.—Shall we go down, Melchior?

MELCHIOR. Let's wait till we've had our tea.

MORITZ.—The leaves are whispering so busily.—It's like hearing Grandmother happily telling the story of the queen that had no head.—She was a fabulously beautiful queen, beautiful as the sun, more beautiful than any other girl in the country. Only she'd had the bad luck to be born without a head. She couldn't eat or drink, couldn't see or laugh, she couldn't kiss. She was able to communicate with her attendants only by means of her soft little hand. With her delicate feet she tapped out declarations of war and sentences of death. Then one day she was conquered by a king who happened to have two heads that got in each other's hair all the year round and quarreled so excitedly that neither let the other get a word in edgewise. So the chief court magician took the smaller of the two heads and placed it on the queen. "And lo! It became her passing well." Whereupon the king married the queen, and the two heads no longer got in each other's hair but kissed each other on brow, cheeks, and lips, and lived many years in happiness and joy. . . . What damn nonsense! Since the vacation I can't get the headless queen out of my head. If I see a beautiful girl, I see her without a head, then suddenly I myself seem to be a headless queen. . . . Perhaps I'll get me another head, though.

Enter MRS. GABOR *with the steaming tea, which she places on the table in front of* MORITZ *and* MELCHIOR.

MRS. GABOR. Here you are, boys, I hope you enjoy it.—Hello, Mr. Stiefel, how are you?

MORITZ. Fine, thanks, Mrs. Gabor.—I was just listening to the goings-on down in the park.

MRS. GABOR. You don't look at all well.—Are you feeling ill?

MORITZ. It doesn't mean a thing. I've been to bed rather late the last few times.

MELCHIOR. Just think: he worked all through the night.

MRS. GABOR. But you shouldn't do such things, Mr. Stiefel. You must look after yourself. Consider your health. School is no substitute for health.—Plenty of walks in the fresh air! At your age that's more important than accuracy in Middle High German!

MORITZ. I'll take plenty of walks. You're right. And one can work while walking. Why didn't I think of that myself?— Even so, I'd have the written work to do at home.

MELCHIOR. You can do the written work with me; that will make it easier for us both.—Did you know Max von Trenk has died of brain fever, Mama?—This morning Hänschen Rilow came to Rektor Sonnenstich from Trenk's deathbed. To report that Max had just died in his presence.—"Really?" said Sonnenstich, "don't you still have two hours' detention to do from last week?—Here's the ticket for the school porter. See to it that the matter is finally settled! The whole class will attend the funeral!"—Hänschen was stunned.

MRS. GABOR. What's that book you have there, Melchior?

MELCHIOR. *Faust.*

MRS. GABOR. Have you read it?

MELCHIOR. Not to the end.

MORITZ. We're in the Walpurgisnacht scene.

MRS. GABOR. If I were your age, I'd have waited another year or two.

MELCHIOR. I never found so much in a book before, Mama. It's beautiful. Why shouldn't I read it?

MRS. GABOR.—Because you don't understand it.

MELCHIOR. You can't know that, Mama. I realize I'm in no position to get all the . . . grandeur of it—

MORITZ. We always read together. Amazing how much more you understand.

MRS. GABOR. You're old enough to know what's good for you, Melchior. Do whatever you can answer to yourself for. I shall be the first to welcome the time when you give me no further reason to hold things back.—I only wanted to point out that even the best can be dangerous when one lacks the maturity to interpret it correctly.—But I'd always rather put my trust in *you* than in "disciplinary measures." ——If either of you need anything else, come over and call me, Melchior. I'll be in my bedroom.

Exit.

MORITZ.—Your mother means the business with Gretchen.

MELCHIOR. Why, we only spent half a second on it.

MORITZ. Faust himself can scarcely have dismissed it more cold-bloodedly.

MELCHIOR. After all, artistically speaking, this outrage isn't the high point of the play.—Suppose Faust just promised to marry the girl and then left her; as I see it he wouldn't be a bit less to blame. As far as I'm concerned, Gretchen could die of a broken heart.—To see the frantic way everyone always fastens on to the subject, you'd think the world revolved around penis and vagina.

MORITZ. To be quite frank, Melchior, since I read your essay, I feel that it does.—It fell at my feet in the first days of the vacation. I had Ploetz's *History* in my hand.—I bolted the door and skimmed through the flickering lines as a frightened owl flies through a burning forest.—I think I read most of it with my eyes shut. Your explanations sounded like a series of dim recollections, like a song that one had hummed happily to oneself as a child and then heard on the lips of another as one lay dying. Heartbreaking!—I was the most strongly affected by what you wrote about girls.

I can't get rid of the impression it made. Believe me, Melchior, to have to suffer wrong is sweeter than to do wrong. To have to let oneself undergo so sweet a wrong undeservedly seems to me the essence of all earthly bliss.

MELCHIOR.—I don't want my bliss given to me as charity.

MORITZ. But why not?

MELCHIOR. I don't *want* anything I haven't had to fight for.

MORITZ. Can you still call that enjoyment, Melchior?—Girls enjoy themselves, Melchior, like the gods in *their* bliss. And a girl's nature is self-protective. A girl keeps herself free of everything bitter till the last moment, and then has the pleasure of seeing all heaven break over her. She hasn't stopped fearing hell when suddenly she notices paradise in full bloom. Her feelings are as fresh as water springing from the rock. She takes up a chalice, a goblet of nectar, which no earthly breath has yet blown upon and—even as it flickers and flares—drains it! By comparison, a man's satisfaction seems to me shallow, stagnant.

MELCHIOR. Think of it as you like, only keep it to yourself.— I don't like to think of it . . .

SCENE 2

A living room.

MRS. BERGMANN, *her hat on, a shawl around her shoulders and a basket on her arm, enters through the center door with a beaming face.* Wendla!—Wendla!

WENDLA, *appears in her bodice and petticoat at the side door, right.* What is it, Mother?

MRS. BERGMANN. You're up already, child?—That's a good girl!

WENDLA. Have you been out already?

MRS. BERGMANN. Be quick and get dressed, you must go down to Ina's. You must take her this basket!

WENDLA, *dressing herself completely in the course of what follows.* You were at Ina's?—How is Ina?—Still no better?

MRS. BERGMANN. Just think, Wendla, the stork paid Ina a visit last night. Brought her a little boy.

WENDLA. A boy?—A boy!—Oh, that's wonderful!——*That* explains the never-ending influenza!

MRS. BERGMANN. A splendid boy!

WENDLA. I must see him, Mother!—So I'm an aunt for the third time—aunt to a girl and two boys!

MRS. BERGMANN. And what boys!—That's what comes of living so near the church!—It's only two and a half years ago that she went up the altar steps in her muslin dress.

WENDLA. Were you there when it brought him?

MRS. BERGMANN. It had just flown away.—Wouldn't you like to pin a rose on your dress?

WENDLA. Why didn't you get there a little sooner, Mother?

MRS. BERGMANN. I think he brought something for you too—a brooch or something.

WENDLA. It's a real shame.

MRS. BERGMANN. But I'm telling you he brought you a brooch!

WENDLA. I have enough brooches . . .

MRS. BERGMANN. Then be satisfied, child. What else do you want?

WENDLA. I should so terribly like to know whether he flew through the window or down the chimney.

MRS. BERGMANN. You must ask Ina. Ha, ha, you must ask Ina, dear heart. Ina will give you all details. Ina talked to him a solid half hour.

WENDLA. I shall ask her when I go over.

MRS. BERGMANN. Mind you don't forget, my angel! I should like to know myself whether it came through the window or down the chimney.

WENDLA. Or had I better ask the chimney sweep?—The chimney sweep must know best if it comes down the chimney or not.

MRS. BERGMANN. Not the chimney sweep, child! What does he know of the stork?—He'd tell you all sorts of nonsense he doesn't believe himself. . . . Wh—what are you staring at down in the street?

WENDLA. A man, Mother. And he's three times the size of an ox! With feet like steamboats!

MRS. BERGMANN, *rushing to the window.* Impossible!—Impossible!

WENDLA, *quickly.* He's holding a bedstead under his chin and fiddling "The Watch on the Rhine" on it.——Now he's turning the corner . . .

MRS. BERGMANN. Oh, you're just a big baby still, Wendla. To startle your silly old mother like that!—Come, take your hat. I shall be surprised if you ever learn sense.—I've given up hope.

WENDLA. So have I, Mother darling. It's sad I haven't learned sense.—Here I have a sister married two and a half years. I myself am an aunt three times over. And I haven't the slightest idea how it all comes about. . . . Don't be angry, Mother darling! Who in the world should I ask but you? Please tell me! Tell me, Mother! Don't scold me for asking, I'm ashamed. Just answer. How does it happen?—You can't seriously expect me to believe in the stork—at fourteen.

MRS. BERGMANN. Good gracious child, the things you think of! —I really couldn't!

WENDLA. Why not?—It can't be nasty when everyone is so pleased about it.

MRS. BERGMANN. Oh—oh God preserve me! I'd deserve to be . . . Go and put on your coat, girl, put on your coat.

WENDLA. I'm going . . . What if your daughter goes and asks the chimney sweep?

MRS. BERGMANN. It's enough to drive one crazy!—Come, child, come here. I'll tell you! I'll tell you everything . . . Merciful providence! But not today, Wendla, tomorrow, day after tomorrow, next week. Whenever you like, dear heart . . .

WENDLA. Today. Now. This minute.—Now that I've seen *you* so upset, *I'm* not likely to calm down.

MRS. BERGMANN.—I can't, Wendla.

WENDLA. Why not?—See, I'll kneel at your feet and put my head in your lap. You can put your apron over my head and talk and talk as if you were quite alone. I won't flinch, I won't cry out, I'll take what comes!

MRS. BERGMANN.—Heaven knows it's not my fault, Wendla

. . . Well, I'll tell you how you came into the world.—Are you listening, Wendla?

WENDLA, *under the apron.* I'm listening.

Pause.

MRS. BERGMANN, *beside herself.*—I can't do it.—I couldn't answer for it!—I deserve to be in prison—I deserve to have you taken away from me . . .

WENDLA, *under the apron.* Courage, Mother!

MRS. BERGMANN. Well then, listen . . .

WENDLA, *under the apron, trembling.* Oh dear, oh dear!

MRS. BERGMANN. To have a child—you understand what I'm saying, Wendla?

WENDLA. Quick, Mother, I can't bear it any longer.

MRS. BERGMANN.—To have a child—one must love the man—to whom one is married—love him as only a husband can be loved. One must love him so much, one must love him, Wendla, as you at your age are incapable of loving . . . Now you know.

WENDLA, *getting up.* God in Heaven!

MRS. BERGMANN. Now you know what trials lie before you!

WENDLA.—And that's all?

MRS. BERGMANN. So help me God!——And now take the basket and go over to Ina's. You'll get chocolates and cakes there.—Come, let's have another look at you. Laced boots, silk gloves, sailor blouse, roses in your hair. . . . But that little skirt is definitely too short for you, Wendla.

WENDLA. Have you got the meat for dinner, Mother?

MRS. BERGMANN. May the Lord bless and keep you!—When I have time, I'll put a strip of flouncing on it.

SCENE 3

HÄNSCHEN RILOW, *with a light in his hand, bolts the door behind him and lifts the lid.*

HÄNSCHEN. Hast thou prayed tonight, Desdemona?

He pulls a reproduction of Palma Vecchio's "Venus" out of his shirt.

You don't seem to be at your prayers, fair one—contemplatively awaiting whoever might be coming—as in the sweet moment of dawning bliss when I saw you in Jonathan Schlesinger's shop window—these supple limbs are just as beguiling still, the gentle arch of the hips, these firm young breasts—how intoxicated with happiness the great Master must have been when the fourteen-year-old original lay before his very eyes on the sofa!

Will you also visit me in dreams sometimes?—I'll receive you with outstretched arms and kiss you till your breath gives out. You'll take me over like the rightful mistress entering her deserted castle. The gate and all the doors are opened by unseen hands while the fountain joyously begins to plash in the park below.

"It is the cause!—It is the cause!"—This frightful pounding in my breast tells you how far from frivolously I murder you. My throat contracts at the thought of my solitary nights. By my soul, child, I swear it is not satiety that sways me! Who would dare boast that he was sated with *you?*

But you suck the marrow from my bones, you crook my back, you steal the light from my young eyes.—Your inhuman modesty makes excessive claims upon me. Your unmoving limbs wear me down.—It was you or I; and the victory is mine.

If I were to count them, the dear departed with whom I have fought the same battle here? "Psyche" by Thumann, another legacy from that dried up Mademoiselle Angélique, the rattlesnake in the paradise of my childhood. Correggio's "Io." Lossow's "Galatea." Then a "Cupid" by Bouguereau. "Ada" by J. van Beers—I had to abduct Ada from a secret drawer in father's bureau before I could include her in my harem. A trembling, twitching "Leda" by Makart that I happened on under my brother's school notebooks. Seven! O blooming candidate for death, seven have trod this path to Tartarus before you! Let that be a comfort to you, and do not seek with those looks of supplication to turn my torments to excesses!

You are dying, not for your sins, but for mine.—Only to defend myself from myself do I—with a bleeding heart——

commit this seventh wife-murder. Is there not something tragic in the role of Bluebeard? I believe that all his murdered wives together suffered less than he did strangling any one of them.

But my conscience will rest easier, my body will gain in strength, when you reside no more, you devil, within the red silk cushions of my jewel box. To your place in that voluptuous love-nest I'll admit Bodenhausen's "Lurlei" or Linger's "Forsaken Maiden" or Defregger's "Loni"—they'll help me to recover in short order! Another three months maybe, and your unveiled Jehoshaphat, dear heart, would have begun to eat at my brain like the sun at butter. This separation of bed and board was overdue.

Phew! There's a Heliogabalus in me, I feel it. *Moritura me salutat.*—Girl, girl, why do you press your knees together? —At this late date?—On the threshold of inscrutable eternity? ——One twitch, and I'll release you.—One feminine movement, one sign of lust, of sympathy, my girl, and I'll frame you in gold and hang you over my bed!—Have you no inkling that it's only your chastity that drives me to excesses? —Woe unto ye, inhuman ones!

. . . One never fails to note that she's had an exemplary education.—But then—so have I.

Hast thou prayed tonight, Desdemona?

My heart! I'm having convulsions!—— Nonsense!—St. Agnes also died on account of her abstinence, and she wasn't half as naked as you are!—One more kiss on the blooming body, the budding, child's breast, the sweetly rounded—the cruel knees . . .

It is the cause, it is the cause, my soul.
Let me not name it to you, you chaste stars!
It is the cause!—

The picture falls into the depths. He closes the lid.

SCENE 4

A hayloft.—MELCHIOR *is lying on his back in the new-mown hay.* WENDLA *climbs the ladder.*

WENDLA. So this is where you've crept off to?—Everyone's looking for you. The wagon has gone out again. You must help. A thunderstorm is coming up.

MELCHIOR. Keep away!—Keep away from me!

WENDLA. What's the matter with you?—Why are you hiding your face?

MELCHIOR. Get out of here!—Or I'll throw you down on the threshing floor!

WENDLA. Now I'm certainly not going.

Kneels down beside him.

Why don't you come with us to the meadows, Melchior?— It's dark and stuffy in here. Even if we do get wet to the skin, what do *we* care!

MELCHIOR. The hay smells so wonderful.—The sky must be as black as a pall.—All I can see is the poppy gleaming at your breast—and I can hear your heart beating—

WENDLA.——Don't kiss me, Melchior!—Don't kiss me!

MELCHIOR.—Your heart—I hear it beating—

WENDLA. People love each other—if they kiss — — — — — don't, don't——

MELCHIOR. There is no such thing as love! That's a fact.—It's all just selfishness and self-seeking.—I love you as little as you love me.—

WENDLA.——Don't!——Don't, Melchior!——

MELCHIOR.——Wendla!

WENDLA. Oh, Melchior! — — — — — — — don't — — don't — —

SCENE 5

MRS. GABOR, *seated, writing.*

MRS. GABOR.

Dear Mr. Stiefel,

Having for twenty-four hours considered and reconsidered all that you have written to me, I take up my pen with a heavy heart. I am unable, I give you my sacred word on it, to provide you with the cost of a passage to America. I have not so much money at my disposal, and even if I had, it

would be the greatest conceivable sin to place in your hand
the means of acting on a sudden whim so grave in its consequences. You would do me a bitter injustice, Mr. Stiefel,
if you were to attribute this refusal to lack of love. On the
other hand, it would be the most brutal violation of my
duty as a motherly friend were I to let myself be persuaded
by your temporary loss of control into losing my own head
and blindly following my own first impulse. Should you
wish it, I will gladly write to your parents. I will try to
convince them that in the course of the term you have done
all you could. You have so used up your strength——I shall
point out——that a strict judgment on your failure would be
not only unjustifiable but in the highest degree prejudicial
to your mental and physical health.

Frankly, Mr. Stiefel, your veiled threats to take your own
life, should you be refused the means of escape, have
slightly alienated my sympathies. Let a misfortune be never
so undeserved, one should not permit oneself to be driven
to forbidden measures. The way in which you seek to make
me, who have never shown you anything but good will, responsible for a possible dreadful misdeed on your part could
all too easily be interpreted by the hostile as attempted
blackmail. I must confess that such behavior in you, who
otherwise seem so aware of your duty to yourself, is the last
thing I would have expected. Meanwhile, I am firmly convinced that you were too much under the influence of the
initial fright to be fully aware of what you were doing.

And so I confidently hope that these words of mine will find
you already in a more controlled frame of mind. Accept
the matter as it stands. In my opinion, it is quite impermis-
sible to judge a young man by his school reports. We have
too many examples of very bad students making splendid
people, and on the other hand of excellent students acquit-
ting themselves indifferently in life. At all events, I give you
my assurance that, as far as it lies in my power, your failure
shall change nothing in your relationship with Melchior. It
will always be a pleasure to me to see my son associating
with a young man who, however the world may judge him,
has been able to win my fullest sympathy.

So, chin up, Mr. Stiefel!—Such crises of one kind or another
confront each of us and must be overcome. If everyone
had recourse to poison or the dagger there would soon be
no human beings left in the world. Let me hear from you
again soon. With warmest greetings from your still devoted
motherly friend,

Fanny G.

SCENE 6

The BERGMANNS' garden in the morning sunlight.

WENDLA. Why did you slip out of the room?—To look for violets!—Because Mother can see me smiling.—Why can't you
keep your lips together?—I don't know.—I really don't know,
I can't find the words . . .

The path is like a plush carpet—not a pebble, not a thorn.
—My feet don't touch the ground. . . . Oh, how sweetly I
slept last night!

This is where they were.—I feel as solemn as a nun at Com-
munion.—Sweet violets!—All right, Mother dear, I'm ready
now for the penitential robe.—Oh God, if only someone
would come that I could embrace, that I could tell the
whole story to!

SCENE 7

*Dusk. The sky is slightly overcast. The path winds through
low brush and reeds. From a little distance the murmur of
the river can be heard.*

MORITZ. It's better this way.—I don't belong. Let the rest of
them knock their heads together.—I'll close the door behind
me and step out in the open.—Pay for the privilege of being
kicked around? I never pushed before. Why should I now?
—I've signed no contract with the Almighty. People will
make of this what they want to make of it. I've been driven
to it.—I don't hold my parents responsible. All the same
they must have been prepared for the worst. They were old
enough to know what they were doing. I was an infant
when I came into the world, or no doubt I'd have been

smart enough to become someone else.—Why should I suffer because everyone else was already there?

One would have to be a perfect fool . . . if someone makes me a present of a mad dog I give him his mad dog back again. And if he doesn't want to take his mad dog back, well, I'm human, and . . .

One would have to be a perfect fool.

One is born entirely by chance. And if, after mature consideration——oh, it's enough to make one want to shoot oneself!

—At least the weather's being considerate. It's been looking like rain all day, but it's kept fine after all.—An unusual peace reigns. In all Nature, not a discordant note. Earth and sky—one transparent cobweb. Everything seems to be feeling fine. The whole landscape's as sweet as a lullaby. "Sleep, princeling, sleep," as Fräulein Snandulia sang. Pity she holds her elbows so ungracefully.—— The last time I danced was at the party on St. Cecilia's day. Fräulein Snandulia only dances with "eligible" men. Her silk dress was cut low back and front. Down to her belt behind and, in front, so low you could almost pass out.—She couldn't have been wearing a slip . . .

— —

—That might be something that could still hold me.—More for curiosity's sake.—It must be an extraordinary sensation ——it must feel like being swept away by a torrent——I won't tell anyone I've returned with the job not done. I shall act as if I've taken part . . . There's something to be ashamed of in having been human without getting to know the most human thing of all.—You were in Egypt, dear sir, and did not see the Pyramids?—

I mustn't cry again today. I mustn't think of my funeral. ——Melchior will put a wreath on my coffin. Pastor Kahlbauch will condole with my parents. Rektor Sonnenstich will cite examples from history.—I don't suppose they'll give me a gravestone. I should have liked a snow-white marble urn on a column of black granite—fortunately I won't miss it. Memorials are for the living, not the dead.

I'd need a year to say good-by to everyone in my thoughts.

I mustn't cry again. I'm glad to be able to look back without bitterness. How many happy evenings I've spent with Melchior!—under the willows on the riverbank; at the keeper's cottage; out on the military road where the five lindens are; on the hillside among the peaceful ruins of the Runenburg.——When the time comes, I'll think as hard as I can of whipped cream. It won't hold me up, but it's filling and the aftertaste is pleasant . . . And I thought human beings were a lot worse too. Never found one that wouldn't have wished to do his best. I pitied many—on my own account.

I proceed to the altar like the young man in ancient Etruria whose death rattle purchased his brothers' good fortune in the coming year.—I savor the mysterious terrors of parting, drop by drop. I sob with grief at this my destiny.——Life has given me the cold shoulder. From the other side, kind, grave faces beckon: the headless queen, the headless queen —sympathy awaiting me with soft arms . . . Your commandments are for minors. I have a complimentary ticket in my heart. If you put down the cup, off flies the butterfly, and the mirage stops giving trouble.—But why must you all play fast and loose with the deception?—The mists dissolve. Life is a matter of taste.

ILSE, *her clothes torn, a colored kerchief on her head, grabs him by the shoulder from behind.* What have you lost?

MORITZ. Ilse!

ILSE. What are you looking for here?

MORITZ. Why did you give me such a fright?

ILSE. What are you looking for?—What have you lost?

MORITZ. Why did you frighten me so dreadfully?

ILSE. I've come from the town. I'm going home.

MORITZ. I don't know what I've lost.

ILSE. Then looking for it won't help.

MORITZ. Hell, hell, hell!

ILSE. I haven't been home in four days.

MORITZ.—And quiet as a cat!

ILSE. Because I'm wearing my ballet slippers.—Mother's eyes

will pop when she sees me.—Come with me as far as our house!

MORITZ. Where've you been loafing this time?

ILSE. In the Priapia.

MORITZ. Priapia?

ILSE. At Nohl's, at Fehrendorf's, at Padinsky's, at Lenz's, Rank's, Spühler's—everybody.—Will she be mad? Wow!

MORITZ. Are they painting you?

ILSE. Fehrendorf is painting me as a saint on a pillar. I stand on a Corinthian column. Fehrendorf is a real nut, let me tell you. Last time I trod on one of his tubes of paint. So he wipes his brush in my hair. I give him a whack on the ear. He throws his palette at my head. I upset his easel. He comes after me with his mahlstick, over sofas, tables, chairs, all around the studio. Behind the stove I found a sketch. "Be good, or I tear it up!"—He called a truce and in the end kissed me something terrible—absolutely terrible.

MORITZ. Where do you spend the night when you stay in town?

ILSE. Yesterday we were at Nohl's—day before yesterday at Boyokevich's—Sunday at Oikonomopulos's. At Padinsky's there was champagne. Valabregez had sold his "Sick with the Plague." Adolar drank from the ash tray. Lenz sang "She Murdered Her Child," and Adolar played the guitar to shreds. I was so drunk they had to carry me to bed.—— You still going to school, Moritz?

MORITZ. No, no . . . I'm leaving this term.

ILSE. Quite right, too. Goodness, how time flies when one's earning a living!—Do you remember how we used to play robbers—Wendla Bergmann and you and I and the others? You'd come over in the evening and drink milk fresh from the goat?—What's Wendla doing? I saw her lately watching the floods.—What's Melchi Gabor doing?—Does he still look so solemn?—We used to stand opposite each other in singing lesson.

MORITZ. He philosophizes.

ILSE. Wendla came over not long ago and brought Mother some jam. I was sitting that day for Isidore Landauer. He's using me as Holy Mary, Mother of God, with the infant Jesus. He's an idiot, and disgusting, too. Ugh, like a weather-cock!—D'you have a hang-over?

MORITZ. From last night!—We soused like hippopotami. I came reeling home about five o'clock.

ILSE. One need only look at you.—Any girls there?

MORITZ. Arabella, the beer-nymph of Andalusia!—The land-lord left us alone with her all night . . .

ILSE. One has only to look at you, Moritz!—I never had a hang-over in my life. At the last Carnival I didn't go to bed or take my clothes off for three days and three nights. From the ball to the café, afternoons to the Bellavista, evenings to the cabaret, nights to the ball again. Lena was there, and fat Viola.—The third night Heinrich found me.

MORITZ. Was he looking for you?

ILSE. He stumbled over my arm. I'd passed out in the snow on the street.—Then I moved in with him. Didn't leave for fourteen days—a terrible time! Mornings, I had to put on his Persian bathrobe, and, evenings, I had to walk about the room in a black page outfit—white lace at the neck, knees, and sleeves. Every day he photographed me in a different pose—once on the arm of the sofa as Ariadne, once as Leda, once on all fours as a female Nebuchadnezzar. And all the time he raved about killing, about shooting, suicide, gas fumes. In the early morning he'd bring a pistol into bed, fill it with cartridges, and stick it into my chest. "Wink just once, and I fire!"—Oh, and he would have fired, Moritz, he would have!—Then he'd put the thing in his mouth like a blowpipe. To awaken my self-preservation in-stincts. After which—brrrr—he'd have put a bullet right through my spine.

MORITZ. Is Heinrich still alive?

ILSE. How would I know?—There was a mirror in the ceiling over the bed. Made the little room seem high as a tower and brilliant as an opera house. There you are large as life hanging down from the sky! At night I had ghastly dreams. God, O God, would day ever come?—"Good night, Ilse. When you're asleep, you look lovely for murdering!"

MORITZ. Is this Heinrich still alive?

ILSE. I hope to God not!—One day while he was getting some absinthe I threw my coat around me and crept out onto the street. The Carnival was over. The police pick me up and ask me what I'm doing in men's clothes. They take me to the station. Then Nohl came, and Fehrendorf, Padinsky, Spühler, Oikonomopulos, the whole Priapia! They bailed me out. Transported me in a cab to Adolar's studio. Since then I've been faithful to the gang. Fehrendorf is an ape, Nohl is a pig, Boyokevich an owl, Loison a hyena, Oikonomopulos a camel, yet I love them one and all and wouldn't want to be tied to anyone else if the world was full of archangels and millionaires!

MORITZ.—I must go back, Ilse.

ILSE. Come as far as our house!

MORITZ.—What for?—What for?—

ILSE. To drink warm goat's milk.—I'll curl your hair for you and hang a little bell round your neck.—And we still have a rocking horse you can play with.

MORITZ. I must go back.—I've still got the Sassanids, the Sermon on the Mount, and the parallelepipedon on my conscience.—Good night, Ilse!

ILSE. Sweet dreams! . . . D'you all still go to the wigwam where Melchi Gabor buried my tomahawk?—Brrr! By the time any of you are ready, I'll be on the rubbish heap.

Rushes away.

MORITZ, *alone.* ——A single word would have done it.—

He shouts.

—Ilse!—Ilse!——Thank God she can't hear now.

—I'm not in the mood.—You have to have a clear head and feel good.—A pity to miss such a chance, though, a great pity!

. . . I'll say I had great crystal mirrors over my bed—trained an unruly filly—made her strut across the carpet before me in long, black, silk stockings and black patent-leather shoes and long, black, kid gloves and black velvet round her neck —stifled her with my pillow in a sudden attack of madness . . . when the talk is of lust I shall smile . . . I shall—

SCREAM! I SHALL SCREAM!—TO BE YOU, ILSE!
——PRIAPIA!—UNCONSCIOUSNESS!—IT SAPS MY
STRENGTH!—THIS CHILD OF FORTUNE, CHILD OF
SUNSHINE, DAUGHTER OF JOY UPON MY WAY OF
SORROWS!——OH!—OH!

— —
— —

In the bushes on the riverbank.

How did I get back here? That grassy bank. The king's-
tapers[1] seem to have grown since yesterday. The view
through the willows is the same though.—How sluggish the
river is—like molten lead.—Don't let me forget . . .

He takes FRAU GABOR's *letter from his pocket and burns it.*

—Look at those sparks! "In and out and roundabout!"—
Ghosts!—Shooting stars!—

Before I lit that match, you could still see the grass and a
strip of light on the horizon.—It's got dark now. I won't go
home again now.

[1] I have used this rarer name for Great Mulleins because it is so
precise an equivalent of the German *Königskerzen* and preserves
the sexual connotation here and at the end of Act Three, Scene
2. E.B.

ACT THREE

Faculty Room.—Portraits of Pestalozzi and J. J. Rousseau on the walls. Around a green table over which several gas lamps are burning sit PROFESSORS AFFENSCHMALZ, KNÜPPELDICK, HUNGERGURT, KNOCHENBRUCH, ZUNGENSCHLAG *and* FLIEGENTOD. *At the head of the table on a raised chair,* REKTOR SONNENSTICH. HABEBALD, *the porter, cowers by the door.*

SONNENSTICH. . . . Have any of you gentlemen further remarks to make?——Gentlemen—if we have no alternative but to apply to the Ministry of Education for the expulsion of this delinquent student, it is for the most weighty reasons. It is because we must atone for the evil which has already befallen and equally because we must protect this institution against similar calamities in the future. It is because we must chastise this delinquent student for the demoralizing influence he has exercised upon his classmate; and above all it is because we must prevent him from exercising such influence upon his other classmates. It is, and this, gentlemen, may well be the weightiest reason of all, because we have the duty to protect this institution from the ravages of a suicide epidemic such as has broken out already in various other schools, and which till now has set at nought all efforts to teach the boys—by way of giving them an education—the obligations of an educated existence.——Have any of you gentlemen further remarks to make?

KNÜPPELDICK. I can no longer resist the conclusion that the time has come at last to open a window somewhere.

ZUNGENSCHLAG. The a-a-atmosphere which p-prevails here resembles that of underground ca-ca-ca-catacombs, or the archives of the lawcourts in old Wetzlar.

SONNENSTICH. Habebald!

HABEBALD. Yes, Herr Rektor?

SONNENSTICH. Open a window! There is atmosphere enough outside, thank God.—Have any of you gentlemen further remarks to make?

FLIEGENTOD. If my colleagues wish to have a window open I have nothing against it. All I ask is that it should not be the window immediately behind my back.

SONNENSTICH. Habebald!

HABEBALD. Yes, Herr Rektor?

SONNENSTICH. Open the other window!——Have any of you gentlemen further remarks to make?

HUNGERGURT. Without wishing to contradict our Rektor, I should like to remind him of the fact that the other window has been bricked up since last autumn.

SONNENSTICH. Habebald!

HABEBALD. Yes, Herr Rektor?

SONNENSTICH. Let the other window remain closed! I feel compelled, gentlemen, to put the matter to a vote. May I ask those who are *for* the opening of the only window in question to rise?
He counts.
—One, two, three.—One, two, three.—Habebald!

HABEBALD. Yes, Herr Rektor?

SONNENSTICH. Let window number one likewise remain closed. —I for my part am convinced that the prevailing atmosphere leaves nothing to be desired.—Have any of you gentlemen further remarks to make?——Gentlemen!—In the event of our omitting to apply to the Ministry of Education for the expulsion of this delinquent student, the Ministry of Education will hold *us* responsible for the misfortune which has descended upon us. Of the various schools afflicted with suicide epidemics, those at which twenty-five per cent of the students have fallen victims to the epidemic have been suspended by the Ministry of Education. It is our duty as custodians of this institution to protect it from such a shattering blow. It grieves us that we are in no position to regard the other qualifications of the delinquent student as mitigating circumstances. While a lenient procedure might be justifiable in relation to the delinquent student, in relation to this institution, endangered as it is at the moment in the most serious way, it would *not* be justifiable. We find ourselves under the necessity of judging the guilty lest we, the innocent, should ourselves be judged.—Habebald!

HABEBALD. Yes, Herr Rektor?

SONNENSTICH. Bring him up!

Exit HABEBALD.

ZUNGENSCHLAG. If the p-prevailing a-a-atmosphere is authoritatively regarded as leaving little or nothing to be desired, I would like to propose that during the s-summer vacation the other window be b-b-b-b-b-b-bricked up!

FLIEGENTOD. If our good colleague Zungenschlag considers our premises to be inadequately ventilated I should like to propose that our good colleague Zungenschlag have a ventilator installed in his frontal cavity.

ZUNGENSCHLAG. I d-d-don't have to put up with that sort of thing!—I d-don't have to put up with insolence!—I am master of my f-f-f-f-five senses!

SONNENSTICH. I must ask our colleagues Fliegentod and Zungenschlag to observe a measure of decorum. The delinquent student would seem to be already on the threshold.

HABEBALD *opens the door and* MELCHIOR, *pale but composed, steps before the assembly.*

SONNENSTICH. Come nearer the table!—After Rentier Stiefel had been informed of his son Moritz's impious misdeed, the bewildered father searched his son Moritz's effects in the hope of learning thereby the occasion of this loathsome crime. He thus chanced, in a place which has no bearing upon the matter in hand, on a document which, without entirely explaining the loathsome crime, nevertheless provides an unfortunately all too adequate explanation of the criminal's morally deranged predisposition. The document in question is a treatise twenty pages long in dialogue form, entitled *Copulation,* equipped with life-size illustrations and teeming with shameless indecencies, a document that would meet the most extravagant demands of an abandoned libertine, a connoisseur in pornographic literature.—

MELCHIOR. I . . .

SONNENSTICH. Please hold your tongue!—As soon as Rentier Stiefel had handed over to us the document in question and we had promised the bewildered father to make the author known to him at any cost, the handwriting was compared with the handwriting of all the fellow students of the impious deceased, and in the unanimous judgment of the entire teaching staff, as well as in the expert opinion of our respected colleague in calligraphy, it betrayed the profoundest similarity to your own.—

MELCHIOR. I . . .

SONNENSTICH. Please hold your tongue!—Regardless of the overwhelming fact of such a resemblance, recognized, as it is, by unimpeachable authorities, we feel ourselves entitled to abstain for the time being from taking action in order thoroughly to interrogate the culprit on the crime against decency with which he is charged and on the impulse to self-destruction which arose therefrom.—

MELCHIOR. I . . .

SONNENSTICH. You are to answer the precisely formulated questions which I am about to put to you one by one with a simple and unassuming "yes" or "no."—Habebald!

HABEBALD. Yes, Herr Rektor?

SONNENSTICH. The dossier!——I must ask the secretary, Professor Fliegentod, to transcribe the proceedings, as far as possible word for word, from this point on.

To MELCHIOR.

Are you familiar with this document?

MELCHIOR. Yes.

SONNENSTICH. Do you know what this document contains?

MELCHIOR. Yes.

SONNENSTICH. Is the handwriting of this document yours?

MELCHIOR. Yes.

SONNENSTICH. Was the indecent document born in your brain?

MELCHIOR. Yes.—Please point out to me one indecency, Herr Rektor.

SONNENSTICH. You are to answer the precisely formulated

questions which I put to you with a simple and unassuming "yes" or "no."

MELCHIOR. What I wrote is fact, no more, no less. Facts well known to you.

SONNENSTICH. Scoundrel!!

MELCHIOR. Please show me one offense against morals in the document.

SONNENSTICH. Do you imagine I shall let myself be made a clown of by you?—Habebald . . . !

MELCHIOR. I . . .

SONNENSTICH. You have as little respect for the dignity of your assembled teachers as you have sense of decency! You are flouting the instinctive human feeling for modesty and discretion! You are flouting the moral order itself!—Habebald!

HABEBALD, *placing a volume before him.* Here, Herr Rektor.

SONNENSTICH, *taking the volume up.* But this is Langenscheidt's *Agglutinative Volapuk in Three Hours!*

MELCHIOR. I . . .

SONNENSTICH. I call upon the secretary, Professor Fliegentod, to close the minutes!

MELCHIOR. I . . .

SONNENSTICH. Please hold your tongue!!—Habebald!

HABEBALD. Yes, Herr Rektor?

SONNENSTICH. Take him downstairs!

SCENE 2

A cemetery in streaming rain. PASTOR KAHLBAUCH *stands before an open grave, with his umbrella up. On his right* RENTIER STIEFEL *and the latter's friend* ZIEGENMELKER *and* UNCLE PROBST. *On his left* REKTOR SONNENSTICH *and* PROFESSOR KNOCHENBRUCH. *Boys from the school complete the circle. At a little distance* MARTHA *and* ILSE, *by a half-ruined gravestone.*

PASTOR KAHLBAUCH. . . . For he who denies the grace with which the Eternal Father has blessed those born in sin shall die the death of the spirit!—He who has lived and worked for evil in self-willed carnal denial of the honor which is God's due shall die the death of the body!—But he who lightly casts from him the cross which the All-merciful has laid upon him for his sins, verily, verily I say unto you, he shall die an eternal death!—

He throws a spadeful of earth into the grave.

Let us who dutifully plod the path of thorns praise the Lord, the All-bountiful, and thank him for the inscrutable disposition of His grace. For as surely as this person died a threefold death, as surely will our Lord God lead the righteous to bliss and everlasting life.—Amen.

RENTIER STIEFEL, *his voice strangled with sobs, throws a spadeful of earth into the grave.* The boy was no son of mine!—The boy was no son of mine!—I never liked him—from the beginning.

REKTOR SONNENSTICH *throws a spadeful of earth into the grave.* Suicide, as the weightiest conceivable transgression against the moral order, is the weightiest conceivable proof of the existence of the moral order, in that the suicide, by saving the moral order the necessity of passing judgment, *ipso facto* confirms the existence of the moral order.

PROFESSOR KNOCHENBRUCH *throws a spadeful of earth into the grave.* Debased, deformed, debauched, depraved, and degenerate!

UNCLE PROBST *throws a spadeful of earth into the grave.* I wouldn't have believed my own mother if she'd told me a child could treat his parents so basely!

FRIEND ZIEGENMELKER *throws a spadeful of earth into the grave.* Could treat a father thus who for more than twenty years, early and late, had entertained no thought but the welfare of his child!

PASTOR KAHLBAUCH, *pressing* RENTIER STIEFEL's *hand.* We know that all things work together for good to them that love God. I Corinthians 12:15.—Think of the disconsolate mother, and seek to replace what she has lost with love redoubled.

REKTOR SONNENSTICH, *pressing* RENTIER STIEFEL's *hand.* We'd probably have been unable to give him his promotion in any case.

PROFESSOR KNOCHENBRUCH *presses* RENTIER STIEFEL's *hand.* And if we *had* given him the promotion he'd have flunked out next spring sure enough!

UNCLE PROBST, *pressing* RENTIER STIEFEL's *hand.* Above all, your duty now is to think of yourself. You are a *pater familias* . . . !

FRIEND ZIEGENMELKER, *pressing* RENTIER STIEFEL's *hand.* Entrust yourself to my guidance!—Wretched weather, enough to make the bowels quake!——If you don't hit back with a hot grog, and quick, it gets you right in the heart!

RENTIER STIEFEL, *blowing his nose.* The boy was no son of mine . . . the boy was no son of mine . . .

Exit RENTIER STIEFEL, *accompanied by* PASTOR KAHLBAUCH, REKTOR SONNENSTICH, PROFESSOR KNOCHENBRUCH, UNCLE PROBST *and* FRIEND ZIEGENMELKER. *The rain abates.*

HÄNSCHEN RILOW *throws a spadeful of earth into the grave.* Rest in peace, honest fellow!—Give my greetings to my everlasting brides of sacrificial memory and commend me most devotedly to God in all His grace, O Simple Simon!—I daresay they'll put a scarecrow on your grave in memory of your angelic simplicity . . .

GEORG. Has the pistol been found?

ROBERT. No need to look for any pistol!

ERNST. Did you see him, Robert?

ROBERT. It's a damned fraud!—Who saw him?—Who?

OTTO. That's just it: they'd thrown a sheet over him.

GEORG. Was his tongue hanging out?

ROBERT. His eyes!—That was why they'd put the sheet over him.

OTTO. Horrible!

HÄNSCHEN RILOW, *to Robert.* Are you positive he hanged himself?

ERNST. They say he had no head left at all.

OTTO. Nonsense!—Rubbish!

ROBERT. I had the rope in my hands!—I've never seen a hanged man yet who didn't have to be covered up.

GEORG. He couldn't have taken himself off in a nastier way!

HÄNSCHEN RILOW. Hell, do you expect hanging to be pretty?

OTTO. Matter of fact, he owes me five marks. We made a bet. He swore he could keep his place.

HÄNSCHEN RILOW. It's your fault he's where he is. You called him a show-off.

OTTO. Bosh! I have to grind all night, too. If he'd done his Greek Lit. he wouldn't have needed to hang himself.

ERNST. Done your essay, Otto?

OTTO. Only the introduction.

ERNST. I can't think what to say.

GEORG. Weren't you there when Affenschmalz assigned it?

HÄNSCHEN RILOW. I shall fix myself up with something out of Democritus.

ERNST. I shall see if I can find something in Meyer's *Lexicon*.

OTTO. Have you done the Virgil for tomorrow?——

The Schoolboys leave.—MARTHA *and* ILSE *approach the grave.*

ILSE. Quick, quick!—The gravediggers are coming.

MARTHA. Wouldn't it be better if we waited, Ilse?

ILSE. What for?—We can bring fresh ones. Fresh ones and then more fresh ones.—There are plenty where these came from.

MARTHA. You're right, Ilse!—

She throws a wreath of ivy into the grave. ILSE *opens her apron and lets fall a profusion of fresh anemones on the coffin.*

I shall dig up our roses. I'll get beaten in any case.—Here they'll really grow!

ILSE. I'll water them whenever I come by. I'll bring forget-me-nots from the brook, and irises from home.

MARTHA. It will be a glorious display! Glorious!

ILSE. I was just across the bridge there when I heard the shot.

MARTHA. Poor kid.

ILSE. And I know why he did it too, Martha.

MARTHA. Did he say something?

ILSE. "Parallelepipedon!" But don't tell anyone.

MARTHA. Cross my heart!

ILSE.—Here's the pistol.

MARTHA. So that's why no one could find it.

ILSE. I took it out of his hand when I came by next morning.

MARTHA. Give it to me, Ilse!—Please give it to me!

ILSE. No. I'll keep it as a souvenir.

MARTHA. Ilse, is it true he's in there without a head?

ILSE. He must have loaded it with water.—The king's-tapers were sprinkled all over with blood. His brains were hanging from the willow branches.

SCENE 3

MR. *and* MRS. GABOR.

MRS. GABOR. . . . They needed a scapegoat. They couldn't allow these spreading accusations to fall on themselves. So now that my child has had the misfortune to fall foul of these fogies at the right moment, I, his own mother, am supposed to finish the hangmen's work for them?—Heaven forbid!

MR. GABOR.—For fourteen years I have observed in silence your "intelligent" methods of bringing up children. They were at variance with *my* ideas. My own conviction has always been that a child is not a plaything, that a child is entitled to our most solemn and serious attention, but I told myself that if the charm and intelligence of one parent *could* replace the serious principles of the other, then, possibly, they might deserve to do so.——I'm not reproaching you, Fanny, but do not stand in my way when I seek to make good the wrong that you and I have done our boy!

MRS. GABOR. I shall stand in your way as long as there's a drop of warm blood in my veins! My boy will be lost in a Reformatory. A criminal nature might be improved in such a place, I don't know. I do know this: a good boy would only be turned into a criminal by such a place—as surely as a plant dies without sun and air. I am not aware of having done wrong. Today, as always, I thank Heaven for having shown me the way to give my child an upright character and a noble mind. What has he done that's so terrible?— It would not occur to me to try to excuse a fault—but it wasn't his fault they turned him out of school. Even if it *was,* he's atoned for it. Maybe you understand all this better than I do. Theoretically you may be right. But I can't let my only child be hounded to death!

MR. GABOR. That doesn't depend on us, Fanny.—It's a risk we have accepted, just like our happiness. Whoever's not strong enough for the march falls by the wayside. And it isn't the worst thing, after all, if what's inevitable comes in good time. Leave it to Heaven to protect us from it! Our duty is to strengthen the weak of will as long as reason can find a way.

—"It's not his fault he was thrown out of school." If he had *not* been thrown out, that wouldn't have been his fault either, I suppose.—You are too lighthearted. You only see childish naughtiness when it's a case of a fundamental flaw in the character. You women are not qualified to judge of such matters. Anyone who could write what Melchior wrote must be rotten to the core; the very marrow is affected; a halfway healthy nature would be incapable of such a thing. None of us are saints, each one of us strays from the straight and narrow path, but there's a principle involved. This was no unintentional lapse, but the documentation, with horrifying clarity, of a purpose openly entertained, a natural drive toward immorality for its own sake. This piece of writing is evidence of that extreme degree of spiritual corruption which we lawyers describe as "moral depravity."—Whether anything can be done for such a state of mind I cannot say, but if we are to keep alive the last ray of hope, if we are to keep our consciences as parents of the person in question unstained, it is time to take a stand. We must be serious at long last.

—Let's not go on quarreling, Fanny. I know how hard it will be for you. I know that you idolize him because your own great gifts are mirrored in his. Be stronger than yourself! Show yourself selfless for once where your son is concerned!

MRS. GABOR. How can I get anywhere against an attitude like that?—It takes a man to talk like that! It takes a man to let himself be fooled by dead words! It takes a man to see no further than his nose this way!—Melchior has always been impressionable, I saw that from the start, and acted according to my conscience and my best judgment. But are we responsible for accidents? Suppose a tile should fall on your head tomorrow and a friend of yours—your father, say—should walk all over you instead of tending your wounds? —I'll not see my child murdered before my very eyes. What is a mother for?—It's just outrageous, I can't believe it! What has he written, for heaven's sake? That he should write such things—doesn't it prove how utterly artless he is, how childlike, how stupid, how innocent? To find moral corruption here, one must have the soul of a bureaucrat, one must be wholly ignorant of human nature, one must . . . Say what you want. If you put Melchior in a Reformatory, it is over between us. Then let me see if—somewhere in the world—I can't find a way to snatch my son from his destruction!

MR. GABOR. You'll have to resign yourself to it—if not today, tomorrow. Coming to terms with misfortune isn't easy for anyone. I'll be at your side. If your courage threatens to give out, I'll do everything in my power to comfort you. The future looks so gray and overcast. If I lost you too, it would be the end.

MRS. GABOR. Never to see him again! Never again! He can't stand crudity, he'll never get used to the filth of it, he'll cut himself loose—with the ghastly example of Moritz always before him!—And if I see him again—the joy of spring in his heart—his bright laughter—everything about him—his child's determination to fight for the right and the good—oh, his heart was pure and clear as the morning sky—it was my most precious possession . . . If there's an injustice here that cries out for expiation, turn against me, do what you like with me, I'll take the blame, but keep your frightful hands off my child!

MR. GABOR. He has gone wrong.

MRS. GABOR. He has not gone wrong!

MR. GABOR. He has gone wrong!!——I'd have given anything to spare you this, I know how you love him.——This morning a woman came to see me. She was beside herself. She could hardly speak. She held this letter in her hand. It's addressed to her fifteen-year-old daughter. She told me she'd opened it out of foolish curiosity, the girl not being home. In this letter Melchior tells the fifteen-year-old child that what he's done is leaving him no peace, he has sinned against her, et cetera, et cetera, but that naturally he'll answer for everything, she mustn't take it to heart even if there are consequences, he's already taking steps to help her, his expulsion will make things easier, what was an error at the time may yet turn out for the best—and a lot more.

MRS. GABOR. Impossible!

MR. GABOR. The letter was written *for* him. It's a forgery—a fraud. His expulsion is the talk of the town, and someone's helping him to exploit that fact. I haven't spoken yet with the boy—but look at the handwriting! Look at the style!

MRS. GABOR. What a rotten, shameless trick!

MR. GABOR. I'm afraid you're right.

Pause.

MRS. GABOR. No. No! Never!!

MR. GABOR. It'll be better for us.—The woman wrung her hands and asked me what she should do. I suggested she might stop her fifteen-year-old daughter from hanging around haylofts. Luckily she left the letter with me.—If we now send Melchior to another school where he's not even under parental supervision, we'll have a repetition of the same case in three weeks: another expulsion—he'll make a habit of it—the "joy of spring" can be lasting.—So what should I do with the boy, Fanny? Tell me.

MRS. GABOR. The Reformatory.

MR. GABOR. The . . . ?

MRS. GABOR. Reformatory.

MR. GABOR. There above all he will find what was wrongly withheld from him at home: iron discipline, principles, and a moral compulsion to which he must in all circumstances submit.—What's more, a House of Correction isn't the abode of horror that you imagine: the emphasis is laid on developing Christian thoughts and Christian feelings. There at last the boy will learn to desire the good, not just the interesting. As for conduct, he will learn to ask what is lawful, not just what is natural.——Half an hour ago I got a letter from my brother confirming this woman's statement: Melchior confided in him and asked for 200 marks to flee to England . . .

MRS. GABOR, *covering her face.* Merciful heaven!

SCENE 4

Reformatory—a corridor.—DIETHELM, REINHOLD, RUPRECHT, HELMUTH, GASTON, *and* MELCHIOR.

DIETHELM. Here's a twenty-pfennig piece.

REINHOLD. What of it?

DIETHELM. I put it on the floor. You all stand round it in a circle. The one that hits it, gets it.

RUPRECHT. Aren't you joining in, Melchior?

MELCHIOR. No, thank you.

HELMUTH. The Joseph!

GASTON. He couldn't, oh no! He's here for a vacation!

MELCHIOR, *to himself.* It's not smart of me to stay out. They all watch me. I'll have to join in. You crack up if you don't. —They're killing themselves, that's what prison's done for them.—If I break my neck, good. If I make a getaway, also good. I can't lose.—Ruprecht is getting to be my friend. He knows the ropes here.—I'll reward him with the story of Thamar, daughter-in-law of Judah, Moab, Lot and his daughters, Queen Vashti, Abishag the Shunammite . . . He has the sorriest face in the outfit.

RUPRECHT. I've got it.

HELMUTH. Here *I* come!

GASTON. Day after tomorrow maybe.

HELMUTH. Look!——Now!——O God, O God . . .

ALL. Summa cum laude! Summa cum laude!

RUPRECHT, *taking the coin.* Thank you very much!

HELMUTH. Give it here, you bastard.

RUPRECHT. You pig!

HELMUTH. You jailbird!

RUPRECHT *strikes him in the face.* There!

He runs away.

HELMUTH, *running after him.* I'll kill him!

THE REST, *on their trail.* After him! Give it to him! Get going! Get going!

MELCHIOR, *alone, turning toward the window.*—That's where the lightning conductor comes down.—You have to wrap a handkerchief around it.—When I think of *her,* the blood rushes to my head. And Moritz—it's as if I had lead in my shoes.——I'll go to a newspaper office. "Pay me by the hundred, I'll sell papers—collect news—write—local stuff— ethical questions—psycho-physical . . ." It's not so easy to starve any more. Luncheonettes, temperance cafés.—The building is sixty feet high and the stucco's coming off . . . She hates me—she hates me because I took her freedom away. Whatever I do about it now, it remains rape.—I can only hope, gradually, over the years . . . In one week's time it's a new moon. Tomorrow I'll grease the hinges. By Saturday I must somehow find out who has the key.—Sunday evening, during the service, a cataleptic fit—God grant no one else falls sick!—It all stretches out before me as if it had already happened. I can get over the window sill without trouble—swing—hold—but you have to wrap a handkerchief round it.——Here comes the Grand Inquisitor.

Exit left. Enter DR. PROCRUSTES *at right with a* LOCKSMITH.

DR. PROCRUSTES. . . . I know the windows are on the fourth floor and that nettles have been planted underneath. But what do degenerates care about nettles?—Last winter one climbed out of a skylight on us, and we had all the trouble of picking him up, carting him off, interring him . . .

THE LOCKSMITH. Do you want the grating of wrought iron?

DR. PROCRUSTES. Wrought iron, yes. And, since it can't be set in, riveted.

SCENE 5

A bedroom.—MRS. BERGMANN, INA MÜLLER, *and* DR. VON BRAUSEPULVER.—WENDLA *in bed.*

DR. VON BRAUSEPULVER. How old are you actually?

WENDLA. Fourteen and a half.

DR. VON BRAUSEPULVER. I've been prescribing Blaud's pills for fifteen years, and in a large number of cases I've had the most striking successes. I prefer them to cod-liver oil or iron tonics. Begin with three or four pills a day and increase the dose as rapidly as you can stand it. In the case of Fräulein Elfriede Baroness von Witzleben I ordered the dose increased by one pill every three days. The baroness misunderstood me and increased the dose by three pills every day. After scarcely three weeks she was able to accompany her mama to Pyrmont for an after-cure. From tiring walks and extra meals I shall excuse you. In return for which, my dear child, you must be all the more diligent in taking exercise, and you must ask for food as soon as your appetite returns. Soon thereafter the palpitations will cease, not to mention the headaches, shivering, giddiness—and these terrible digestive disturbances of ours. Eight days after the cure began, Fräulein Elfriede Baroness von Witzleben ate a whole roast chicken garnished with potatoes in their jackets—for breakfast.

MRS. BERGMANN. May I offer you a glass of wine, Herr Doktor?

DR. VON BRAUSEPULVER. Thank you, my dear Mrs. Bergmann. My carriage is waiting. Don't take it to heart. In a few weeks our little patient will be as fresh and lively as a gazelle. So take comfort!—Good day, Mrs. Bergmann. Good day, dear child. Good day, ladies. Good day!

MRS. BERGMANN *escorts him to the door.*

INA, *at the window.*—Your plane tree is changing color again already.—Can you see it from your bed? A short-lived splendor, hardly worth the joy we feel to see it come and go.—I must be going soon too. Müller'll be waiting for me outside the post office, and I have to go to the dressmaker first. Mucki is getting his first pair of trousers, and Karl's going to have a new woolen suit for the winter.

WENDLA. Sometimes I feel so happy—all joy and sunshine. I never dreamt one's heart could be so light. I want to go out and walk in the meadows in the evening sun, look for primroses by the river, sit down on the bank and dream . . . And then I get the toothache and feel as if I must be going to die tomorrow. I go hot and cold, it gets black in front of my eyes, and the monster flies in again.——Every time I wake up I see Mother crying. Oh, that hurts so much—I can't tell you, Ina!

INA.—Shall I put your pillow a little higher for you?

MRS. BERGMANN, *coming back.* He thinks the vomiting will die down, and then it will be all right to get up again . . . I think it would be better for you to get up soon, too, Wendla.

INA. The next time I drop in, you'll be bouncing about the house again, I'm sure.—Good-by, Mother. I simply must go to the dressmaker's. God bless you, Wendla, dear.

Kisses her.

Get better quickly!

WENDLA. Good-by, Ina.—Bring me some primroses when you come again. Good-by! Give my love to the boys.

Exit INA.

What did he say when he was outside, Mother?

MRS. BERGMANN. He didn't say anything.—He said Baroness von Witzleben had a tendency to faint, too. He said it was usual with anemia.

WENDLA. Did he say I had anemia, Mother?

MRS. BERGMANN. You're to drink milk and eat meat and vegetables as soon as your appetite comes back.

WENDLA. Mother, I don't think I have anemia . . .

MRS. BERGMANN. You have anemia, child. Calm yourself, you have anemia.

WENDLA. No, Mother. I know it, I feel it, it's not anemia, it's dropsy . . .

MRS. BERGMANN. You have anemia. Didn't he say you had anemia? Calm yourself, child. You'll get better.

WENDLA. I won't get better. I've got dropsy. Oh, Mother, I'm going to die!

MRS. BERGMANN. You're not going to die, child . . . Merciful Heavens, you're not going to die!

WENDLA. Then why do you cry so terribly?

MRS. BERGMANN. You're not going to die! It's not dropsy! You're going to have a baby, Wendla! A baby! Why have you done this to me?

WENDLA.—I haven't done anything to you.—

MRS. BERGMANN. On top of all, don't deny it, Wendla!—I know everything, I just didn't have it in me to speak about it.— Wendla, my Wendla . . . !

WENDLA. But it's impossible, Mother: I'm not married.

MRS. BERGMANN. Great God above—that's just it, you're not married. That's the dreadful thing!—Wendla, Wendla, Wendla, what have you done?

WENDLA. I don't know, Heaven knows I don't know. We were in the hay. . . . I never loved anyone but you, Mother, you!

MRS. BERGMANN. My precious—

WENDLA. Why didn't you tell me everything, Mother?

MRS. BERGMANN. Child, child, let us not make each other's hearts any heavier! Pull yourself together. Don't despair! How could I tell such things to a fourteen-year-old girl? It'd have been the end of the world. I've treated you no different than my mother treated me.—Let's place our trust in God, Wendla, let's hope for mercy, and do our part. Look, *nothing* has happened yet, and if we're not faint-hearted God won't forsake us.—Be brave, Wendla, be brave! ——One may be sitting by the window with one's hands in one's lap because everything has turned out for the best after all, and then trouble comes, and you feel your heart breaking inside you . . . Why are you trembling, Wendla?

WENDLA. Someone's at the door.

MRS. BERGMANN. I didn't hear anything, dear.

Goes to the door and opens it.

WENDLA. I did. Very clearly.——Who can it be?

MRS. BERGMANN.—No one——Schmidt's mother, from Garden Street.——You've come at the right time, Mother Schmidt.

SCENE 6[2]

VINTAGERS—*men and women alike—in the vineyard.—In the west the sun is sinking behind the mountain peaks. The clear sound of bells from the valley below.* HÄNSCHEN RILOW *and* ERNST RÖBEL, *at the uppermost vine trellis, beneath the over-hanging cliffs, rolling in the drying grass.*

ERNST.—I've been overworking.

HÄNSCHEN. Let's not be sad.—Pity, the way time flies.

ERNST. You see them hanging there and can't do anything about it. And tomorrow they're in the wine press.

HÄNSCHEN. I find hunger unbearable, but fatigue is just as bad!

ERNST. I can't manage any more.

HÄNSCHEN. Just this one shining muscatel!

ERNST. I can stretch my stomach just so much.

HÄNSCHEN. When I bend the spray, it swings from my mouth

[2] Another Wedekind translator, Eric Vaughn, points out that there is an analogy between this scene and Act II, Scene 4. The sexual activity of the two boys is indicated by much the same method as that of Wendla and Melchior. But Wedekind, it seems to me, has respected the taboos of bourgeois society to this extent—that there is much more symbolism in the homo- than in the heterosexual scene. Then again, the scene-on-stage begins toward the end of the actual drama in the vineyard: the kiss is not a climax but something closer to an aftermath. Mr. Vaughn thinks the Pastor is no Pastor but a Reverend Father of the Roman Church, the little lady being, not a wife, but a housekeeper. This interpretation would make of Wedekind a highly clinical observer of a certain type of homosexual fantasy. I myself am prepared to believe that Ernst will not turn out a homosexual at all, but that summer and autumn will leave spring quite far behind. E.B.

to yours. Neither of us need move—just bite the grapes off and let the stalk spring back to the vine.

ERNST. You make a good resolution. "But lo! the strength that fled is renewed again."

HÄNSCHEN. Add the flaming firmament—and the evening bells —I don't ask much more of the future.

ERNST. I sometimes see myself as already a worthy pastor with a good-natured homebody for a wife, a voluminous library, and duties to perform—positions to hold—in every sphere of society. Six days for meditation; on the seventh, one opens one's mouth. When you take your walk, schoolboys and girls shake hands with you. And when you return home, the coffee is steaming, a big cake is served, and girls bring apples in through the garden door.—Can you imagine anything finer?

HÄNSCHEN. What *I* imagine is half-closed eyelashes, half-opened lips, and Turkish draperies!—Look, I don't believe in their grand manner: our elders pull their long faces to hide their stupidities from us. Among themselves they call each other dunderheads just like us. I know that.—When I'm a millionaire, I'll build a monument to the Lord God.— Think of the future as a bowl of milk with sugar and cinnamon on it. One man knocks it over and bawls, another churns it up and sweats. Why not skim it? Or don't you believe one can learn to?

ERNST.—Let's skim it!

HÄNSCHEN. And leave what's left for the hens.—I've got my head out of many a noose before . . .

ERNST. Let's skim it, Hänschen!—How can you laugh?

HÄNSCHEN. Are you starting over?

ERNST. Somebody has to start.

HÄNSCHEN. When we think back in thirty years to an evening like this maybe it will seem indescribably beautiful.

ERNST. How does it get this way—all by itself?

HÄNSCHEN. Why shouldn't it?

ERNST. If one were alone—one might burst out crying.

HÄNSCHEN. Let's not be sad!

He kisses him on the mouth.

ERNST *kisses him.* I left the house thinking I'd just speak to you and go right back.

HÄNSCHEN. I was waiting for you.—Virtue's not a bad suit of clothes, but you need quite a figure to fill it.

ERNST. It still hangs pretty loose on *us.*—I wouldn't have known contentment if I hadn't met you.—I love you, Hänschen, as I have never loved a living soul . . .

HÄNSCHEN. Let's not be sad.—When we think back in thirty years, maybe we'll just make a joke of it.—And it's all so beautiful now. The mountains glow, grapes hang down into our mouths, and the evening wind caresses the cliffs like a playful little flirt . . .

SCENE 7

A clear November night. Dry leaves rustle on bushes and trees. Ragged clouds race across the moon.—MELCHIOR *climbs over the graveyard wall.*

MELCHIOR, *jumping down inside the wall.* The wolves won't follow me here.—While they're searching the brothels I can catch my breath and see how I'm doing. . . . My coat's in rags, my pockets are empty, just about everything is a threat to me . . . I must try to push on through the forest by day . . .

I've stepped on a cross.—The flowers would have frozen anyhow. The ground is bare all around.—In the kingdom of the dead!

Climbing through that skylight wasn't as hard as the journey: this was the one thing I was unprepared for.

I'm suspended over the abyss—the ground has fallen away beneath my feet, it's faded clear away.—I wish I'd stayed there!

Why must it be she?—Why not the one who was to blame? —Inscrutable Providence!—I would have broken stones and starved . . . !

—What keeps me going?—Crime follows crime. Deeper and

deeper in the mire. Not even the strength left to put an end to it . . .

I wasn't bad!—I wasn't bad!—I wasn't bad . . .

No mortal ever wandered among graves so full of envy—Pah—I wouldn't have the courage! Oh, if only madness would overtake me—this very night!

I must look over there among the most recent ones.—The wind whistles a different note against every stone—a symphony of distress.—The decaying wreaths are torn in half. They dangle in pieces by their long ribbons around the marble crosses—a forest of scarecrows. Scarecrows on every grave. Each more horrible than the last. Tall as houses. The very devils run from them.—How coldly the gilt letters glitter! . . . The weeping willow groans and runs over the inscription with giant fingers . . .

A praying cherub—A tablet—

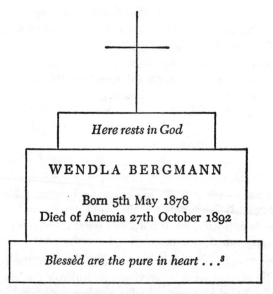

Here rests in God

WENDLA BERGMANN

Born 5th May 1878
Died of Anemia 27th October 1892

Blessèd are the pure in heart . . .[3]

[3] This is how the German editions, presumably following Wedekind's MS., have presented these lines. As no audience could be expected to read such an inscription, we must imagine either that Melchior reads it aloud or that (in a highly expressionistic production)

A cloud casts its shadow on the earth—how it rushes and howls—it is massing in the east like an army on the march.

—Not a star in the sky.

—Evergreen around that little plot. Evergreen?—— Wendla . . .

And I am her murderer.—I am her murderer!—Nothing is left but despair.—I mustn't cry *here*. I must get away— away—

MORITZ STIEFEL *comes stomping over the graves, his head under his arm.* One moment, Melchior. This opportunity will not be repeated in a hurry. You've no idea how everything is bound up with time and place . . .

MELCHIOR. Where have *you* come from?

MORITZ. By the wall there. You knocked my cross over. I lie by the wall.—Give me your hand, Melchior . . .

MELCHIOR. You are *not* Moritz Stiefel!

MORITZ. Give me your hand. You'll live to thank me. Things aren't going to be easy for you. It is a strangely lucky encounter.—I came over on purpose . . .

MELCHIOR. Don't you sleep, then?

MORITZ. Not what you people call sleeping.—We sit on church steeples and rooftops . . . anywhere . . .

MELCHIOR. Without rest?

MORITZ. For the fun of it.—We haunt Maypoles and solitary forest shrines.—We hover over crowds, gardens, public fairgrounds, places where disasters happen.—Indoors, we cower in the chimney corner or behind the bed curtains.—Give me your hand.—We have no truck with each other, but we see and hear all that goes on in the world. We know that what men do and strive for is folly, and we laugh about it.

MELCHIOR. What good does that do?

MORITZ. What good does it have to do?—We can't be got at— not by anything—not by good, not by bad. We are 'way high

---

the inscription is suddenly made legible to the public by enlargement and projection. Another oddity is the date of Wendla's death in view of the fact that Wedekind says he wrote the play "Autumn 1890 to Easter 1891." E. B.

above all earthly goings-on, each for himself alone. We have nothing to do with each other because it's boring to do so. We none of us still cherish anything that we might lose later. We are above the battle—both the weeping and the laughter. We are satisfied with ourselves, and that's the whole story.—The living we despise unspeakably, we can hardly even pity them. Their doings cheer us up. Being alive, they are not really to be pitied. We smile at their tragedies, each of us for himself, and make our observations on the subject.—Give me your hand. If you give me your hand, you'll fall down laughing at the emotion with which you give me your hand.

MELCHIOR. Doesn't that disgust you?

MORITZ. We're above such disgust. We smile.—I was among the mourners at my funeral. A most entertaining experience! That's what being above it all means, Melchior. I bawled with the best of them, and then slipped over to the cemetery wall to hold my sides laughing. Only by being above it all like us are you in a position to swallow all the hogwash . . . There must have been quite a bit of laughter at *my* expense before I soared aloft.

MELCHIOR. I have no wish to laugh at myself.

MORITZ. . . . The living are truly not to be pitied.—I admit this would never have occurred to *me* either, but now it's inconceivable to me that men can be so naïve. I've seen right through the whole swindle. Not the smallest cloud remains.——How can you even hesitate, Melchior? Give me your hand. Before you can turn round, you'll be sky-high above yourself.—Your life is a sin of omission.

MELCHIOR.—Can you forget, you people?

MORITZ. We can do anything.—Give me your hand.—We can deplore youth that takes its timidity for idealism and age that dies of a broken heart rather than surrender its superiority. We see emperors tremble at a street ballad, and beggars at the mention of the last trump. We look through the actor's mask and watch the poet putting his mask on in the dark. We see that this man is contented in his beggary. In the weary and heavy-laden we descry the capitalist. We observe lovers and see that they blush before each other, sensing that they are deceived deceivers. We see parents bringing children into the world in order to be able to shout at them: "How lucky you are to have such parents!" and we see the children go and do likewise. We can eavesdrop on the innocent in their love-starved loneliness, on the two-bit whore reading Schiller . . . We see God and the Devil trying to put each other out of countenance, and in our hearts we cherish the unshakable awareness that they're both drunk . . . This is peace, Melchior, contentment.—You need only offer me your little finger.—Your hair may be white as snow before another such opportunity presents itself.

MELCHIOR. If I agree, Moritz, it will be from self-contempt. I see myself as a pariah. All that gave me courage is in the grave. I can no longer regard myself as deserving of noble emotions. I can't conceive of anything that could stand between me and doom. To myself I am the most execrable creature on earth . . .

MORITZ. Why do you hesitate . . . ?

Enter a MAN IN A MASK.

THE MAN IN THE MASK, *to* MELCHIOR. You're trembling with hunger. You're in no position to judge.

To MORITZ.

Go away!

MELCHIOR. Who are you?

THE MAN IN THE MASK. That will become clear.

To MORITZ.

Get going!—What do you think *you're* doing here?—Why don't you have your head on?

MORITZ. I shot myself.

THE MAN IN THE MASK. Then stay where you belong. Your time is past. Don't molest us with the stench of your grave. How can you? Just look at your fingers. Pah! They're crumbling already.

MORITZ. Please don't send me away . . .

MELCHIOR. Who are *you*, sir?

MORITZ. Don't send me away. Please! Let me join you for a

while. I won't cross you in any way.——It's so gruesome down below.

THE MAN IN THE MASK. Then why do you prate about being above it all?—You know quite well that's all humbug—sour grapes. Why do you lie so assiduously, you bogy?——Well, if it's such a priceless boon, stay for all I care. But refrain from empty boasting, my friend—and please leave your dead hand out of the game.

MELCHIOR. Are you going to tell me who you are, or not?

THE MAN IN THE MASK. Not.—I suggest that you place yourself in my hands. I would give your survival my best attention.

MELCHIOR. You are—my father?

THE MAN IN THE MASK. Wouldn't you know your father by his voice?

MELCHIOR. No.

THE MAN IN THE MASK.—At the moment your father is seeking solace in the doughty arms of your mother.—I will unlock the world to you. Your loss of equilibrium arises from the misery of your present position. With a warm dinner in your belly you'll laugh at it.

MELCHIOR, *aside*. They can't both be the devil.

Aloud.

After what I am guilty of, a warm dinner cannot give me back my peace of mind.

THE MAN IN THE MASK. That depends on the dinner!—I can tell you this much: that little girl would have given birth splendidly. She was superbly built. It was Mother Schmidt's abortion pills that did for her.——I will take you among men. I will give you the opportunity to enlarge your horizon in the most amazing way. I will acquaint you, without exception, with everything of interest that the world has to offer.

MELCHIOR. Who *are* you? Who *are* you?—I can't entrust myself to a man I don't know.

THE MAN IN THE MASK. You can't get to know me unless you entrust yourself to me.

MELCHIOR. You think so?

THE MAN IN THE MASK. It *is* so.—Anyhow, you have no choice.

MELCHIOR. At any moment I can give my friend here my hand.

THE MAN IN THE MASK. Your friend is a charlatan. "We are above the battle, we smile." Put a penny in a man's pocket, and he'll stop smiling. Your humorist friend is the most pitiful creature in all creation. And the most deplorable.

MELCHIOR. Whatever *he* may be, you tell me who *you* are or I give this humorist my hand.

THE MAN IN THE MASK. Well?

MORITZ. He's right, Melchior. I was bragging. Accept his guidance. Make use of him. If he's masked, he's masked, you know where you are with him.

MELCHIOR. Do you believe in God?

THE MAN IN THE MASK. It all depends.

MELCHIOR. Could you tell me who invented gunpowder?

THE MAN IN THE MASK. Berthold Schwarz—alias Konstantin Anklitzen, a Franciscan monk, in about 1330, at Freiburg im Breisgau.

MORITZ. If only he hadn't!

THE MAN IN THE MASK. Then you'd have hanged yourself.

MELCHIOR. Where do you stand on morality?

THE MAN IN THE MASK. Fellow!—You take me for some little pupil of yours?

MELCHIOR. What *should* I take you for?

MORITZ. Don't quarrel!—Please don't quarrel. What good does it do?—What's the point of our sitting together, two alive and one dead, here in the churchyard at two o'clock in the morning, if we're going to quarrel like a bunch of drunks?—It should be a pleasure to me to be present at these negotiations.—If you want to quarrel, I'll put my head under my arm and go.

MELCHIOR. Still the same timid old Moritz!

THE MAN IN THE MASK. The ghost is not wrong. One should not leave one's dignity out of account.—I take our morality to be the real product of two imaginary factors. The imaginary factors are "I ought to" and "I want to." The product is called "morality." Its reality is undeniable.

MORITZ. If only you'd told me that before!—My morality drove me to my death. I took up the murderous weapon for my parents' sake. "Honor thy father and thy mother that thy days may be long." In my case, the old saying has been made to look rather silly.

THE MAN IN THE MASK. Don't permit yourself illusions, my friend! Your parents would no more have died of it than you need have. Strictly considered, they would have raged and thundered solely from physical need.

MELCHIOR. That may be true as far as it goes.—But I can assure you, sir, that if I'd gone ahead and given Moritz my hand just now, only my morality would have been responsible.

THE MAN IN THE MASK. You didn't—because you're not Moritz!

MORITZ. I don't believe the difference is so essential. You might have happened on me too, honored stranger, as I was trudging through the alder plantations with the pistol in my pocket.

THE MAN IN THE MASK. Then you don't remember me? Even at the last moment you were hesitating between death and . . . life.—Incidentally, in my opinion this is hardly the place to prolong so searching a debate.

MORITZ. It's certainly getting cold, gentlemen.—They may have dressed me in my Sunday suit, but I'm wearing neither shirt nor shorts.

MELCHIOR. Farewell, dear Moritz. Where this man is taking me I don't know. But he *is* a man . . .

MORITZ. Don't hold it against me that I tried to kill you, Melchior. Put it down to lingering affection.—I'd gladly moan and groan for the rest of my life if I could go out with you one more time.

THE MAN IN THE MASK. To each his own: to you the soothing consciousness that you possess *nothing*, to you the enervating doubts about *everything*.—Farewell.

MELCHIOR. Farewell, Moritz! Thank you very much for appearing to me. How many untroubled, happy days we've had in the fourteen years! In the years ahead, things may go well with me or badly, I may become a different man ten times over, but, come what may, I shall never forget *you . . .*

MORITZ. Thanks, thanks, dear heart!

MELCHIOR. . . . though I live to be an old man with gray hair, you may still be closer to me, Moritz, than all the living.

MORITZ. Thank you.—Good luck on your journey, gentlemen. —Don't let me keep you.

THE MAN IN THE MASK. Come, my boy!

He puts his arm in MELCHIOR's *and withdraws with him over the graves.*

MORITZ, *alone.*—So here I sit with my head on my arm.—— The moon hides her face, unveils herself again, and looks not a bit the smarter.——So I shall go back to my little plot, set up my cross that that madcap trampled down, and, when everything is in order, I shall lie on my back again, warm myself with the putrefaction, and smile . . .

THE UNDERPANTS

A Middle-Class Comedy
by

CARL STERNHEIM

English version by
Eric Bentley

Characters

THEOBALD MASKE
a petty official

LUISE MASKE
his wife

GERTRUD DEUTER
a neighbor

FRANK SCARRON
a writer

BENJAMIN MANDELSTAM
a barber

A STRANGER

THE TIME: *About* 1910.
THE PLACE: *Germany. Maske's living room.*

A Note on the Style: The German original is deliberately bizarre. Few of the oddities have any exact English equivalent: Any *traduttore* becomes a *traditore* by sheer necessity. All I can plead in self-defense is that I have tried to steer a middle course between the over-literal and the over-free. For while a literal rendering would be grotesque to the point of unreadability, to rewrite Sternheimian rococo into the standard colloquial English of 1959 would be evading the issue. One would earn the praises of those who value fluency—but not of those who value Carl Sternheim.

E. B.

ACT ONE

Enter THEOBALD *and* LUISE.

THEOBALD. I'll go clear out of my mind!

LUISE. Put the stick down.

THEOBALD, *beating her.* Disgraced! The whole neighborhood prattling about it! "Frau Maske's lost her underpants!"

LUISE. Ow! Ouch!

THEOBALD. In the open street. The Kaiser himself might have seen it. And me just a petty official.

LUISE, *screaming.* That's enough!

THEOBALD. Can't you tie your ribbons and button your buttons before you leave home? Your inner life's nothing but dreams and fantasies and excesses, your outer life is lasciviousness and irresponsibility.

LUISE. I tied a good hard double knot.

THEOBALD, *bursting out laughing.* A good hard double knot. What low-down sort of chatter is that? A good hard——all right, *there's* a good hard double smack on the ear! The consequences! Think of the consequences! But I don't dare. Dishonored! Run out of the service, out of my job . . .

LUISE. Oh, cool off.

THEOBALD. I'm furious.

LUISE. You're innocent.

THEOBALD. Guilty! Guilty of having a wife that's a slattern, a trollop, a moon-gazer.

Beside himself.

Where is the world?

He takes her head and beats it on the table.

Down here in the pots and pans! Down on the dusty floor of your room! Not in the sky! Do you hear me? Is this chair unbesmirched? No. Dirt! Has this cup a handle? I touch the world. It breaks open! There are holes in it! Holes in this life of ours! Appalling! Think of that, woman. Auspicious fate gave me a position that brings in 700 thaler.

Shouts.

700 thaler! Enough for a couple of rooms, decent food, to buy clothes, provide heat in winter. We can manage a ticket to the theatre. Good health spares us doctors and druggists. Heaven smiles on our existence. That's where you come in with *your* way of doing things and utterly destroy a life the gods have blessed. Why no heat yet? Why is this door open, that one shut? Why not the other way round? Why isn't the clock going?

He winds it up.

Why do the pots and pans leak? Where is my hat, where has an important document got to, and how can your pants fall down in the open street? How could they?

LUISE. You knew me as a young girl.

THEOBALD. So?

LUISE. And you liked me to be dreaming.

THEOBALD. What else should a young girl do with her time? That's what she's made for. Reality's something she should keep away from. But now you've bumped into it. The dream is over!

LUISE. Yes.

THEOBALD. Look how deeply moved I am, Luise.

LUISE. Oh, I quite believe you, husband.

THEOBALD. In the open street.

LUISE. I still can't understand it.

THEOBALD. Laughter and grimaces! Street urchins! Young bucks! I shall go clear out of my mind.

LUISE. There you go again.

THEOBALD. My heart froze inside me. I am averse to anything sensational—you know that. Do I permit you a hat, a dress in the latest fashion? You have to dress to disadvantage, and why? Because your attractive face is *too* attractive for my modest place in the world. Your eyes, your bosom are too great a challenge. If I could only get you to see that every scandal is caused by the failure of two factors—which should combine in a single phenomenon—to, um, combine.

LUISE. Oh, stop it. I've had as much as I can take.

THEOBALD, *loudly.* Two factors which should combine in a single phenomenon—my position and your appearance—have failed to combine.

LUISE. I can't do anything about that. God made me this way.

THEOBALD. It isn't God's fault. It's the fault of a shameless education that takes a girl's hair and makes it wave, that takes a girl's bosom, which would otherwise be harmless, and pushes it out through her bodice. A plague on matchmaking mothers!

LUISE. Mother was a very respectable person.

THEOBALD. And if I lose my job?

LUISE. Why should you?

THEOBALD. And the Kaiser riding by, as they say? God in heaven!

LUISE. Theobald!

THEOBALD. One quiver of his eyebrows, and I'm finished. I'd sink into the dust, never to rise again. Misery, shame, hunger would bring me down in sorrow to the grave.

LUISE. You're torturing me.

THEOBALD, *his head in his hands.* Oh, oh, oh!

LUISE, *after a pause.* Would a leg of mutton and string beans be all right?

THEOBALD. On the open street! How lucky we have no children yet. To have this hanging over them!

LUISE. I thought of fixing some raspberries.

THEOBALD. And His Majesty!

LUISE. Father says he's sending some more wine.

THEOBALD. How many bottles?

LUISE. A case.

THEOBALD. Have we any left?

LUISE. Five bottles.

THEOBALD. Hm. Leg of mutton. And just the right amount of salt . . . Woman, demons are forever at work in our souls.

If we don't exert the full force of our will and get the better of them—impossible to tell how far they will go with us . . . Raspberries. With cream. But where will you get the cream at such short notice?

LUISE. Fräulein Deuter will let me have some.

THEOBALD. Think so?—Women and clothes, tsk, tsk, tsk . . .

He sits in an armchair at the window and takes the newspaper. LUISE *is busy at the fireplace.*

Another thing. They say that sea serpent has turned up again—in the Indian Ocean.

LUISE. Gracious heavens above, is it possible?

THEOBALD. It's in the *News*.

LUISE. Tsk, tsk.

THEOBALD. Thank God there are few living things in that part of the world. Few or none.

LUISE. What does such a beast live off?

THEOBALD. Well, the experts disagree. It must be horrible to look at. I prefer places where one's safety is provided for. Like our town. One should restrict oneself to what is one's own, and hold it fast, though the price be unceasing vigilance. What have I in common with this serpent? What can it do to me but excite my imagination? And what's the good of that?

He rises.

If one has one's little apartment, everything in it is familiar. One put it together piece by piece. One came to value it all, to cherish it. Does one have to fear that the bird will burst out of its cage and go for the dog? That the clock will spit fire? No. It strikes seven as it has done for three thousand years whenever it was seven. I call this Order. One likes it. One even *is* it.

LUISE. Surely.

THEOBALD. To ruin a holiday for me with such excitement! Pray that we keep what we have. And see to the roast. I must be off again now to hear the latest gossip about this confounded incident.

LUISE. Are you all right again now?

THEOBALD. The good Lord has put me in mind how fortunate we've been up to now. And remember, the tulips need watering. Pray, Luise!

He disappears through the hall door and down the steps.

LUISE *has followed him onto the landing and looked after him.* Neighbor!

FRÄULEIN DEUTER, *from below.* Is that you, Frau Maske? Good morning.

LUISE. Did you hear about my accident?

DEUTER *appears above.* It couldn't have been much.

LUISE. Will you come in for a moment?

DEUTER. I'll take the liberty.

LUISE *comes back with* FRÄULEIN DEUTER.

From what Frau Kiesewetter says, they were pure linen and looked very nice and quite reputable.

LUISE. Yes—

DEUTER. But you'd sewn on your initials in red, and they're doing them in white these days. Still, only a couple of people even saw it, because the Kaiser was driving by, and everyone was looking at him. Is it true the ribbon broke?

LUISE. When I was straining to see the coachman.

DEUTER *laughs.*

LUISE. What a thing to happen! There was this white hem peeping out from under my skirt. I didn't dare move an inch.

DEUTER. Your dear husband's beside himself?

LUISE. Right off his rocker. The old song and dance about woman's lasciviousness.

DEUTER. They say you looked charming.

LUISE. Who said that?

DEUTER. Frau Kiesewetter. I suppose a few gentlemen turned their heads and were duly astonished.

LUISE. I acquitted myself honorably. One careful pace forward, and I was clear of them. I bent down, and in the twinkling of an eye they were under my shawl.

DEUTER. Of course, by tomorrow they'll be saying the whole thing was a well-planned piece of coquetry.

LUISE. Evil tongues!

DEUTER. But a woman with your looks can just laugh at them.

LUISE. My husband would rather die than hear such gossip.

DEUTER. There are things your husband will have to get used to.

LUISE. Why, Fräulein Deuter?

DEUTER. The sun shines, and mankind wants to take a walk.

LUISE. What?

DEUTER. Dear good little Frau Maske, your husband is someone I simply can't abide.

LUISE. My beloved Theobald!

DEUTER. Oh dear!

LUISE. I mean it.

DEUTER. Oh, all right.

LUISE. Fräulein Deuter, do you think you could spare a little jug of cream?

DEUTER. For you, anything. Isn't your first wedding anniversary coming up this week?

LUISE. The day after tomorrow.

DEUTER. And no sign of life? No little one on the way?

LUISE. Oh . . .

DEUTER. Can that be accidental? From what I know of Herr Theobald . . .

LUISE. Now you be quiet.

DEUTER. I'll get you the cream.

Exit DEUTER. *After a moment* SCARRON *comes very quickly up the stairs.* LUISE, *who had stayed on the landing, cries out.*

SCARRON. Did I frighten you? Do you know me?

LUISE. Who are you looking for?

SCARRON. I'm at the right apartment.

LUISE. This is the house of—

SCARRON. Yes, and who else?

LUISE. My husband will be back at any moment.

SCARRON. Before he comes we must have said everything.

LUISE. Sir!

SCARRON. May I speak in metaphors, lady? Risk a big statement without further circumlocution? No. Forgive me. I got far too excited, too little master of a soul which even now was mine but which at this moment is dancing along the hallway.

LUISE. Someone's coming. They mustn't see us together.

SCARRON *disappears up the stairs.*

DEUTER *comes in with a jug.* There! Your clothes—above all your underwear—count for a great deal. At the same time, a lot can be done with a ribbon, a little bow. Oh, I could show you things. It's not always a matter of clothes when we find favor. You have lovely eyes. So long though, we'll talk another time. Today we'd better not let ourselves be caught at it, little coquette.

She runs laughing back down the stairs. Enter SCARRON.

LUISE. You have a wish?

SCARRON. Lady, if you want to know, I have a pretext.

LUISE. Make it short.

SCARRON. This morning, on the main avenue of the Tiergarten——

LUISE. Oh Heaven!

SCARRON. Rapture came rushing through all my limbs. A young lady——

LUISE *turns away.*

SCARRON. I believe in miracles. For months I have dashed through the streets in a frenzy—in search of miracles. I have turned a hundred street corners, flashed round them, expecting to find a miracle. And now I've found one. Under a linden tree. Bound by untoward circumstance to that bright green trunk, bathed in sunshine, a helpless, brown body beneath bewildered eyes. Amid the foolish, greedy crowd, an enchanting martyrdom. O dazzling jest of God! I quivered, I positively twitched, with life! What I suffered in the three seconds before you reached down, took from me what till then I thought I loved and brought me, lady, to the very threshold of you. I haven't yet learned to speak your language. The something that is between us till now is but a movement of the blood. When are you going to tell me what the words are that do you good—so that I can speak them?

LUISE *makes a gesture.*

SCARRON. I know: you cannot admit such breathless emotion into your life till it is licensed by considerable further acquaintance. Permit me a moment of silent worship.

A moment of silence. SCARRON *sits with his eyes closed.*

LUISE. Sir!

SCARRON. You don't know who I am?

LUISE. I think I've seen you.

SCARRON. When?

LUISE. This morning.

SCARRON. When else? Only then?

LUISE. Only then. The places you prefer I am a stranger to. My life is lived within these four walls.

SCARRON *walks right up to her.* LUISE *retreats.*

SCARRON. Hear one man's fate.

LUISE. I'm afraid to.

SCARRON. From today, I shall desire you with all the strength of my soul: it is such bliss to say so that I do not even ask your opinion—whether you'd like to send me to the devil or, alternatively, invite me back.

LUISE. The gall of the man! Stand up.

SCARRON. I am so full of conviction, even my limbs express certitude. They refuse to stand up. Kill me, lady. But let me remain kneeling.

LUISE. For Heaven's sake. What if my husband comes in?

SCARRON. Brown. They're chestnut brown. I'll take the two rooms announced for rent in your window. You glow like a chestnut in charcoal. Let us take it as settled. The discussion is over.

LUISE. A gentleman of such distinction—at our place? Who would believe it?

SCARRON. Once out of doors again, I promise never to return except in the attire of the simplest citizen.

LUISE. You stir me to the depths.

SCARRON. As you do me—to depths below depths.

LUISE. Renting those rooms.

SCARRON. If I should wish . . .

LUISE. What if he comes in?

SCARRON. Just introduce me.

LUISE. As who?

SCARRON. Herr Scarron. Between the first sound of his key in the lock and his actual entrance there are seconds in which to rise.

LUISE. You at our place!

SCARRON. Where?

LUISE. Bedroom and living room, O God.

SCARRON. Simply, "O God." That is everything. Why do you tremble?

LUISE. No!

SCARRON. I am a church bell. My clapper hangs limply down. But just strike me, and I'll sound all the fine sounds you have in your throat! Enough. I'm going. When shall I return?

LUISE. He's bound to be back soon.

SCARRON. You'll expect me then?

LUISE *is silent.*

SCARRON. You'll expect me then?

LUISE. Yes.

They stand before the ladder. SCARRON *rushes out.* LUISE *climbs the ladder as in a dream, stays at the top for a moment. Enter* DEUTER.

DEUTER. The door open? Heavens, what are you doing up there in the sky?

LUISE. The curtains . . .

DEUTER. You couldn't reach the curtains if your arms were twice as long. Besides, you'll be losing your——No, I'm joking. But that ribbon is hanging, so you're bound to fall over it when you get down. You are certainly a supersensual person, I've known it quite a while.

LUISE. Oh, stop scoffing.

DEUTER. Who's the lucky man, little woman? Or rather god among men? You've known a long time I'm not the sort of neighbor that murders reputations. Shall I tell you right out what I want from you?

LUISE. Help me down.

DEUTER. Stay where you are: the position is good for the purpose. I am full of the lust for life, but my face isn't right for it, I know. You, on the other hand, are blessed with such an appearance, I would count it the fullest satisfaction of my desires could I but see or hear at close quarters whatever satisfaction life brings to you.

LUISE. I don't understand.

DEUTER. Do you like me?

LUISE. Certainly.

DEUTER. You instinctively know I'll stand by you forever?

LUISE. You won't do me any harm.

DEUTER. What was he after?

LUISE. Just imagine!

DEUTER. A nobleman! I'd give ten years of my life. What excuse did he have?

LUISE. Oh, he had a real reason. He saw me this morning.

DEUTER. In all your glory?

LUISE. That's right.

DEUTER. What a treat! Oh, you bring joy to many. I suppose he rose to the bait like a tiger?

LUISE. He was quite impetuous.

DEUTER. He shook at the tree of the world and overpowered you!

LUISE. He's renting the rooms from us.

DEUTER. Marvelous! You'll go far, I see that.

LUISE. Catch me.

She jumps down.

DEUTER, *kissing her.* I'll deck you out in a special style. On top you'll still be the old Cinderella—for Herr Theobald. But underneath you'll be a white dream with a pair of brightly colored ruffles he'll never forget—a red one at the knee as a barrier. Now listen. Six meters of fine batiste will make six pairs of pants. I'll borrow a pattern, neat as a new pin, we'll leave no stone unturned. Four meters of fine bobbin lace for the petticoats.

LUISE. What are you dreaming of? I'm an honest wife.

DEUTER. But he's a hero, a stormer of barricades!

LUISE. Oh! You're a regular procuress!

DEUTER. I agree. There are no better jobs available when you're out there with your back to the wall.

LUISE. But what nonsense it all is! You know very well my husband will wring his neck the first time he gives me a look.

DEUTER. O simplicity! A husband can have a dozen eyes, and his wife can just fill them with sand, if she really wants to.

LUISE. Let's drop this.

DEUTER. Too late. In the gray twilight of your domesticity romance sits at the window looking out. The master of the house has had a year at his disposal. Why hasn't he made use of it, and filled your veins with his masculine might? Why aren't you running around twice your normal size and listening to little sounds within? Where is God's blessing on this marriage?

LUISE. We were cheated of it. A child would be beyond our means.

DEUTER. In view of this dereliction of sacred duty a judge has arisen—in you.

LUISE. I came within a hair's breadth of standing before you this day a virgin. It isn't his fault if I'm not.

DEUTER. Barbarian!

LUISE. "On 700 a year?" he says every day.

DEUTER. Lift up your eyes to the throne of grace! Man is entitled to his happiness, so one may help him to it with a quiet heart. Put your hand in mine.

LUISE. Heaven knows, we see eye to eye.

DEUTER. Hoho! Your lord and husband will have to be quite a fellow to change things now.

LUISE. For Heaven's sake, the mutton!

DEUTER. Who?

LUISE. For lunch, I mean.

DEUTER. *You're* having mutton too?

LUISE. I *was* having mutton. I forgot it, talking.

DEUTER. Wait a minute. Suppose *my* mutton strays into *your* oven. Then there's beans. Shall I attend to it?

LUISE. How good you are! What about yourself?

DEUTER. A fried egg will do me. Be right back.

Runs off. LUISE *goes to the window, takes down the Room For Rent board, makes a fire in the grate while humming: "Früh wann die Hähne krähn."*[1] *Then she goes to the mirror and looks at herself, then back to the grate, humming on.* DEUTER *comes back with the pan.*

On the fire, quick. It's almost ready. Add one touch of butter and a pinch of salt.

LUISE. What do I owe you?

DEUTER. Listen. I've often wanted to tell you. Your husband is a machine. If you get in his way you'll be run over. But since, like all steam rollers, he always announces his coming, it's easy to get out of his way. Just to make sure of things, though, I'm offering my services as a signalman, flag in hand. If you want me to hold your husband up, I hold up my flag. In the meanwhile you have time to clear the tracks.

LUISE. The soul is free, I can feel mine stirring within me, and you have talked away my every reservation. No bonds for me, no bridle, no servitude, no upraised finger! Forward to freedom! You help me.

DEUTER. Only if you take what I say to heart, happy little fool. Let your sovereign reason take charge of the abundant opportunities provided by your husband's absence between nine and three. In his hours of leisure, just do your duty. And nothing can go wrong. Your nobleman will have to have his supposed working hours precisely when your hus-

---

[1] From *The Forsaken Maiden,* words by Mörike, music by Hugo Wolf. C. F. Manney's translation reads: "When crows the cock at morn/ Ere the starbeams dwindle/ Must I arise, forlorn/ Hearthfire to kindle."

band sleeps. In this way you keep them from meeting and avoid embarrassments. That's enough for now. Shall I do the shopping?

LUISE. But bring roses instead of violets, and make it eight meters instead of six.

DEUTER. Theobald will have to be a Cyclops to escape his fate, a veritable giant. What else have you in your heart?

LUISE. Don't judge me.

DEUTER. I wouldn't know how. For me there were always just wishes. For every old unfulfilled wish, two new ones.

LUISE. It's as if a great weight had fallen off my shoulders.

DEUTER. It's as if one were a child again.

LUISE. And nothing had happened yet . . .

DEUTER. As if the young girl were to come . . .

LUISE. And dream . . .

DEUTER. And long . . .

LUISE. And, O miracle! Give . . .

They take each other's hands and dance in a ring, singing: Ring Around a Rosy.[2] *While they're still laughing,* DEUTER *runs out.*

Quick! Raspberries, come forth! What did he say his name was? Two spoonfuls of sugar. What a world he brings with him! I see an image: a woman, in a veil, lying there below, he is bending over her, she is stretching out her foot. . . . Father must give me a pair of shoes. Well, now to lay the table, it's past three o'clock.

She laughs.

THEOBALD, *entering with* MANDELSTAM. Now what's this monkey business with the furnished-room ad in the window?

LUISE. As soon as you approve, the rooms are rented.

THEOBALD. Oho!

To MANDELSTAM.

[2] The German verses could be given this approximate rendering:
Round and round again
Go the children twain
Dancing under the elderbush.
What are they doing? Hush, hush, hush.

What do you say? Oh, don't worry, you have my promise. But the situation *is* critical.

To LUISE.

For how much?

LUISE. Fifteen thaler.

THEOBALD. Inclusive?

LUISE. Exclusive.

THEOBALD, *to* MANDELSTAM. Think of that: fifteen thaler exclusive.

MANDELSTAM. I don't understand.

THEOBALD. Exclusive of coffee. Isn't it enough to make your hair stand on end? If only I hadn't set foot out of doors!

To MANDELSTAM.

Greed of gold is not in my nature, the lodger as a human being weighs equally in the scales, but—are you a barber, Herr—

MANDELSTAM. Mandelstam.

THEOBALD. Semitic?

MANDELSTAM. No, no.

THEOBALD. Would you turn toward the light?

MANDELSTAM. Stam. With one M.

THEOBALD. German, myself. I make no noise about this Jewish thing. It's best to keep the Red Sea between them and me, that's all.

MANDELSTAM. Just what *I* think.

THEOBALD *presses his hand.* Good for you. Now to business. You were prepared to pay five thaler for the smaller room?

MANDELSTAM. With coffee.

THEOBALD. But now there's someone who could use both rooms for fifteen thaler. Let me put it this way: I am Herr Mandelstam and put the question to you, Herr Maske. In your own interest and that of your family, what will you, what can you do?

MANDELSTAM. Your calculations favor the other fellow. But you approved me, and I'm counting on you as a man of your word. To be disappointed in such a matter would be more than a young man like me could bear.

THEOBALD. What are you thinking of? Could the nation that produced Friedrich Schiller produce an apostate?

MANDELSTAM. You like Schiller?

THEOBALD. I make no claim to be a literary expert of course.

MANDELSTAM. Wagner, not Schiller, is the man of our time.

THEOBALD. To remove all possible doubt, I too should like to name a name: Martin Luther.

MANDELSTAM. Very good.

LUISE. Can I serve now?

THEOBALD. May I invite you to a bite of lunch?

MANDELSTAM. I'll take the liberty.

They sit.

THEOBALD. Give me your hand. Well, you look like a fine fellow to me, quite innocent of the trouble you're causing.

MANDELSTAM. I lost my parents at an early age. I live from the work of my hands.

THEOBALD. And that keeps you going?

MANDELSTAM. Three years with the same employer.

THEOBALD. Very good.

MANDELSTAM. In the evenings every penny I've saved goes for Wagner. I've seen *Lohengrin* three times.

THEOBALD. Good God!

MANDELSTAM. A seventh heaven of delight.

THEOBALD. One must also take walks. Stretch one's legs. Health, health . . .

MANDELSTAM. Oh, certainly. Health . . .

THEOBALD. What's this, what's this? Let me have some more beans. Now speak right out.

MANDELSTAM. Oh, I'm sure you can guess the rest. Not that I can have any very specific trouble.

THEOBALD. But?

MANDELSTAM. My mother was always delicate. Undernourished too. My father used to drink a bit more than he could stand.

THEOBALD. The devil!

MANDELSTAM. If I'd brought a completely healthy body into the world, believe me, I should have made other plans for myself.

THEOBALD. Hear that, Luise?

LUISE. Yes.

THEOBALD. Oh yes, health and strength come first. Feel this thigh. The biceps.

MANDELSTAM. Gigantic.

THEOBALD. Life is my horse, young man: I ride it with those biceps. I can lift a hundredweight. I can pick you up with one arm and wave you in the air. If my muscles rub up against someone, oh, he knows it, he knows it! You need feeding and caring for, young fellow. What do you say to boarding with us?

MANDELSTAM. If it isn't beyond my means, I should be glad to.

THEOBALD. What do you think, Luise? Do you feel no emotion? How much must we ask?

LUISE. That is no matter to settle all in a moment.

THEOBALD. Not a word from me, my boy: this is woman's sphere! Talk it over with her, I won't put a spoke in the wheel.

To Luise.

Bring me a cigar to celebrate with, Luise.

LUISE. You were going to bring some home. There are none left.

THEOBALD. All the commotion drove it from my mind. I'll run over and get some. Can the other lodger be relied on to rest content with one fine big room?

LUISE. He's coming by at quarter past three. Talk with him.

THEOBALD. If it's for a period of time one might buy a screen and, so to say, make two rooms out of one. Much could also be done with a curtain. But if he won't?

MANDELSTAM. I have your word.

THEOBALD. By heaven, you'll have your room, O Aryan Mandelstam! I'll be right back.

Exit. A moment of silence.

MANDELSTAM. Pardon me . . .

LUISE. I wonder you don't want to see the room. It seems to mean a lot to you, to live in this particular house. Do you work for Lämmerhirt across the way?

MANDELSTAM. No. I work on the Linden Strasse.

LUISE. That's fifteen minutes' walk from here. Strange. Wouldn't you be smarter to——

MANDELSTAM. I have my reasons.

LUISE. Are you nearsighted? You look at me so.

MANDELSTAM. Oh, Frau Maske!

LUISE. What's the matter with you? You're blushing all over!

MANDELSTAM. Harbor no unjust thoughts about me! Don't find me strange, even!

LUISE. Oh, your secrets don't bother me.

MANDELSTAM. Since this morning I have only one secret. Salvation to be relieved of it!

LUISE. Then confide in my husband.

MANDELSTAM. The last man in the world! I'd forfeit his sympathy forever. It carries no stigma, and concerns, not me, but you . . . yes, you more than anyone else in the world.

LUISE. Me? What do you mean, me?

She has stood up.

MANDELSTAM, *getting up.* Pardon me.

LUISE. Speak.

MANDELSTAM. It wasn't my fault, but . . .

LUISE. Please!

MANDELSTAM. I've never been in a position like this in all my life. Yes, yes, I'll tell you. Your underpants——

LUISE. What?!

MANDELSTAM. This morning—your——

LUISE. Silence!

THEOBALD, *returning.* The decision?

LUISE. I want to talk it over with you.

THEOBALD. Fine.

To MANDELSTAM.

For now, you're in. Would you like a cigar?

MANDELSTAM. I don't smoke.

THEOBALD. Only one lung left? Have you taken a good look at my chest? Abundant room in it for everything neatly side by side. Come over here. Stand in front of me. Arms out sideways. Trunk backwards bend! Slowly. Lower. Just listen. We'll have to have a very serious talk about this.

MANDELSTAM. I'm exhausted.

THEOBALD. Spitting and snorting like a bellows. But, but——

The bell rings. THEOBALD *goes to the door.*

LUISE, *quickly, to* MANDELSTAM. It was an unworthy action, to come here.

MANDELSTAM. Don't scold.

LUISE. Get out!

SCARRON *enters.* I had the honor of stating my business to the lady.

THEOBALD. My wife informed me that you need two rooms. But, knowing nothing of your offer, I gave the smaller room here to Herr Mandelstam, who in any case comes of a good German family.

SCARRON. Oh!

LUISE. Herr Mandelstam was just saying, though——

MANDELSTAM. No. No, I've decided to stay.

THEOBALD. Yes, we know.

To SCARRON.

There is a very distinct possibility of your being satisfied with the fine big room that is left. Six and a half meters by five! Wouldn't you like to take a good look at it and let us know your well-considered opinion?

He leads him to the door and into the room.

LUISE, *to* MANDELSTAM. Your conduct is unworthy. I shall have to tell my husband.

MANDELSTAM. And of course I can't stop you. Still, I request you not to, or I'll have to ask Herr Maske the following question: "What can have caused the noble Herr Scarron to seek lodgings in a house like this except——"

LUISE. You know him?

MANDELSTAM. I had the honor of dyeing his hair. Twice.

LUISE. That's just libel!

MANDELSTAM. He certainly wouldn't remember a thing like that, but as for me, I know all about him.

LUISE. What causes *you* to do all this?

MANDELSTAM. This morning I was rereading *The Flying Dutchman*. You remember Senta, the heroine? You are a dreamer like her, Frau Maske. I was still reading when I saw you coming with your husband. I sat there, and you passed by, not six feet in front of me. All of a sudden——

LUISE. Only six feet! Infuriating! Anyway, your behavior is no concern of mine. I utterly despise you—that is all.

THEOBALD *and* SCARRON *come back.*

THEOBALD. Herr Scarron agrees. He values the room's good points and will pay twelve thaler. Further, he doesn't expect to use the room for more than a few hours daily.

SCARRON. Yes, indeed.

THEOBALD. For certain important writing assignments which he cannot complete in all the hubbub of the street where he lives.

SCARRON. No, indeed.

THEOBALD. I was able to assure him we would do everything to make his stay with us a pleasant one. My wife, worthy sir, has the capability, tenderness, and complaisance that you'd expect of a girl from one of the best middle-class families. Living in all the certitude of a fine heritage, we may on occasion give way to pride. At the same time we would not shrink—especially my wife would not—from the performance of a kindness.

SCARRON. I'm very, very glad. Yes, indeed.

THEOBALD. To touch, finally, on this question of next-door neighbors: Herr Mandelstam, who in any case comes of a good German family, as I think I told you, is out of the house all day at business. So we can share our attention

between you, giving it without stint during the day to Herr
Scarron, and the rest of the time to Herr Mandelstam. Then
too: on this side there's an alcove that's lit by a window in
our bedroom wall. Whatever Herr Scarron cannot get into
his room he can keep there. We'll hang a curtain so you'll
know we can't see! The conveniences, gentlemen, are halfway up the stairs. Now, I'm sure, everything must be in
beautiful shape. I will forthwith give you your keys—one to
the house, one to the apartment—and all is set for you to
regard the place as at all times your own. Just for form's
sake, I must ask you, Herr Scarron, if the work you'll be
doing here would in any way tend to overthrow the government by force? Is it in any way subversive? I am a civil
servant.

SCARRON. In no way, sir. You have my word of honor.

THEOBALD. I accept it. I feel it—man to man. For you, as for
every German, the word "honor" still has a wealth of
meaning.

MANDELSTAM. Till tomorrow morning then.

THEOBALD, *to* SCARRON. The lease is for one year.

SCARRON. Agreed.

THEOBALD. Till tomorrow.

SCARRON, *bowing.* Frau Maske!

THEOBALD. Till tomorrow.

SCARRON *and* MANDELSTAM *leave.*

LUISE. The barber is an unpleasant boor.

THEOBALD. Because he doesn't reek of perfume like the other
one?

LUISE. He will bring his sickness into this house and a thousand kinds of uncleanliness!

THEOBALD. I wouldn't say he had any special sickness. He's
shiftless, delicate, no marrow, no spunk, if you ask me.
From living in hostelries with sufferers from malnutrition.
But we'll soon fix that. For the rest, my dear Luise, you
keep quiet these next few days, and cut out the tongue
work, or I'll whack you so hard on your backside, you won't
be able to speak for weeks. Be thankful if the mess you
made of things today seems to be without consequences.

It's to be hoped that you fully realize how utterly happy your life is. What inherited good health means must have become faintly apparent to you if you took half a look at that miserable, hollow-cheeked figure of a barber. But for that matter if you will look the other fellow in the eye, well combed, immaculately dressed as he is, you can hardly fail to notice that behind a pretended assurance he only half conceals a will that has been thoroughly undermined. Believe me, my own, what I said about conscience and honor revealed in him a man of no convictions. Even so he signed a lease for a year.

LUISE *breaks out in sobs.*

THEOBALD, *with a loud laugh.* That's choice! We talk of this funny fellow, and you cry? What's the connection?

He fondles her.

Shall I knock him down for you, you silly thing? Laugh! These two inferior specimens of masculinity that God has sent into our house have really put me in a good humor again. Wasn't he a scream when he stood there saying: "Frau Maske!"? To my Luise, that loses her underpants!

LUISE *sobs more violently.*

THEOBALD. "Yes, indeed! Yes, indeed! Yes, indeed!" He's a *parrot!*

He is shaking with laughter.

And in the other corner, that soapsuds angel gasping for air! Anyone who wouldn't die laughing at all this simply doesn't know delicious humor when he sees it!

ACT TWO

THEOBALD, *coming out of the alcove.* So that's that: the curtain is up.

MANDELSTAM, *at the coffee table.* Why didn't you hang it on your side?

THEOBALD. To convince him that no one wants to pry.

MANDELSTAM. If he's of the same school of thought, well and good.

THEOBALD. His short answers to me—his reticence—suggest that he is.

MANDELSTAM. Just his pride in his higher station.

THEOBALD. And *that* brought him here? A quiet workroom could also be found in better-class homes.

MANDELSTAM. What does the man do, actually?

THEOBALD. You avoid calling him by name. To hear him talk, I conclude it's an experience—of the heart . . .

MANDELSTAM. An adventure.

THEOBALD. He called it an experience. You have an unhappy habit of substituting one word for another. It's an intimate experience that he wants to put in writing.

MANDELSTAM. I see. An experience.

THEOBALD. But if you say it that way, you'll get off the track again.

MANDELSTAM. You are very precise.

THEOBALD. It follows. Inexactitude is a detour. From nine in the morning till three in the afternoon I handle official documents. Can I permit myself inexactitude?

MANDELSTAM. Well, a man talks without thinking. I have to entertain my clients as I take the razor to them. Make sure they don't notice when I cut them or slice off the wrong piece of beard. No time for thought. Words are what I need. Any words—just so there's no interruption.

THEOBALD. So you're the victim of your profession!

He laughs.

MANDELSTAM. An experience! Probably a love story.

THEOBALD. Possibly. Do you have to be at work before eight on Saturdays?

MANDELSTAM. Have to be? I choose not to be. The boss himself comes no earlier. The apprentice can shave the riffraff that come before that.

THEOBALD. Hm. Then at least you take an early morning walk. If I were as uncertain of my health as you, I would build up my strength by all possible means.

MANDELSTAM. A lot of walking wears me out.

THEOBALD. At first. I should like you to see your present condition with complete clarity.

MANDELSTAM. Why?

THEOBALD. So that you know where you stand.

MANDELSTAM. If adequate measures are beyond my means, what can the truth do for me?

THEOBALD. A thousand devils, man, what good are lies?

MANDELSTAM. Well, after all, my God, it's all lies—everything.

THEOBALD. You are a card. Ho, ho, ho! A pessimist. Lies? Just lies, eh?

MANDELSTAM. Don't laugh. I'll give you the evidence.

THEOBALD, *laughing.* Fine. Where?

MANDELSTAM. Wherever you like. Everywhere. Everybody.

THEOBALD, *laughing.* Yourself included?

MANDELSTAM, *in a state.* Certainly.

THEOBALD. Herr Scarron?

MANDELSTAM. Him too.

THEOBALD. My wife?

MANDELSTAM. Definitely.

THEOBALD. I myself?

MANDELSTAM. Assuredly.

THEOBALD, *roaring.* You're a fighting cock! A living miracle,

and well worth the money! You're no barber! You're a baron
in disguise. Sneaking in here to be my wife's lover.

MANDELSTAM, *snorting with rage.* Herr Maske!

THEOBALD. A human bombshell! With intestines like powder
kegs!

LUISE *comes out of the bedroom.*

Luise, leave the odors of your middle-class background behind you. Mandelstam is a baron. Your lover. Ho, ho, ho!
And the world is all lies. Basta.

MANDELSTAM. At this point, Herr Maske, I must earnestly
beg——

THEOBALD. No, no, dear friend. As sure as you're unsteady on
your pins and shave men's beards off, as certain as I think
of nothing but the fact that both columns in the account
book should say the same thing, that Herr Scarron writes
love stories, and that my wife belongs to me—so sure is the
evidence of my own eyes—so sure is it that your dreams are
only lies—of which phenomenon my diagnosis is: liver, lung,
or stomach. I shan't rest till I've given you certainty on the
point. Are you coming along?

MANDELSTAM. No, thank you. In ten minutes.

THEOBALD. Well, don't be offended. Your hour may yet strike.
You may yet convince me. Not in this life, I'm afraid. But
no hard feelings on that account. I must be running. You
still don't wish . . . ?

MANDELSTAM. Thanks, no.

THEOBALD. Very well. See you soon.

Exit THEOBALD.

MANDELSTAM. He certainly makes it easy for a man.

LUISE, *taking his measure.* He? For a man?

MANDELSTAM. Such credulity is ludicrous.

LUISE. He places his trust where best he can.

MANDELSTAM. One day his eyes will be opened—with a
vengeance.

LUISE. To the doings of certain people he brings under his
roof.

MANDELSTAM. My meaning exactly.

LUISE. With their transparent pretexts.

MANDELSTAM. Which a child could see through. "To set down a love story far from the noisy street!"

LUISE. If you're going to insult me, I'll call for my husband.

MANDELSTAM. Call away. He's still on the stairs. Get thoroughly on my nerves, I'm not at the end of my resources yet. Why does he laugh at me all the time? Why the contemptuous pity in his tone? By what right, may I ask, do you despise me? For my part, I don't mind admitting I have a certain feeling about you. Not one, however, that would allow me to approach you with anything but the utmost respect.

LUISE. No one's stopping you.

MANDELSTAM. Yes. You are. Do you think I could be a party to such proceedings—an accomplice of such goings-on? Could I stand calmly by while another man makes a conquest of you? At this very table I swear to prevent it with every means in my power!

LUISE. What time was it you have to be at work on Saturdays?

MANDELSTAM. You underestimate me, Frau Maske. An oath has just been taken. As God is my help, you will not reach your goal!

LUISE, *slowly.* You are a child.

MANDELSTAM. Say, rather, a human being in a state of exaltation . . . Heaven is my witness!

LUISE. A regular child. You're getting excited about nothing. Nothing at all.

MANDELSTAM. I permit no man to despise me!

LUISE. You're getting quite out of breath. What about a nice cup of coffee? Honey and roll come with it.

MANDELSTAM. When one has nobody in the wide world.

LUISE. Go ahead with the sugar.

MANDELSTAM. One *has* nobody in the wide world.

LUISE. The honey's from my father's. Two miles from here, he has a little house in the country.

MANDELSTAM. When one has hardly known one's parents.

LUISE. As a rule I'm quite stingy with it.

MANDELSTAM. One is so absurdly alone. No roots in the soil. Nothing to hold a man up.

LUISE. You need caring for a little bit? There's a lot of nervousness around these days. If only you weren't so wild!

MANDELSTAM. I'm not.

LUISE. Violent men I just cannot respect. I like obedient, pliant natures. Well-behaved children.

MANDELSTAM. To a man who never knew a mother, that is the one thing necessary!

LUISE. The *one* thing? I'll believe that when I see it.

MANDELSTAM. This I affirm, Frau Maske, by the memory of my late mother who is looking down on us now: Never shall I overstep the boundary that you prescribe!

LUISE. Not that I'd have anything against you.

MANDELSTAM. After all, it wasn't my fault—what I saw yesterday.

LUISE. I forbid you to mention that ever again. Not a syllable. I was terrified at the way you turned up here. I foresaw unpleasant discussions with my husband.

MANDELSTAM. As if I wouldn't stand by you with my dying breath.

LUISE. Good. With the passage of time, then, we shall perhaps become friends.

MANDELSTAM. And Herr Scarron?

LUISE. What is that fop to me?

MANDELSTAM. A fop. I agree. At that, you might deceive me. Though by no means a novice, I haven't had enough experience of women to judge. Really.

LUISE. He may have his own reason for being here. It is not impossible. But you are reckoning without me, sir. You take for granted an understanding between us. I am outraged. Do you think I'm so blind I can't see what I'd be to this spoiled Don Juan—one more easy conquest that he can set aside in as little time as it took him to think of possessing her? You think I'd sacrifice my reputation and all the advantages of my position to gratify the desires of another?

MANDELSTAM. The looks he gave you permitted me to guess——

LUISE. Looks that are given without our leave are mere presumption.

MANDELSTAM. *I* shall never presume! Grateful for small mercies. Made happy by the lightest breath.

LUISE. Good. Let's leave it all to time.

MANDELSTAM. But don't expect to deceive me.

LUISE. What light clothes you're wearing! Put something else on, it's raining.

MANDELSTAM. When you say that! You make me well and strong in a moment! I don't even notice the weather. I'm going to take my scarf off.

LUISE. No, no! Prevention is better than cure!

MANDELSTAM. The way you say that!

LUISE. Would you like a sandwich to take to work?

MANDELSTAM. You think of everything!

LUISE. I tell myself: it could only do you good.

MANDELSTAM. I don't need to eat. I dream of heaven, and earthly troubles cease to bother me. If the idea appeals to you, sometimes, of an evening, we could read *The Flying Dutchman* together.

LUISE. Is it a love story?

MANDELSTAM. The greatest of love stories. Hear what the Dutchman says about Senta:

> If in such torment, in such error,
> Love-longing comes and speaks to me
> Then can I cry: An end to terror!
> This is my journey's end! I'm free!

LUISE. Nice. Now be off, or you'll be late.

MANDELSTAM. Wait for the ending:

> Though without hope, alas, I be,
> I give myself, O Hope, to Thee!

You should hear that with the music. It goes right through you.

LUISE. See you at noon.

MANDELSTAM. At noon! At noon!

Exit MANDELSTAM.

DEUTER, *entering immediately*. Who's that giddy fellow?

LUISE. A dangerous fellow. A nuisance. Another of those who saw what shouldn't have been on view yesterday. He sneaked in here on the same pretext as our friend. They're sharing the rooms.

DEUTER. Well!

LUISE. And the worst is, he hates Herr Scarron and he's a good guesser. He was just swearing that never would he tolerate ——What do you say?

DEUTER. What a song and dance.

LUISE. I believe he's quite capable of carrying the whole tale to Theobald before anything happened. I'm beside myself. Even before, my husband called out to me: "Mandelstam"— that's this barber boy's name—"Mandelstam is your lover!" It was spoken in jest, but it means Herr Scarron must have mentioned such possibilities in earnest. At least he must have steered the boat into those waters.

DEUTER. How've you been handling him up to now?

LUISE. With flattery. I've tried to build up his confidence.

DEUTER. Very good.

LUISE. But . . .

DEUTER. I shall keep him under observation. You see how lucky you are to have me at your side.

LUISE. What's that you've got there?

DEUTER. Guess.

LUISE. Tell me.

DEUTER. The batiste.

LUISE. It's superfine. You're a dear!

DEUTER. You like it?

LUISE. Marvelous. But expensive?

DEUTER. More dignified than silk!

LUISE. I can imagine how it lies along the skin.

DEUTER. Not like your nasty old twill. Twill is not for a body like yours. I'll measure the waist . . . Lift your skirt . . . Sixty-five centimeters . . . Call it sixty-six.

LUISE. Do you have the ribbon yet?

DEUTER. Here.

LUISE. Divine! You're my very best friend. You do all this for me and still so young yourself.

DEUTER. I've honestly given up all hope. Or, it's true, I wouldn't have so much time to devote to you.

LUISE. We must pray for you.

DEUTER. You think it would help?

LUISE. One must try everything—for the Cause.

DEUTER. You've been making strides.

LUISE. Last night was the hour of decision. A sweet dream . . .

DEUTER. Go on.

LUISE. You poor girl.

DEUTER. Not another word or I'll burst out crying.

LUISE. Surely we can find a man for you. What about the barber?

DEUTER. Pah! I'd rather have your husband!

They laugh heartily.

SCARRON *opens the door from outside and comes in.* Divine cheerfulness! I step out of the rain into a tropical sun!

LUISE, *quietly to* DEUTER. Stay.

DEUTER. One minute—then I must go downstairs.

SCARRON. Uninvited—by means of a latchkey—I invade your gay social life and tear it to shreds! Laugh on, ladies. I will take part only if permitted, only if I really belong. What was it all about?

LUISE. Fräulein Deuter——

SCARRON *bows.*

LUISE.—Fräulein Deuter and I were speaking of the barber.

SCARRON. What barber?

LUISE. Mandelstam, of course.

DEUTER. Frau Maske thought him too ugly for her, but recommended him for the post of *my* lover.

LUISE. The word never passed my lips.

DEUTER. But that was what she meant, Heaven knows.

LUISE. I was joking.

SCARRON. You must have been. He is not what one would call a man.

DEUTER. Yet good enough for an old maid.

SCARRON. Who might that be?

LUISE. She's fishing for a compliment.

DEUTER. Nothing of the kind. But what would you say of this material, Herr Doktor? You like it?

SCARRON. Batiste, isn't it? What's it for?

DEUTER. Pants for the young lady. Pardon me: in your circles they are called lingerie.

LUISE. Fräulein Deuter!

DEUTER. I was measuring her when you interrupted.

LUISE. Fräulein Deuter!

DEUTER. Sixty-six centimeters. I call those slim hips, Herr Doktor.

SCARRON. I certainly shouldn't have held up such a sweet transaction.

LUISE. Herr Scarron?

DEUTER. Now I just need the length.

She bends down and measures.

Sixty-three to just below the knee.

LUISE. Enough. What are you doing?

SCARRON. May I—having so indelicately intruded—may I offer a piece of advice? The ladies who know nothing but fashion and finery, who set the tone in all questions of taste, would not, perhaps, have found their way so far down. They would have come to rest at a point some two or three centimeters above the knee.

DEUTER. Then lend us a hand. I counted on getting such information. I was also wondering if our width of eighteen corresponds to the newest cut?

SCARRON. As wide as possible below. At the top, a closer fit.

DEUTER. Then there was the question——

LUISE, *flying to her bosom.* Trude, be quiet, or I'll be angry with you for life.

SCARRON, *to* DEUTER. This important business has been entrusted to you?

DEUTER. If you have the opportunity to admire the finished product—finished and in place—I believe you may wish to pay me a compliment.

SCARRON. How may I earn your friendship?

DEUTER. Please note that I am already at your service.

SCARRON. It is your wish, then, to be the godmother of a happiness which needs a protecting hand more than the bird that is still unfledged?

DEUTER. But which has the will to fly.

LUISE. And doesn't yet know how.

DEUTER. As for me, I'm only half a bird. When the moment came, my courage failed me, and I stayed under the eaves. I won't be able to provide detailed instructions.

SCARRON. Quite unnecessary, I assure you.

DEUTER. Besides, the nestling is bestirring herself. I found her yesterday with wings aflutter—in intuitive contact with the higher regions.

SCARRON. Let us dare to fly!

DEUTER. A hawk is circling on the horizon. Not the fat old owl who is only to be feared at night. A thin and hungry cloud that swoops down, quick as a flash, into the darkest place of hiding.

SCARRON. Who?

DEUTER. A cloud of soapsuds. A lather beater.

SCARRON. The barber.

LUISE. He's lying in wait. He shouted in my face that he'd be on the watch. And that he'd stand for nothing. I am very unhappy.

DEUTER. Now that it's out, I'll be going. Caution!

SCARRON. Thanks!

DEUTER. I will do my worst against him.

Exit DEUTER.

SCARRON. Luise!

LUISE. I'm afraid.

SCARRON. Sit at the table.

LUISE. My feet are giving way under me.

SCARRON. It doesn't matter if someone comes in—I shan't touch
you. At the other side of this table, but more than two
oceans away, I cower in the shadow of the mountain wall.
Sleeping life off, as it were, in the light of your two blue
suns. You send out beams of will power in my direction.
They singe what is nearer, and kindle what is further away,
with a brilliant, joyous warmth. Your fist is clenched; taking
hold of the idea, it proceeds to enjoy it. An idea to make
the heart melt! Your bosom is heaving now. I see the moving
muslin stiffen. And now, from the tree top to the roots, you
shed your leaves, Luise, 'tis a sweet sort of sorrow. You are
struck down by destiny.

LUISE, *like one sleeping, has buried her head in her arms
on the table.*

With father and mother my life began. Brothers and sisters
moved, beckoning, about me, and from my father issued
almost uninterrupted sound. Where did all that go? I could
see only my mother's arm raised in supplication like a
shadow above me. Then, suddenly, I was alone in a storm
that tore up the ground and brought down the sky on my
head. I ran—with a destination but no path. Stand up,
woman, I am entering upon a false passion! But stay! What
I have to say now is quite different. There are wonderful
women in the world, Luise. Blondes covered with pale-red
birthmarks and brunettes covered with down like young
eagles, whose backs undulate, when you excite them, like
the waves of the sea. Many wear rustling adornments and
stones that shimmer like their own fluidities. Others wear
tight trim skirts, and their temper is cool like their skin.
There are blondes covered with down and brunettes covered with pale birthmarks, some dark and humble, some
flaxen-haired and proud. And there are flaxen-haired, humble maidens with cool skin who tell lies in rustling silk as if
their love were fluid like the words that spring from that
love. The sky is full of stars and the nights are full of women.
The world is sublimely beautiful—but . . . !

Large, broken-off gesture. LUISE *has got up.*

You are the most beautiful woman that ever crossed my path. I expect tempests from you, an explosion to melt down my last remains of earth. Rushing into insanity, I will caress my empty carcass at your uplifted feet.

He has gone close to her.

Before you press your hand into mine, Luise, give it a quick look. It is not impossible that God will make words flow from that hand to our martyred country in fine new songs. I love you ardently, Luise, had you noticed?

LUISE. I am yours.

SCARRON. The formula is classic. A destiny clothed in three words. What humanity! If I could preserve this in my book I should rank with the greatest.

LUISE, *bending forward*. Let me be yours.

SCARRON. Desk, pen, approach your essence! Close to pure, simple Nature, no work of art can fail!

LUISE. Yours.

SCARRON. So be it. In a measure that is greater than either of us. A fire ne'er felt before inflames me. Happiness can elude me no longer. Vibrating with poetic rhythms, I feel myself turn happily away. Turning toward you on my knees. I will preserve your image for mankind. First let me show it to you, and I will claim the full guerdon of your grace.

He runs into his room.

LUISE. Why?

She runs to SCARRON's *door and listens. After a moment or two she plucks up courage and knocks.*

Heavens!

She breathes, listens, and approaches the table from which she lifts MANDELSTAM's *scarf, glancing as she does so at* SCARRON's *door. She raises the scarf to her face. Just at this moment* MANDELSTAM *turns up at the hall door. He is seen pressing his face against it. Then he opens it gently and enters.*

MANDELSTAM. Gracious, my scarf.

He comes close to LUISE.

LUISE. You frightened me. Where did *you* come from?

MANDELSTAM. Why were you frightened?

LUISE. The way you *crept* in here.

MANDELSTAM. Is that my scarf?

LUISE. God knows.

MANDELSTAM, *kissing her.* Luise!

LUISE, *boxing his ears.* Shameless man!

MANDELSTAM. Forgive me.

LUISE *has gone to* SCARRON's *door and knocked.*

SCARRON'S VOICE. Give me five minutes!

LUISE *is bewildered.*

MANDELSTAM. I implore you. Something came over me, it will never happen again. I'll kill myself!

LUISE *starts to go to her room.* MANDELSTAM *faints.*

LUISE. Lord have mercy!

Runs to him.

What? Water?

She brings water and gives it to him.

MANDELSTAM. I feel good.

LUISE. Your chin is bleeding. What kind of a point is that?

MANDELSTAM. That? A gimlet.

LUISE. How could you stick *that* in your trouser pocket? It might have given you a mortal wound!

MANDELSTAM. As long as it touched your heart.

LUISE, *rising.* It would touch anyone's heart. A young man so full of hopes. What nonsense! Lie down on the sofa for a minute.

MANDELSTAM, *lying down.* In any event it will reveal to me what goes on in Herr Scarron's room.

LUISE. You intend to . . .

MANDELSTAM. Bore a hole through the wall. I am crazed with jealousy, Luise, I don't know myself. What was it brought you to this wretch's door? Do not misjudge me: despite my weakness, I will murder him.

LUISE. What right . . . ?

MANDELSTAM. I love you, Luise!

SCARRON, *coming quickly out of his room.* Color, tone, all the various values realized to the last detail. No one can ever take them away from me. I come—all love and gratitude——

He sees MANDELSTAM.

Excuse me.

THEOBALD, *entering quickly.* How are you, gentlemen?

ACT THREE

The remains of the evening meal are on the table, about which all are sitting.

THEOBALD, *to* MANDELSTAM. It was very hard for your employer to get through all the work without you this afternoon. He said you might have put your indisposition off to some day other than Saturday.

MANDELSTAM. The first afternoon I've missed in three years.

THEOBALD. He hopes you'll be all right again by the day after tomorrow at the latest. There's all of Sunday in between.

MANDELSTAM. Even a dog wants to rest if anything's not quite kosher with him.

THEOBALD. Kosher? Hm. As you wish. Incidentally, I had a long discussion with a colleague who has the same condition to complain of as yourself. He knows the inside of his poor, ruined body like his account books. He even goes to work with Latin names.

He has stood up and gone to the back.

MANDELSTAM, *eagerly following.* For the life of me, I don't see any basis for the comparison.

SCARRON, *quietly, to* LUISE. I forbid you to stare all the time at that clod.

LUISE. I can't help feeling sorry for him.

SCARRON. All lies. He's an incorrigible ruffian, a highwayman. He deliberately ruined our afternoon and——

THEOBALD. It is first and foremost a matter of the nerves even if the other organs—one more, the other less—are also infected. If I understood him correctly we must regard each nerve as a fine tube surrounded and protected by a second tube. In debilitated persons, this second, protective tube peels off like bark from trees—am I right, Herr Scarron?

SCARRON. More or less. As far as I know.

THEOBALD. Yes. And it is hard beyond all expectation to repair the damage once it is done.

MANDELSTAM. How in the world do you conclude that my nerves—it's outrageous—without having seen more of me . . .

THEOBALD. Be calm. I don't want to excite you. Surely people must have commented on the state of your nerves before now?

MANDELSTAM. Never.

THEOBALD. I will consult a completely unbiased observer. Mr. Scarron: how does our friend strike you?

SCARRON. As typically neurasthenic.

MANDELSTAM. Ha!

THEOBALD. You see? There are of course other factors, as I said. With this other man it's the stomach that's ruined by long years of inadequate nourishment. With you, I would guess it's the lungs.

LUISE. You mustn't scare Herr Mandelstam, Theobald.

THEOBALD. On the contrary, I am trying to arm him against disaster. If possible, to prevent disaster.

LUISE. But he utterly denies having any serious illness.

MANDELSTAM. Absolutely.

THEOBALD. So much the better. I regard it as my simple duty.

MANDELSTAM. And I regard it as inconsiderate to tell such things to a sensitive person. Naturally, they weigh on him, they work away on him . . .

THEOBALD. Even if they have no bearing?

MANDELSTAM. Is there a window open?

THEOBALD. Ever so slightly.

MANDELSTAM. May I close it?

He does so.

LUISE. You'd better put your scarf on.

MANDELSTAM. Many thanks.

SCARRON, *to* THEOBALD. As far as your sick colleague goes, I find this saying extremely helpful: whatever is weak and unfit must yield to the healthy and the strong!

LUISE. Of course it's for the mighty to support the weakling. Religion teaches that.

SCARRON. The religion of other centuries. Not ours.

THEOBALD *hands* MANDELSTAM *a newspaper.* Read!

SCARRON. We are beyond all that. Into the moldy, musty atmosphere of past centuries, heavy with pity as it is, we have brought a good stiff breeze!

MANDELSTAM. Read what? My eyes aren't focused.

THEOBALD, *showing him.* At the bottom there. They say the sea serpent has turned up again in Indian waters.

MANDELSTAM, *furiously.* What do I care?

THEOBALD. It may distract you.

SCARRON, *to* THEOBALD. Has the name of Nietzsche reached your ears?

THEOBALD. In what connection?

SCARRON. He teaches the gospel of the age. He shows that the boundless mass of men find a purpose in the individual who is blessed with certain energies. Strength is the highest happiness.

THEOBALD. Strength is certainly a happiness. I learned that in school, and those under me had to suffer for it.

SCARRON. I mean, of course, not only brutal, physical strength. Above all: spiritual energies.

THEOBALD. Yes, of course.

MANDELSTAM. I only noticed this morning that my room faces the northeast.

THEOBALD. One moment. Yes, you are right.

MANDELSTAM. Even for the strongest of men, that would hardly be advantageous.

SCARRON, *to* LUISE. The sloppy dog will have to be taught the Master Morality. Tonight I shall do everything in my power to reach you.

LUISE. For Heaven's sake!

SCARRON. Who do you take me for? Do you think the Evil One Himself is a match for my will power?

LUISE. But wait.

SCARRON. No!

THEOBALD, *who has opened* MANDELSTAM's *door.* Put the bed against the wall opposite the window. Then you'll be sleeping toward the southwest.

MANDELSTAM. I feel the draft on my pillows.

SCARRON, *to* LUISE. This night shalt thou be with me in Paradise.

THEOBALD, *to* MANDELSTAM. Now you exaggerate.

MANDELSTAM *goes into his room. One can see him busy himself with something.*

SCARRON, *to* THEOBALD. Have you never heard of these theories? Do you read so little?

THEOBALD. Hardly at all. Seven hours of official duties. Afterwards I'm tired.

SCARRON. That is deplorable. What are the criteria of your thinking?

THEOBALD. Some of us get along with less thinking than you might imagine.

SCARRON. Yet you live according to a certain scheme?

THEOBALD. Scheme A, Scheme B, Scheme C . . .

SCARRON. That is: you eat, sleep, and copy documents. Where does that lead?

THEOBALD. To a pension—God willing.

SCARRON. Frightful. No interest in politics?

THEOBALD. I was always excited about what Bismarck did.

SCARRON. He's been dead for some time.

THEOBALD. There hasn't been much going on since.

SCARRON. Science?

THEOBALD. Heavens, there isn't much there for the likes of us.

SCARRON. Are you aware that Shakespeare once walked the earth? Do you know Goethe?

THEOBALD. A nodding acquaintance.

SCARRON. For Heaven's sake!

THEOBALD. You take it too hard.

SCARRON. A comfortable philosophy.

THEOBALD. What's wrong with comfort? My life lasts seventy years. With whatever degree of understanding I've managed to acquire, after my own fashion I can enjoy quite a lot of things in that amount of time. As for your higher philosophy and all that, I don't think I could master it if I lived to be a hundred.

LUISE. To think there's to be no more pity in the world!

SCARRON. It simply does not exist.

LUISE. But if I *feel* it . . .

THEOBALD. Don't butt into our conversation.

MANDELSTAM, *returning.* I wonder if Frau Maske could let me have a woolen blanket. I've turned the bed around.

THEOBALD. That was reasonable.

LUISE. I'll go and get one.

She goes into her room.

SCARRON. I judge each man by his contribution to the spiritual development of humanity. The great thinkers, poets, painters, and musicians are our heroes. The layman?—important only insofar as he knows them.

MANDELSTAM. And the great inventors!

SCARRON. Surely—but only to the extent that they enable mankind to circulate the ideas of the geniuses more efficiently.

THEOBALD. And what about sentiment, sir?

SCARRON. What?

THEOBALD. Did I say it wrong? What use have you for the heart?

SCARRON. The heart is a muscle, my dear Maske.

LUISE *returns.*

THEOBALD. Fine. But there's something to it. With females especially.

LUISE, *to* MANDELSTAM. It's big enough to wrap right around you.

MANDELSTAM. Many thanks.

SCARRON. Leave me alone with your simplicity—ultimate problems are under review. Females—women, let us say—are, Heaven knows, a delicious affair, but when a Shakespeare wrestles with the soul of Hamlet, a Goethe struggles for insight into the soul of a Faust, women must stand to one side.

MANDELSTAM. Schwarz wouldn't have been thinking of his wife when he invented the printing press. Neither would Newton. Or Edison. Or Zeppelin.

LUISE. Is that certain?

SCARRON. I'll take my oath on it.

MANDELSTAM. And I'll join you.

THEOBALD. Setting Goethe aside—and Schwarz too, for all I care—even so—if I may put it this way—women have hearts.

SCARRON. A muscle, my dear Maske.

THEOBALD. I know. But they live off that muscle, and make up half the earth's inhabitants.

SCARRON. Well and good. But you are no woman. You should be penetrated with a sense of your dignity as a man. Beside the domestic, friendly element that unites you with your wife, there are also moments in which you feel worlds away from her—moments when sheer masculinity overpowers you and fills you with an almost insane pride!

MANDELSTAM. Wonderfully worded!

LUISE. Not all men are like you.

SCARRON. In their heart of hearts, all, dear lady.

MANDELSTAM. Positively.

THEOBALD. I don't know. There *is* something of the sort, it's true, but, actually, I've always fought against it.

SCARRON. There we have it: he fought against—Nature.

MANDELSTAM. The devil!

SCARRON. What makes man a giant, the gigantic obelisk of creation, whom woman cannot put down, but the transcendent will to knowledge which the profoundest erotic passion cannot paralyze?

MANDELSTAM. "Paralyze" is good.

LUISE. My husband is different.

THEOBALD. Luise, God Almighty, keep away from me with your silly chatter. . . . Speaking from personal experience,

I don't see how it would have helped my marriage if I'd felt more strongly about this difference between the sexes. . . .

SCARRON. Personal gain—we must set aside such considerations. It is incontestable that every step of human progress depends on the strict maintenance of masculinity.

LUISE. Pah!

MANDELSTAM. Who would have thought, ten years ago, that we'd be flying?

THEOBALD. Anyhow, I'm glad to see the two of you so fully in agreement. How pleasant to have lodgers who don't get in each other's hair!

MANDELSTAM. Man stands by man.

SCARRON, *to* MANDELSTAM. Incidentally, you still owe us a statement of your opinion. Up to now you've simply rejected ours.

MANDELSTAM. Zeppelin is no hero then?

SCARRON. Plato and Kant can be dispensed with?

MANDELSTAM. Where should we be without railroad and telephone?

SCARRON. Without his predecessors, Goethe is an absolute impossibility. Would you deny Pontius and Pilate and yet have Goethe stand?

MANDELSTAM. What about Wagner? Mankind's most sacred possession!

THEOBALD, *slowly*. All this aside, there are still a lot of other things. Having children and things like that . . .

MANDELSTAM. Women's affairs yet again!

THEOBALD. Don't shout at me. Have I cast doubt on the accuracy of your facts?

SCARRON. Even a god could not do *that*.

THEOBALD. Yet the two facts I bring from my own experience —that women have hearts and that children are born—get both of you angry.

SCARRON. Incredible! These are platitudes—obvious as . . .

THEOBALD. As what?

SCARRON. No simile comes to mind. Polemics with you are pointless.

THEOBALD. Have a glass of Münchner. Luise, you pour it for Herr Scarron.

SCARRON. Thanks.

THEOBALD. Tomorrow one could go to the Zoological Gardens. They've just acquired a giraffe.

MANDELSTAM *bursts out laughing.* Giraffes!

THEOBALD. What's so funny about it?

MANDELSTAM. I'm having my own thoughts.

THEOBALD. Quite honestly, I'd never have dreamt of taking a look at such a beast. I'm not partial to such freaks and stage tricks of nature. But, since Herr Scarron's put me up to it, I want to do something for my education.

MANDELSTAM *bursts out laughing.*

THEOBALD. Don't get wild, Herr Mandelstam.

SCARRON. You pretend to be so narrow-minded, my friend . . .

MANDELSTAM. When will the scales fall from your eyes?

THEOBALD, *to* MANDELSTAM. Don't overtax your meager resources, Herr Mandelstam.

SCARRON. Should not the presence of a noble young woman be the spur to higher achievement? Raising you above your former station?

THEOBALD. My wife's parents are tailors and have been for generations.

LUISE. Six brothers fell on the field of honor.

MANDELSTAM. Today no one would be so stupid. Getting yourself slaughtered! Ugh!

THEOBALD. The spirit of the age is against it? It isn't modern to love your country?

MANDELSTAM. A while ago you almost made me ill. Now you are making me well again. Despite external handicaps, I feel like another man—strong in the knowledge that there are battalions behind me. That sort of talk leaves us cold. We know the facts: the highest born man in the world descends—like Herr Scarron and myself—from the ape. All men are equal. And anyone can get to the top.

THEOBALD. Anyone who wants to. But there are people for

whom one position is much like another, and the one they already have is the one they prefer. My birth placed me in quite a favorable position, and I feel secure till death in the possession of it—my fellows all over the Fatherland could say the same. Only special merit or extraordinary disgrace could deprive me of this security.

SCARRON. Sir, that is frightful! Slave morality!

THEOBALD, *grinning*. No. It's just that I lose my freedom if the world pays me any particular attention. Inconspicuousness is a magic cloak—under cover of which I give rein to my own real nature.

SCARRON. God forbid this faith of yours should be shared by your fellows!

THEOBALD. As for them, I cannot judge. But I can guarantee that progressive notions are not favored on the higher echelons. One of our bureau chiefs let his wife go off with another man. He wrote later in his deposition that he didn't wish to "take the curb to her"—an expression derived from the stable. Today he sells mineral water at the intersection of Wildenmacher Strasse and Fischer Strasse.

SCARRON. A martyr. His wife must look up to him.

LUISE. His wife looks down on him.

SCARRON. But you are wrong.

LUISE. With all her heart and soul.

MANDELSTAM. I, too, rather doubt it.

THEOBALD. Let's leave it to the two of them, Luise.

MANDELSTAM. I happen to have the evidence in my own past. I lived with little Frau Frühling—they have the restaurant in Ahorn Strasse—the husband permitted the relationship.

THEOBALD. That she is called Frühling and lives on Ahorn Strasse is not to the point.

LUISE *stands up*. Good night.

THEOBALD. You're staying till we all go.

MANDELSTAM. She's worshiped her husband ever since.

THEOBALD. I'll have to drink a schnapps on that. Would anyone like to accompany me to the the Golden Basket for a few minutes?

SCARRON. I am more confused than I can express. I have met this view of life before but never anyone who believed in it!

THEOBALD. Someone of no importance.

SCARRON. And yet someone. And under no circumstances would you cease to believe in it, eh?

THEOBALD. Correct. I don't want to fall off the deep end.

SCARRON. It would be hard, I see that. But one must try!

THEOBALD. Don't trouble yourself about it.

MANDELSTAM. I'm afraid it's a hopeless case.

THEOBALD. Of course, I might see reason over a glass of schnapps in the Golden Basket.

SCARRON. Please! I must beg you to be in earnest about this!

THEOBALD. If I were, I might find many things intolerable that I've been putting up with. I might have to be quite impolite. So come along!

SCARRON. Even if your *point de départ* is a theory of immutable values . . .

THEOBALD. Mandelstam, you come. They have a first-rate Münchner.

MANDELSTAM. Sorry. I must go to bed.

THEOBALD. Each man to his taste.

SCARRON, *gesticulating violently at* THEOBALD's *side*. Even if, with Kant, you assume . . .

THEOBALD *and* SCARRON *exeunt*.

MANDELSTAM. After this conversation, many things will never be the same for me again. To live in the same house with this dolt is hell. True, I have met with dense people before, but such wrongheadedness—disgusting fellow! And his vulgar familiarity because I happened to mention that my constitution wasn't of the strongest! Beside this creature, Herr Scarron seems like God Himself, if the simile is good enough. And what brutality—to take a man whose health one regards as utterly shattered—and saddle him with a room facing northeast!

LUISE. You agreed with Herr Scarron that one should feel pity for nobody.

MANDELSTAM. Pity? Who wants pity? I demand decency, no-

bility of mind—qualities, I must admit, which Herr Scarron
has exemplified in the highest degree.

LUISE. How?

MANDELSTAM. By what he said. Didn't he thrill you? Didn't
you feel what a great, overflowing heart the man has? Isn't
it touching to see how, even now, he tries to knock some
sense into that bonehead? For his pains, he'll get the same
grin that I got when I complained to the master of this
house about the room.

LUISE. We didn't have any other.

MANDELSTAM. Then it was your duty to warn me about this
one.

LUISE. But you demanded it.

MANDELSTAM. In ignorance.

LUISE. You insisted you must have that room to be near my
person.

MANDELSTAM. But if it means my certain death?

LUISE. You exaggerate.

MANDELSTAM *laughs out loud*. Exaggerate! A room facing
northeast—for a man with lung trouble—is like—an adequate
simile does not come to mind. Add to this that the awareness of such a state of affairs cannot but upset my nervous
system. Like the bark on a tree! Peeling away—can't you
see it? You with your sound, solid health—your natural
cheeks look just like make-up.

He runs into his room.

No storm windows! I'll drop dead tonight if I've no woolen
shirt, and mine's in the wash.

He returns.

Do you imagine it takes years to bring a debilitated organ-
ism down to the grave?

He disappears again into his room.

Didn't he say himself his colleague couldn't live more than
three days? In addition to which, the window doesn't close
properly.

He returns.

Now what was that about the tube? It *was* a tube he was talking about, for Heaven's sake. Say something!

LUISE. You were saying it had to do with the nervous system.

MANDELSTAM. I'm utterly confused. Now I have it: he spoke of *two* tubes and how it was impossible to patch them up again.

He again disappears, then shouts.

This hole is contrary to police regulations! Police on every block, but when it comes to a poor fellow like me, why, they leave me to rot in a corner like a mad dog.

He appears again.

What was it the doctor always did? Wait a minute. Look down my throat!

He tears his jaws open.

LUISE. I don't understand such things.

MANDELSTAM. No. This is it.

He hurls himself into a chair and throws one leg across the other.

Hit my knee, here, with the flat of your hand.

When LUISE does so, and his leg jumps upwards, he shouts.

I am lost! Obviously, a whole night facing northeast has been too much for me.

LUISE, *unable to control herself any longer.* But . . .

MANDELSTAM, *beside himself.* And you talk of pity!

LUISE, *close to tears.* You wanted to be near me—more than anything in the world.

MANDELSTAM, *roaring.* It's the grave I'm near! This is monstrous. We must speak further!

He runs into his room, slamming the door behind him and locking it on the other side. LUISE is motionless. DEUTER appears in front of the glass door. LUISE lets her in.

DEUTER. The both of them arm in arm down the street?

LUISE. What kept you so late?

DEUTER. I was at the theatre. A superb play—by Sternheim. I'll tell you about it later. You should have seen *him*. He simply sparkled!

LUISE. Who?

DEUTER. Not the giant, though he seemed all right. Our hero! Radiating manliness and power!

LUISE. Oh . . . !

DEUTER. Theobald got some of his reflected glory. Seemed livelier than usual. Well, the two of you were together all day. Tell me about it. What happened? I burn.

LUISE. Quiet. Mandelstam is home.

DEUTER. Let me look deep into your eyes. Let me take you by the hands, by the arms.

LUISE. Why, Trude?

DEUTER. To drink in your bliss. This is the sofa he sat on, near you, every moment a little nearer. Pressed, finally, against the sofa back, you could retreat no further, you didn't want to, either. Tell what he did.

LUISE. I don't remember.

DEUTER. That's cheating, you little thief. I want an unexpurgated confession. And don't be shy, Luise. I've done more reading than you think, and I dream about more of the same. I didn't see, but just the same I know. How did it begin? He put his arm around you.

LUISE. He was sitting—somewhere.

DEUTER. What about you?

LUISE. At the table.

DEUTER. He came over to you?

LUISE. He stayed where he was.

DEUTER. And?

LUISE. Spoke.

DEUTER. What? Can you repeat what he said? Splendid things.

LUISE. There was a buzzing in my ear.

DEUTER. He exploded over you like a thunderstorm! Hm? That's what I've read. Your body grew weak at the touch of his manly strength. Your legs wouldn't move.

LUISE. I did feel that way. For a moment there I took leave of my senses.

DEUTER. Happy woman! Then?

LUISE. He came over to me.

DEUTER. Luise! And then?

LUISE. Spoke.

DEUTER. And?

LUISE. Said something.

DEUTER. And?

LUISE. Spoke.

DEUTER. After which?

LUISE. What?

DEUTER. When he was through speaking?

LUISE. He left.

DEUTER. He did what?

LUISE. Left.

DEUTER. He called: "I love you!"

LUISE. Yes.

DEUTER. What about you?

LUISE. Same thing.

DEUTER. "I am yours!"

LUISE. Yes, um . . .

DEUTER. You did?

LUISE. With all my heart.

DEUTER. At last. And then?

LUISE. He left.

DEUTER. Where'd he go?

LUISE. Into his room.

DEUTER. You followed?

LUISE. No.

DEUTER. Unhappy woman!

LUISE. When he shut his door I followed. I even dared to knock.

DEUTER. You knocked?

LUISE. But he didn't open.

DEUTER. He shut himself in? . . . I have it: Mandelstam was around.

LUISE. No.

DEUTER. Are you sure? Without your seeing him, maybe? But *he* saw him?

LUISE. Hm.

DEUTER. Think back.

LUISE. Mandelstam did come in right afterwards.

DEUTER. Ha!

LUISE. I've only just realized.

DEUTER. You see! You see! Misjudging my hero! Carried away with emotion, making large, sweeping gestures, he is suddenly aware of the presence of the creeping fox I have so earnestly warned him against. In an instant, speech and gesture fall to normal. Overcome with feeling, yet sparing the loved one, the tender-hearted man takes his leave. And the intriguer's greedy eyes find the lady, quite properly, alone. How right I was! You are in no position to understand him. Didn't he later take the first opportunity that offered to renew his vows of love?

LUISE. He did. He proved to be jealous of the barber.

DEUTER. I formed a clearer picture of him from afar than you did near at hand.

LUISE. But later, talking with the men . . .

DEUTER. What about?

LUISE. I lost him completely. I went outside. I had to cry.

DEUTER. A false conclusion.

LUISE. It was my aversion to my husband that I felt to be false, and my liking for this other man. The misery that took me by the throat as he talked on made me feel everything about me was false and had been since the day I was born.

DEUTER. You understood him just as little as earlier when he spared you. You simply didn't grasp what he had in mind. Trust to my own deep conviction. He is even now preparing the deed that will finally conquer you.

LUISE. I am plunged in despair. I am forever unhappy.

DEUTER. Fainthearted girl! Not in vain does he draw your husband from your side by night. Not for nothing does he fascinate him with the fire of life, and entangle him inextricably in problems and ideas. Had you been with me at the theatre, you would know that happiness stands in your path. There was a man in that play who climbed walls, burst gates open, and set fire to things—just to be near his loved one. The conviction that men have us poor creatures in their power poured forth in a torrent of words. What shall we do, little fool? Any time that we squander in talk is stolen from the waiting hero. . . . Good night . . . One kiss . . . By the bones of the saints, I swear: it shall be . . . Quiet . . . Lie down, hurry, put all the lights out. He is coming!

She hurries out.

LUISE. Is it possible?

She sits motionless for a moment and listens, then goes to the window and looks out, sits down again, stands up, and goes into the bedroom where she lights up. Returning, she begins to get undressed, her face pressed against the hall door. Sounds are heard on the stairs. She puts out the light on stage and stands there trembling. The sound is lost again.

No!

Mechanically she goes on with her unbuttoning. Then she approaches MANDELSTAM's *door and touches the latch—but then returns to her own bedroom door, dragging her feet behind her. And there she stays, lighted from behind, in slip and pants, slowly and repeatedly combing her hair, while at intervals* MANDELSTAM's *regular snoring shakes the air.*

ACT FOUR

THEOBALD *shouts into the bedroom.* That was a sloppy job you did, mending my suspenders! You can't neglect me just because of these two other fellows!

LUISE *comes in and pours him coffee.*

Luckily neither of them is in. Thank God we needn't expect Scarron before noon. After he'd talked at me till two in the morning like someone with hallucinations, he earnestly requested me to take him to his apartment because the bed there is better. I drank five beers and three schnapps. The result—diarrhea.

LUISE. He's not coming.

THEOBALD. I don't see how anyone can sleep like you with a man running back and forth all the time. Where is the honey?

LUISE. There's none left.

THEOBALD. What housekeeping! Please get some. Also I don't like to find your underwear on my chair. Always something for me to lecture you about!

LUISE. Mandelstam made another scene about facing northeast. After which I sank into bed.

THEOBALD. The man is crazy. What's wrong with the north? Or the east either? Does he consider them inferior points of the compass? The sun rises in the east. Painters like their rooms to face the north. And yet a miserable barber expects to include the west and the south for a miserable five thaler?

LUISE. It's true the south would be easier on his weak chest. And you say Herr Scarron won't come today? How is that?

THEOBALD. Your nose is running, please wipe it. What do you mean: how is that? He was drunk and won't be at his best today.

LUISE. Drunk?

THEOBALD. Plastered. He got to be an awful sight to see. Despite his condition, he never gave up the idea that he must convert me. You'd have thought he'd been stung by a tarantula.

LUISE. Heavens!

THEOBALD. That man is an exotic, ornamental plant in the garden of God. Also, his breath smells.

LUISE. Theobald! He used to have—doesn't he at times have something heroic about him?

THEOBALD. As in a novel, you mean?

LUISE. Yes, as in a novel.

THEOBALD. My Lord! Luise, look: he hasn't much ability. Don't you think he should be a good deal more heroic than he is—to make up for the deficiency?

LUISE. Yes.

THEOBALD. These projects aren't serious that he starts up. I believe he's tired already of the whim that brought him here. Not that it matters to me. He took the room for a year, and it's in writing.

LUISE. May I go to church today? It's almost an emergency.

THEOBALD. Certainly, my dove. A very happy thought. Last week, with your pants falling down, was fraught with danger for us both. It's no less than your duty to thank your Maker. Meanwhile, I shall be following to its logical end a resolve of mine that is fraught with consequences.

LUISE. Tell me.

THEOBALD. You are inquisitive. Rightly . . . When you return, Luise. Leave me an hour to mull it over. You'll be astonished.

LUISE. Will I?

She goes into the alcove.

THEOBALD. What are you doing?

LUISE. The curtain should be on our side. Everyone can see in.

THEOBALD. Don't fall off the window sill.

He follows her. One hears him from inside.

The little woman has pretty good calves.

MANDELSTAM *enters, hurriedly sits at the coffee table, starts greedily to eat, goes to the alcove to shut the door.* What?

Recognizing THEOBALD.

Oh, excuse me.

THEOBALD, *embarrassed.* I didn't hear you come in. We're taking the curtain into our room.

MANDELSTAM. You've had breakfast?

He sits.

THEOBALD. Yes.

LUISE *walks across the stage into her bedroom.*

MANDELSTAM. Good morning, Frau Maske.

THEOBALD. You seem to have slept well.

MANDELSTAM. You got me so excited, I was simply overcome with drowsiness. Yes, I slept wonderfully.

THEOBALD, *laughing.* Despite the northeast . . .

MANDELSTAM. Yes, indeed. Although——

THEOBALD. There's an although?

MANDELSTAM. The bed is a good one.

THEOBALD. Better than the softest belly.

MANDELSTAM. Although——

THEOBALD. You hear the street noises?

MANDELSTAM. Not a sound. Although——

THEOBALD. The morning sun disturbs you . . .

MANDELSTAM. I love nothing so much—and yet . . .

THEOBALD. In view of all these advantages, five thaler is too little. You have my wife to thank.

MANDELSTAM. Not that you'd suddenly raise the price, I'm sure?

THEOBALD. Not at present.

MANDELSTAM. I'm afraid you don't make yourself clear. Why don't we set a date?

THEOBALD. Why bind yourself?

Enter LUISE.

MANDELSTAM. Don't I get any honey today?

LUISE. Honey is extra. All over the world.

MANDELSTAM. I thought it was included.

LUISE. Then you thought wrong. At that, the sugar gets used up anyway in no time at all.

To THEOBALD.

So long.

THEOBALD. And take care.

Exit LUISE.

Why bind yourself? If the doctor discovered something more serious and decided that the northeast outlook is hazardous you'd be in a fix. Yes, the bed is good. The mattress is made of a kind of horsehair not found any more—even on thoroughbreds.

MANDELSTAM. Indisputably.

THEOBALD. Morning sun and perfect quiet . . . It so happens we'd decided to exchange that bed for another—just before you came. Fräulein Deuter, who lives downstairs, offered sixty thaler for it in cash.

MANDELSTAM. Never! You must never do it!

THEOBALD *has gone into* MANDELSTAM's *room.* An eiderdown! And my wife went and added a second pillow expressly against my wishes.

MANDELSTAM. All right, to cut a long story short: one year. We understand each other, Herr Maske.

THEOBALD. The state of your health . . .

MANDELSTAM. I feel as strong as a giant.

THEOBALD. Prices rise in this neighborhood from one day to the next. In three months this room will easily be worth eight thaler and not five.

MANDELSTAM. The more excited you get me the less attractive the proposition!

THEOBALD. I'll name my lowest price. Six thaler.

MANDELSTAM. I can't pay it.

THEOBALD. Very well. Nothing doing.

MANDELSTAM. Oh, all right. Just to put an end to all this. The way you can talk of Bismarck and Luther, I'd never have believed it.

THEOBALD. A deal!

MANDELSTAM. One year. And let's put something in writing at once. "Herr Maske rents to Herr Mandelstam until May 15 . . . one room, morning coffee included."

THEOBALD. But no honey.

MANDELSTAM. "For six thaler. The bed now in the room may not be replaced by another." Now sign.

THEOBALD. Now suppose my wife isn't agreeable. She finds you unsympathetic.

MANDELSTAM. But we needn't have anything to do with each other, for Heaven's sake.

THEOBALD. Even so. As she doesn't like to have you here, she may feel inhibited.

MANDELSTAM. Not by me. I'll swear it to her a thousand times over: she doesn't bother me, she can do and not do as she pleases. Don't throw me out on the street! I admit the bed is good. In view of the appalling state of my health—have mercy on me!

THEOBALD. All right. Since you leave me no alternative. I'm no monster.

He signs.

There: Theobald Maske.

MANDELSTAM. Is there a leftover armchair about the place?

THEOBALD. I'd better tear it up. My wife——

MANDELSTAM, *grabbing the paper out of his hands.* The devil take your wife!

THEOBALD. Here's to our life together!

MANDELSTAM. I'll do *my* part.

He looks into his room.

You should have seen the bed in my previous place. A torture chamber. Uninterrupted noise from all sides. Also a small menagerie . . . oh yes, my dear fellow, fleas, bed-bugs. . . . I wrote Richard Wagner's signature on the wallpaper with pins stuck through dead insects.

He laughs.

When I spoke against you last night, I was a little bit carried away. I meant no harm.

THEOBALD. That was more than all right with me. The thing is to agree with Herr Scarron. He pays well. We owe him all kinds of consideration.

MANDELSTAM, *hat on head.* I'll do *my* part.

THEOBALD. Where are you off to today?

MANDELSTAM. The Park Pavilion.

THEOBALD. Wouldn't you be making better use of your day off if you consulted a good doctor?

MANDELSTAM. Not while I feel as I do.

THEOBALD. What's her name?

MANDELSTAM. No one. My last was Frieda. She has an engineer now.

THEOBALD. A fine strapping wench?

MANDELSTAM. Tremendous. Trust me. At the firework display this evening, there'll be more such.

Exit MANDELSTAM.

THEOBALD. It was just an idea in passing—to ask for more rent. A thoroughly feeble brain, that fellow. Eighteen thaler in all. Twelve times eighteen is 180 plus, um . . . 216 thaler for the year. Now I pay 115 for the apartment. 101 are left. I earn 700, that makes 801 thaler and free living quarters. Not bad. It can be done, you see. Great. Excellent. Who's there?

DEUTER *is at the door.*

THEOBALD *lets her in.* Come right in, Fräulein. We were just talking about you.

DEUTER. Who was?

THEOBALD. A barber and I.

DEUTER. A worthless fellow.

THEOBALD. And very much interested in you, it seems.

DEUTER. Leave out the jokes.

THEOBALD. His eyes fluttered gently upwards and he said: "Trude."

DEUTER. How did he know my first name?

THEOBALD. I'm sure I don't know who is lucky enough to be intimate with you.

DEUTER. You're trying to tease me.

THEOBALD. God forbid.

DEUTER. Is your wife in?

THEOBALD. She's at church.

DEUTER. Herr Scarron is out?

THEOBALD. A flowered dress you happened to wear last night seemed to him an admirable subject for conversation. He even thought of a word for you.

DEUTER. Which was?

THEOBALD. *Popote.*

DEUTER. What does it mean?

THEOBALD. I don't know the definition, but the word *has* something. What's that you're holding so tight?

DEUTER. Nothing for you. I find Herr Scarron's description of me absurd. I see nothing nice about it.

THEOBALD. I like it. I think it fits.

DEUTER. As you don't even know what it means . . .

She sits down on the couch.

THEOBALD. It's the sound of the word . . .

DEUTER. The sound?!

THEOBALD. The images it conjures up. Makes you think of little round arms—oh, all sorts of things.

DEUTER. Quite absurd. You call a lady either plain or pretty.

THEOBALD. Let's say: either spindly or *popote.*

DEUTER. Spindly! Oh dear, an old maid like me.

THEOBALD, *who has taken her package and opened it.* Underpants! And what underpants! Pink silk ribbons, material like a spider's web. The woman who wears these and talks of old maids is fishing for a compliment!

DEUTER. You think so?

THEOBALD. Why would a battered old ship sport silken sails?

DEUTER. So as not to seem battered and old.

THEOBALD. In fairy tales only. In real life, they save themselves useless expenditure.

He holds the pants up, spreads them out.

They have zing. And when they fit their owner as if she'd been poured into them, they will give rise to some very pretty notions.

DEUTER. Herr Maske! I don't know this side of you.

THEOBALD. You don't know any side of me. One might even say you and I didn't see eye to eye before today. And it didn't really bother me. But then yesterday you came with that devil of a dress—and today you come in these tricky underpants . . .

DEUTER. *Carrying* them chastely on my arm to show to your wife.

THEOBALD. If all is to be as it should be, they need complementing by white stockings.

DEUTER. The things you think of!

THEOBALD. My good girl, how do you know I haven't been thinking of you—before today? I'm like that. Now you've got me discussing such delicate topics, you'll find I am by no means as indifferent to your many qualities—qualities which, by Heaven, a man can't help noticing—as thus far it may have seemed.

DEUTER. If your wife knew this!

THEOBALD. She knows nothing. I wouldn't permit myself to tell her—it would only trouble her. I do such things very much in secret. And not often, though with great pleasure.

DEUTER. Human beings are only human beings after all.

THEOBALD. Not after all. I began at the age of fourteen.

DEUTER. I'm thirty-two. A girl doesn't have it so easy.

THEOBALD. But almost.

DEUTER. My parents were more strict than I can say. Father beat me for being a minute late, and didn't die till I was twenty-nine.

THEOBALD. That's tough.

DEUTER. Then I came here. But under the eyes of all these old women . . .

THEOBALD. Did you leave your apartment unlocked?

DEUTER. I locked up when I came here. This house is all spies.

THEOBALD. Twenty past ten . . . I have it: one evening I

found myself looking down at you from our windows while
you——

DEUTER. I must go. Your wife will be back.

THEOBALD. Not for another hour.

He stands in the open door of the bedroom.

Do you notice how clearly one can see your room from near
my bed?

DEUTER, *going toward him.* Really?

The door closes behind them. SCARRON *enters by the hall
door after a moment and looks enquiringly about. A knock
at the hall door.* SCARRON *opens it.*

THE STRANGER. They tell me downstairs there's a room for rent
here.

SCARRON. The tenant isn't in. Maybe you should come back
later. But there are no rooms free so far as *I* know.

THE STRANGER. The janitor's wife says the opposite.

SCARRON. Of course I can't tell you for sure.

THE STRANGER. Are there many children in the house? Is there
a piano? Can you tell me these things?

SCARRON. No.

THE STRANGER. Thank you very much. When will the tenant
be back?

SCARRON. I'm afraid I can't say.

THE STRANGER. Good-by.

Exit THE STRANGER. SCARRON *goes into his room.*

THEOBALD, *peeping out of the bedroom.* Who was that?

Goes to SCARRON's *door, listens, and runs to the bedroom.*
Come on. Scarron is back.

DEUTER, *coming.* Do you love me? When shall I see you again?
Today? Early tomorrow morning before you leave?

THEOBALD. Now don't let's overdo it. I'll be thinking over how
things should be arranged. Perhaps, after all, we should fix
on a certain day of the week. I'll make all the arrangements.

DEUTER. Am I to see you only once in seven days? What shall

I do with the others, now that each minute without you seems an eternity?

THEOBALD. Pull yourself together, your impatience may spell disaster. If you can only be content with a few times, the pleasure of each particular time will be the greater.

DEUTER. But . . .

THEOBALD. Not another word. And I'll send my wife downstairs if you want to talk with her.

DEUTER. Actually, I've nothing to say to her now.

THEOBALD. So much the better. And remember: no scowling at her! No snide remarks for her to overhear!

SCARRON, *entering.* Good morning all! There was an elderly man here with a full beard. He wanted to rent a room.

THEOBALD. Ah! This business has possibilities. We are making headway!

DEUTER. I'll be going.

THEOBALD. Maybe I should have let Mandelstam go.

DEUTER. Where did I leave my parcel?

SCARRON *hands her the underpants wrapped in paper.*

Voilà! Thank you so much, Herr Scarron. Good morning.

Exit DEUTER.

THEOBALD. Are you better?

SCARRON. You left me for dead in my doorway—you have the right to ask. But what happened will very much surprise you. The need to elude the grasp of a senseless theory became more imperative than the demands of my prostrate body. And so—as you staggered off home . . .

THEOBALD. Don't worry about me. Just a little bellyache.

SCARRON. The clarity of your view of things had struck me most forcibly and, exhausted as I was, brought into doubt the accumulated conclusions of many years.

THEOBALD. The view of a petty official, Herr Scarron.

SCARRON. A view that, for me at least, was an event—an event that required me to re-establish the truth of my own gospel without a moment's delay.

THEOBALD. In the middle of the night?

SCARRON. God was merciful. As I ran up and down the river-bank—my brain confused and affrighted—all of a sudden I saw a shadow following me.

THEOBALD. Oh!

SCARRON. When I came to a standstill, there before me towered—a woman.

THEOBALD. Towered?

SCARRON. Don't interrupt. She stared at me out of vacant eyes.

THEOBALD. I'll be damned.

SCARRON. The quest for bread and God in human form! Those first minutes! That exquisite eloquence of the eyes! She administered more than a sacrament: she poured herself into me, body and soul, she let me into the secret of her thousand shames. Understand this, my dear fellow: it was a miracle. Never was chastity so fervently close to me—running around with children, kneeling before the madonna—as with this whore. I soon reached a conclusion: your view that values are immutable—for that, surely, is your view of life in a nutshell . . .

THEOBALD. It is?

SCARRON. Yes, it is. And it was proved forever invalid by this woman. Year after year I had maintained, nay, strengthened my faith in humanity's power to develop. Year after year I had endeavored to educate and improve my own powers of understanding. Now I knew: it was not in vain.

THEOBALD. You knew?

SCARRON. I followed her to her miserable dwelling, and there in the light of a quavering lamp I drew from her locked and bolted breast such a confession of high, new, undreamt-of Greatness that I fell on my knees beside her straw mattress . . .

THEOBALD. She was already on the straw?

SCARRON. And uttered prayers full of a fearful strength and humility. I wouldn't have lifted my head even if she'd trodden on it with her thorn-torn feet.

THEOBALD. Which happens sometimes.

SCARRON. How far from appreciating such a feeling you are,

all of you! Every hour she sacrificed her body to the baseness of men, and every day she raised herself, by her sorrow, nearer to the Omniscient One.

THEOBALD. These girls are very goodhearted.

SCARRON. When the morning sun surprised us, she found me unworthy of her.

THEOBALD. But you did pay?

SCARRON. I shall not take offense at your question: we are oceans apart. How you'd laugh if I told you I wouldn't have *dared* ask her to marry me!

THEOBALD, *worried*. You still haven't slept? You seem in a bad way.

SCARRON. There will be no sleep for me till I see this woman's soul so clearly that I can re-create it for all mankind. Would you believe that, yesterday, I was intending to make you, Herr Maske, the hero of a work of art? Today I feel with greater conviction than ever before: the artistic viability of any object depends solely upon that object's psychological volume.

THEOBALD. Viability? Psychological volume?

SCARRON, *smiling*. Poor fellow! I forgot. You must have difficulty following me?

THEOBALD. I got some of it. You were with a woman last night.

SCARRON. An angel.

THEOBALD. A fallen angel.

SCARRON. You are a philistine.

THEOBALD. You're not going to tell me about psychological volume?

SCARRON. Nothing is immutable. Not even good and evil—thank God.

THEOBALD. Man alive, that sounds dangerous!

SCARRON. It is. Thus have I lived, and thus will I die. . . . And there's something I hope you won't take amiss: I shall have to leave you.

THEOBALD. But you signed a lease for a year.

SCARRON. I'll honor it. I'll pay you twelve times twelve thaler in advance—a hundred and fifty

Which he pays.

—and I've no objection in the world if you wish to rent the friendly little place all over again. Your personality—however auspicious in your own sphere of life—might affect my next project unfavorably. You understand?

THEOBALD. This is six thaler too much.

SCARRON. Think nothing of it.

THEOBALD. You're an unusual character.

SCARRON. A man of action, that is all: I can leave nothing unfinished. That is why I am drawn to this woman—irresistibly. I must be the intimate witness of her life and her milieu. It is my God-given duty to plumb human relations to the depths. Accustomed as I am to the heights, I must consent to descend into the abyss. Who knows what unheard-of joys await me?

THEOBALD. You're a bit of a rascal.

SCARRON, *severely.* Unheard-of joys—and unlimited torments!

THEOBALD. *I* see! One should take care not to fall too low too soon. A certain regularity is required.

SCARRON. A certain *ir*regularity is required. Or I'd hang myself.

THEOBALD. One can be irregular—with a certain regularity.

SCARRON. In a short time I hope to send you a book that will make you sit up.

THEOBALD. And if you have a well-to-do friend who needs a room, send him to us. What you need first, though, is a couple of hours' sleep.

SCARRON. Herr Maske!

THEOBALD. You do.

SCARRON. Well, Heaven knows, it may be sound advice. I begin to feel a little fatigue. Good luck go with you!

THEOBALD. You'll be with us again sometime.

SCARRON. Where can I find a cab in this neighborhood? That damned winding staircase.

THEOBALD, *laughing.* Your poor old legs! But you'll sleep it off.

SCARRON, *encountering* THE STRANGER *in the doorway.* Here's the gentleman who wanted the room.

Exit SCARRON.

THE STRANGER. The janitor's wife told me you were bound to be home. You have a room free now, I hear?

THEOBALD. As chance will have it, yes. Twelve thaler, breakfast included.

THE STRANGER. Expensive.

THEOBALD. A large room. See for yourself.

THE STRANGER. Any pianos in the vicinity? Little children? A sewing machine? Canaries?

THEOBALD. Nothing in that line at all.

THE STRANGER. You keep cats or dogs?

THEOBALD. No.

THE STRANGER. You have marriageable daughters?

THEOBALD. No.

THE STRANGER. You're a married man: is your wife young?

THEOBALD. Yes.

THE STRANGER. Flirtatious?

THEOBALD. There'd be hell to pay.

THE STRANGER. So you're constantly on the watch?

THEOBALD. Absolutely . . . The conveniences are halfway up the stairs.

THE STRANGER. I reduce personal contacts to the minimum. The maid will knock three times before entering. Instead of coffee, I shall take tea, which I supply myself. I suffer from constipation, but that is my affair.

THEOBALD. Your affair entirely.

THE STRANGER. Under these conditions, I'll come here for a trial period of one month. I can give notice as late as the fifteenth. My name is Stengelhöh, my field is science.

THEOBALD. Agreed.

THE STRANGER. When the maid comes in, her clothes must be proper: nothing torn, nothing transparent. My things will be here in one hour. Good morning.

THEOBALD. Good morning, Herr Stengelhöh.

Exit THE STRANGER.

I'll take out "Joseph Before Potiphar" and hang instead "Boa Constrictor in Combat with Lion."

He gets a picture from his bedroom and carries it over to what had been SCARRON's *room. Enter* LUISE.

Did you see Herr Stengelhöh on the stairs? A man with a full beard?

LUISE. I believe so.

THEOBALD. He's our new lodger. The business is making headway. Nothing can stop it. He takes tea, which he'll supply, and his field is science.

LUISE. Scarron?

THEOBALD. Ah yes, Scarron. I saw through him. He is tired of us. He's vanished, never to return, after paying one year's rent in advance. He expressed a wish to be cordially remembered to you. I could tell you other things about him, but Heaven preserve one's wife from such ridiculous fanfaronades. He was a clown and a poltroon, he stank of violets. Mandelstam, on the other hand, is staying for a year, and I'll fix it so he'll barber me for nothing. Did it do you good, going to church?

LUISE. The dear old Holy Catholic Church, Theobald.

THEOBALD. No empty dream, you're right.

LUISE. We've been married just one year today.

THEOBALD. How time flies!

LUISE. What shall I cook for you?

THEOBALD. I know very well you have a tasty pork roast tucked away somewhere.

LUISE. I'll serve it with sauerkraut.

THEOBALD. You might risk adding an onion. And now I'm going to come right out with my big secret: those two men that stumbled on this apartment, so to speak, have put us in a position finally to—to what, Luise?

LUISE. I don't know.

THEOBALD. You don't even guess.

Gently.

I can manage it now: I can give you a child. What do you say?

LUISE *starts cooking in silence.*

Handle him with kid gloves. He's peculiar, Stengelhöh. He wishes to have no personal relationships here. Asked if you were flirtatious. Suffers from constipation.

He runs around the room.

The clock isn't wound up—as usual—for all my appeals. The flowers need water.

He pours some on them.

Fräulein Deuter was here an hour ago. Wanted to show you some underpants she's made herself. They're using snap buttons now instead of ribbons. Look into it. With these snaps, the confounded incident that gave us so much trouble need never have happened. With you so lascivious, it's good we can avoid big trouble at so little expense.

He sits at the window and takes a newspaper.

Behind the wallpaper of life, so to speak, strange things happen. I still have that bellyache. Mustn't go on the spree in future . . . Snaps . . . The human race invents something good and sensible once in a while. I believe I read you this before: They say the sea serpent has turned up again in Indian waters.

LUISE, *mechanically.* Good Lord! And what does such a creature live off?

THEOBALD. The experts disagree. And anyway I find reports of weird things like that repulsive. Repulsive.

A SOCIAL SUCCESS

by

MAX BEERBOHM

Characters

TOMMY DIXON
aged 30, clean-shaven, debonair

THE DUCHESS OF HUNTINGTON
handsome, a widow, aged 40

THE EARL OF AMERSHAM
*full-bodied, sleek, red-faced man of 53. Fair hair
turning grey, small fair moustache*

THE COUNTESS OF AMERSHAM
pretty, romantic-looking woman of 29. Dark hair

HENRY ROBBINS
*three or four years older than Tommy. Rather stiff
and formal. Long, serious face, clean-shaven*

HAWKINS
valet acting as butler

SCENE: *Drawing-room of* TOMMY DIXON's *flat in Mount Street.*

TIME: *1913. Between 11 and 12 p.m.*

The room is of a conventionally luxurious kind. Facing you is a wide bay-window with drawn curtains. Between the window and the door there is a threefold screen of Spanish leather. In front of the window is a writing-table, with a telephone. Book-shelves in plenty. Bright fire in grate. Along the mantelpiece and all around the mirror, a serried array of invitation-cards, big and little. Two arm-chairs near fire, Also a low table with the inevitable Tantalus and syphons, a bottle or two of mineral water, cigarettes, etc.

At a large round table (in the middle of your side of the room) the game of poker is being played. TOMMY *(facing you) has on his right side* LADY AMERSHAM, *and on his left the* DUCHESS. *Next to the* DUCHESS *is* LORD AMERSHAM; *next to whom, on* LADY AMERSHAM's *right, is* HENRY ROBBINS. TOMMY *has a goodly pile of counters before him, interspersed with banknotes and gold. There is also a large "pool" in the middle of the table. The four other players have but a few counters apiece.*

As the curtain rises these four players are taking up the cards dealt them by TOMMY.

TOMMY, *fingering the remainder of the pack.* Cards, Duchess?

DUCHESS, *sighing as she lays down her cards.* Hopeless.

TOMMY. Amersham?

LORD A., *laying down his cards.* Pass.

DUCHESS, *fingering the pool.* And such a pool!

TOMMY. Robbins?

ROBBINS, *shaking his head.* I must pass.

TOMMY. Come! I can't be left to rake all this in!

Persuasively.

Lady Amersham!

LADY A., *after a slight tremor.* Two cards, Tommy.

Takes the two cards, utters a little cry of relief. TOMMY *looks at his own cards.*

TOMMY. H'm, I'll stay as I am.

DUCHESS. What cards he has!

Looks fondly at him.

TOMMY. Yes, it's too bad to ask you all here, and then . . .

LADY A., *pushing forward her counters.* I stake my all!

TOMMY, *with a shrug of the shoulders.* Sorry. Raise you a fiver. Can't help it.

LADY A., *holding out her hand to her husband.* Two fivers, Jack.

LORD AMERSHAM *produces banknotes from pocket-book, and passes them to his wife, not taking his eyes off* TOMMY, *whose hands are below the level of the table.*

LADY A. *lays down one note on table and says to* TOMMY. There.

She lays down the other.

See you for a fiver.

TOMMY. Four aces.

He shows his cards.

LADY A., *ruefully.* Oh . . .

DUCHESS. Didn't I . . .

LORD AMERSHAM *meanwhile has leapt to his feet.*

LORD A., *leaning across the table with forefinger outstretched to* TOMMY, *and in a voice hoarse with passion.* You scoundrel!

TOMMY. W-what?

LADY A. Jack!

ROBBINS. Really!

DUCHESS. The man's mad!

LORD A. How did you come by the ace of clubs?

TOMMY, *vaguely.* How did I . . .

LORD A. How did *I*, sir?

Turns up his own cards, confronting TOMMY *with ace of clubs.*

LADY A., *faintly.* Don't call him "sir"!

ROBBINS. It must have got in out of the other pack.

LORD A., *relentlessly.* The other pack's pink. This one's green. This card of mine has a green back: so has—our host's.

TOMMY, *pursing his lips, and gazing wide-eyed at* LORD AMERSHAM'S *ace.* H'm.

DUCHESS, *to* LORD A. You don't—you can't mean——
She rises from table.

LADY A. Mean what?

LORD A. I mean that I have been watching him very narrowly for the past half-hour, and . . .

TOMMY, *springing to his feet.* A pretty thing to do—watching a man under his own roof, and then slandering him and . . . and . . .

LORD A. Undo your sleeve-links! Lay bare your arm!

TOMMY, *staggering back, stammering.* You seem to—to forget there are ladies present.

ROBBINS, *who has also risen, to* LORD A. You don't mean . . .

LORD A. I mean that I'm going to see if that was the only ace the fellow had up his sleeve.
He darts round the table (in front of the DUCHESS, *who has retreated a few steps) and seizes* TOMMY *by the left arm.*

LADY A., *her hands clasped in agony.* Tommy, say it isn't true!

TOMMY, *wrenches his arm out of* LORD AMERSHAM'S *grip; then sullenly.* Wouldn't make much difference what I said. May as well own up and . . .
With a broken laugh. . . .
make a—clean wrist of it. It's what they call "a fair cop."
Produces a card from left-hand shirt-cuff and throws it on table.
Ace of hearts.
Two cards from right-hand shirt-cuff.
Ace of spades. Ace of diamonds.
Feels in breast pocket of coat.
Other court cards.
Throws down these.
That's the lot.

Hang-dog he stares down at table. ROBBINS *and the two women have slowly retreated further and further away from him.* LADY AMERSHAM *now buries her face in her hands.* THE DUCHESS *gazes up in petrified agony to the ceiling.* ROBBINS *stands with chin sunk on breast.*

LORD A., *bringing clenched right hand down on open palm of left.* And this—this is the man we—we've broken bread with! This is the man we've all of us for the past few years been calling Tommy till, damn it, I hardly remember his surname. . . . Dixon, that's it. . . . Dixon the card-sharper.

A low wail escapes from LADY AMERSHAM.

Enid, my darling, go and get on your cloak. This . . .

With increasing horror.

. . . is the man I put up for Bains's—the one remaining club that *nobody* can get into—and got him in. You'll send in your resignation to-night, sir.

ROBBINS *utters a groan.*

TOMMY. Don't you try to bully *me!* I'm a member of Bains's and there I'll stick—till they expel me.

LORD A. I'll go straight there—Enid, you can drop me there—and I'll tell every man in the place.

To TOMMY.

And there'll be an end of *you!*

Simultaneously TOMMY *presses button of electric bell in wall behind him. Another groan from* ROBBINS.

LORD A., *turning on* ROBBINS. As for you, Mr. Roberts——

ROBBINS. Robbins.

LORD A., *to* TOMMY. You had the impudence to-night to ask me to second your friend for the Club. . . .

TOMMY. And you said that any friend of mine . . .

LORD AMERSHAM *makes an explosive sound.* HAWKINS *meanwhile has appeared in answer to the bell.*

TOMMY. The lift, Hawkins.

Exit HAWKINS.

LORD A. I won't set foot in your lift. Enid, my darling, come—by the staircase. Duchess, I'm unspeakably . . .

DUCHESS, *moving with them to the door.* I feel that the very staircase is polluted.

Makes a gesture as to gather up her skirt, and audibly inhales between her teeth.

I should like to be carried to my car.

Exeunt the DUCHESS *and* LORD *and* LADY AMERSHAM. TOMMY *stands motionless, with bowed head and clenched hands.* ROBBINS *stands on the other side of the room, with arms folded, looking him up and down. At sound of the slammed front-door he moves slowly towards the door of the room, still gazing sternly at his friend, and goes out, shutting the door after him.* TOMMY *looks at the door, delightedly clasps his hands, beams, looks around, and anon begins to pirouette gracefully around the room. As he reaches the table where the glasses and decanters are, he stoops down (facing you), and airily pours some whisky into a tumbler, then some Apollinaris. As he does so, the door opens noiselessly, revealing* ROBBINS *in hat and overcoat.* ROBBINS *gives a violent start, strides down the stage. Just as* TOMMY *raises the tumbler to his lips* ROBBINS *from behind grips his friend's wrist with one hand and firmly removes the tumbler with the other.* TOMMY, *confounded, returns his stare.* ROBBINS, *not relaxing his grip, raises the tumbler to his nostrils, sniffs it, looks quickly round from it into his friend's eyes.*

ROBBINS. Arsenic?

He quickly sniffs tumbler again, then with another piercing and probing glance at TOMMY.

Strychnine?

Sniff and glance repeated.

Hydrochloric? . . . Anyhow . . .

He carefully inverts the tumbler and spills its contents to the carpet.

. . . that's the place for it.

TOMMY. You haven't much feeling for my carpet, old boy.

ROBBINS. A human life—even the life of a man who has sunk so low as you—is more sacred to me than any carpet.

TOMMY. Ah, you see, you don't derive an income from carpets. *I do.* This is one of Dixon's extra double-pile hand-woven, and . . .

ROBBINS. That's what makes it all the more horrible that you have . . .

Gesture to card-table.

. . . done *that* . . . If you had been a *poor* man. . . .

TOMMY. I can't see that that would have been any excuse.

ROBBINS. I am glad you are not lost to all sense of decency. . . . In the old days, when we had those rooms in the Temple——

TOMMY. Happy days!

ROBBINS. Ah, if you'd only stuck to the Bar! If your father had only lived . . .

TOMMY. And left me to shift for myself—yes. It's that con-founded unearned increment that has undermined me. Good-night, old man. Rising barristers can't afford to asso-ciate with card-sharpers.

ROBBINS, *with a groan.* How long have you been——?

Gesture to card-table.

TOMMY. Well, as a matter of fact, to-night was my debut.

ROBBINS, *throws back head, and sighs deeply.* When I think of the splendid social position you'd made for yourself—made without effort—the great houses you had the run of—the great people and the gay and noble who . . . To-night, when I heard the Duchess calling you "Tommy" . . . Charming woman, the Duchess.

Meditatively removes hat from head.

It was very good of you to ask me to-night, Tommy. . . . And Lord and Lady Amersham—what charming people! The best type of our old English——

TOMMY. You're becoming maudlin, old boy.

ROBBINS. Ah, Tommy, I can't take those people so lightly as you do. Perhaps that's the reason why they never seem to follow me up. . . . When I think of you dragging out a mis-erable existence in some shady foreign watering-place . . .

TOMMY. I shall do nothing of the sort.

ROBBINS. You mean . . . ?

Pointing to tumbler.

TOMMY. You certainly are maudlin. As if a fellow can't have a simple whisky and Apollinaris without being suspected of suicide!

ROBBINS. Then I didn't save your life?

Points down to the stain on carpet.

There wasn't a drop of . . . ?

TOMMY. If you doubt my word . . .

Gesture to telephone.

. . . ring up the Home Office and ask them to send round the Public Analyst, to analyse the carpet.

ROBBINS, *in a constrained voice, staring down at the stain.* Oh, . . . well, . . . I'm glad.

TOMMY. Don't take it so hard, Robbins. You showed great presence of mind and good feeling, and all that. But some-how . . .

Mixing another drink for himself.

. . . you chaps with trained legal faculties are always so awfully wide of the mark. . . . Now mind!

Indicating tumbler.

This is for *me*. I will not have you debauching my carpet.

Takes a deep draught.

As for dragging out a miserable existence in a shady foreign watering-place that you've found in the pages of Thackeray —nonsense! I shall stay just where I am.

ROBBINS. And face the music? Tommy, I shall stand by you.

TOMMY, *with a queer look.* That's the worst of old friends— no shaking 'em off!

ROBBINS. Tommy!

TOMMY. I'm sorry.

Lays hand on ROBBINS' *shoulder.*

I don't mind old friends. Hang it, no: I don't want to be a hermit. Freedom!—that's all I wanted. And now . . .

Flings wide his arms, gazing up beatifically.

. . . I've got it!

ROBBINS. Freedom? Of course there'll be no question of gaol.
But to be publicly branded, as . . . Freedom? Freedom
from what?

TOMMY. Why, from the whole cursed dog's-life I've been leading. Freedom to sit down cosily and lead my own life. Tranquillity, independence, quiet fun. Books. Pipes. D'you know,
Robbins, I haven't been able to settle down to a book since
. . . heaven knows when . . . ever since I got caught up
into that infernal social merry-go-round. To-night I've
jumped off. Jolly neatly, too. Pleasing air of finality about
the whole thing.

ROBBINS. Tommy, this bravado is more heart-rending than if
you . . .

TOMMY. Bravado? When a man's just brought off a very delicate and ticklish job which he——

ROBBINS. You *didn't* bring it off. You were found out.

TOMMY. Robbins, you're hopeless. How many more times must
I tell you that my object was just *to* be found out?

ROBBINS. *To* be found out?

TOMMY. You lawyers aren't able to understand the simplest
statement unless it's made on oath in a witness-box by a
man whom you can browbeat. . . . *To* be found out. . . .
Mind you, I only tell you this in strictest confidence. You
must swear not to——

ROBBINS. I never betray a confidence. But do you ask me to
believe . . . What possible motive——

TOMMY. Haven't I told you my motive was to get right out of
Society, as it is called?

ROBBINS. Society as it is *called?* Society is Society. And—
surely there are other ways of getting out of it than . . .

TOMMY. No, there aren't.

ROBBINS. You could have gone away—settled quietly down in
the country—Cornwall——

TOMMY. But I love London. Not a drop of Cornish blood in
my veins. Never happy away from London. Never do get
away from it properly. It's in my bones.

ROBBINS. Well, what was to prevent you from leading a quiet
life here in London, if you really wanted to?

TOMMY. Ah, there speaks the man who isn't a social success!

ROBBINS. You needn't remind me of that.

TOMMY. My dear chap, I'm only congratulating you. . . . A social success is a man who can't call his soul his own. Might as well be a trapped rabbit. Better. Agony not so prolonged. Moment he shows his face—"Can you lunch to-morrow?" If he stays at home—"Trr-trr-trr": telephone bell: "Can you lunch to-morrow?" Oh, that eternal "Can you lunch to-morrow?"!

ROBBINS. Very easy to say you're sorry you're engaged.

TOMMY. Oh, of course, I always said that—and horribly true it was. "Then can you lunch the next day?"—"Next day? No, I'm afr——" "Then the day after?"—"That's Thursday, isn't it? N-n——" "Then Friday? Or *any* day next week?" And there one is. They've no shame.

ROBBINS. But if you had said firmly—if you had given them to understand, once and for all——

TOMMY. I'm not that sort of fellow. I can't hurt people's feelings: I'm not a boor. If I were, I should never have been a social success. It was my confounded easygoing amiability and general niceness that got me into Society—and prevented me from getting out.

ROBBINS. But——

TOMMY. Oh, I did what I could. All sorts of things. I went in for a diet of sea-weed biscuits. No good. All the hostesses instantly had sea-weed biscuits for me. Sea-weed biscuits became the rage. There were sea-weed luncheons, sea-weed dinners, sea-weed suppers. Last summer, at the Foreign Office reception, I pretended to be drunk. Not a soul there but refused to see anything at all strange about me. There was a time when I used to sit in the bow-window of Bains's, wearing a motor-cap and a frock-coat. They all admired my splendid moral courage. My dear fellow, I've tried scores of ways. This . . .

Gesture to card-table.

. . . was the only way out. Desperate remedy? Desperate disease. And here I am—cured.

Finishes his whisky and Apollinaris.

By the way I'm sorry about Bains's. I should like to have got you in.

ROBBINS, *gloomily*. Oh, I should never have got in.

TOMMY, *consolingly*. No.

ROBBINS. Then why did you put me up?

TOMMY. Well, you were always saying you'd like me to. And —there it was: my amiability again. Unable to say "No."

ROBBINS, *nods his head, sinks down onto edge of arm-chair, and heaves a deep sigh*. I had often wondered—forgive an old friend's frankness—what it was that people saw in you. *I've* always liked you. But why should every one else? "Tommy"—"Tommy" to every one. Nobody ever called me Harry.

TOMMY. Is your name—er—Henry?

ROBBINS. There! After all these years! You didn't even know my Christian name.

TOMMY. I knew your initial was H.

ROBBINS. You never called me H.

TOMMY, *kindly*. H.

ROBBINS. Thanks, old fellow.

TOMMY. Odd! When Amersham called me "Dixon" to-night, I felt I must go down on my knees for sheer joy and gratitude. *Rolls it over his tongue.*
"Dixon."

ROBBINS, *gloomily*. "Dixon the card-sharper." That's how you'll go down to posterity.

TOMMY. Think so? I shall be satisfied if the name sticks to me while I live! . . . It was my being "Tommy" to the husbands as well as to the wives that always sickened me. . . . I've a sense of honour.

ROBBINS. Do I understand that you were in the habit of be-having dishonourably?

TOMMY. Oh, no. Only, *I'm* the sort of fellow who happens to be attractive to—I know it sounds fatuous—but attractive to —well, to the *sillier* sort of women, don't you know?

ROBBINS. *Married* women?

TOMMY. Well, lots of silly women get married. There's no competitive examination. But not necessarily *married* women.

Waves his hands vaguely.

Widows. All kinds.

ROBBINS. *All* widows?

TOMMY. The *sillier* sort of widows—like the Duchess.

ROBBINS, *rising from arm-chair.* You really mean that the—there was a chance of your becoming a—a sort of Duke?

TOMMY. I think there was a sort of danger. May have been. . . . One never knows where one is with those people. They've such a lot of time to waste, and there's so much make-believe. . . . The married women, they don't want you to make love to them. But they want you to *want* to make love to them, all the time. And if they think you're making love to anyone else—or if they think anyone else is *wanting* you to *want* to—then there's a deuce of a row. And of course a man's one idea is to avoid rows. Only, the wear and tear of avoiding a row is worse than the row itself. And of course there always *is* the row, anyway. . . . *Was,* at least. *Was!*

ROBBINS, *after a pause.* I'd no idea how much you were sacrificing.

TOMMY. No?

Fingering the strewn cards on the table.

I say, I'd no idea how much I was winning. The struggle for freedom is a jolly lucrative thing.

Gathering up notes and gold.

What shall I do with it all? Can't send it back to those people. Look like climbing down. . . . How much did you lose?

ROBBINS, *waving away proffered banknote.* Send it all to some charity.

TOMMY, *pocketing the notes and gold.* Right. To-morrow morning. Society for the Relief of Decayed Card Sharpers or Something. . . . I say: here's the ace of clubs—*and* the other one. These I must have framed and glazed. Big white margin, with suitable inscription. Gilt frame, with bird of freedom perched on it.

Carries the two aces around as though seeking the place where they would look best on the wall.

Look at *those* cards!

Inclusive gesture to the invitation cards over the mantel-piece.

Waste-paper! . . . Look at that telephone! Mute for evermore.

TELEPHONE-BELL: "Trr-trr-trr!" *Both men start and stare at telephone.*

TOMMY, *raising a finger.* Hark to the swan-song!

TELEPHONE-BELL: "Trr-trr-trr, trr-trr-trr."

TOMMY. Pathetic, isn't it?

Goes across to writing-table and raises the receiver.

Halloa! Yes.

An instant later, with a violent start.

Duchess? Duchess of—*Huntington?* . . . Yes, of course I knew your v-voice, but . . . *What?*

His face becomes positively blank with horror.

You're sorry you . . . What? . . . Worse things in the world than cheating at . . . But, my dear woman . . . What? . . .

Stares wildly at Robbins.

But . . .

Covers receiver with one hand, and, turning to ROBBINS, *asks in a hissing whisper,*

"What shall I say?"

Puts it back to his lips.

Fact is I—I'm married already—years ago—unfortunate en-tanglement . . . N-no. No chance of a divorce. Lost sight of her. Living somewhere in the wilds of New Zealand. *Absolutely* respectable. N-no, to-morrow I can't. Lunching with Robbins—my friend, H. Robbins. . . . Come round to you in the morning? Well, I . . . Well . . . No, not tea, I have to go out to tea . . . Y-yes, I could come in later, I suppose—d-delighted—but——

At about the middle of this monologue, the electric bell of the front-door has sounded, audible through the open door of the drawing-room. ROBBINS *has made a gesture at hearing it.* TOMMY *has done likewise. At the word "but"* HAWKINS *ushers in* LADY AMERSHAM, *who flings herself past him into the room. Exit* HAWKINS.

LADY A., *to* ROBBINS. Where——

Sees TOMMY, *who stands stupefied, receiver in hand.*

Tommy, my dear—dear——

ROBBINS, *much embarrassed, takes his hat and moves towards door.*

TOMMY: Robbins! Don't *go*—don't!

To LADY A.

What on earth . . .

LADY A. Tommy, I think I must have been mad. The whole thing was so sudden. Forgive me. Don't—don't look at me like that. In your hour of need I turned from you. As if there weren't heaps of things worse than cheating at cards! Though all the world condemn you—Tommy, the old life is over: I throw in my lot with you.

Throws her cloak from her shoulders, letting it fall to the ground.

For ever.

ROBBINS *awkwardly picks up cloak and stands holding it on his arm.*

TOMMY. For—forev——

LADY A., *with quick suspicion.* Who are you telephoning to?

TOMMY, *mechanically dropping receiver onto its groove.* Enid, for heaven's sake—think of Amersham. . . .

LADY A. I think of the man whom Amersham has exposed, ruined, hounded down—the man I——

TOMMY. But, Enid, he was quite right——

LADY A. According to his own lights, yes. Oh, I don't judge him. Who am I that I should cast the first stone at him—I, who deserted you just when——

Buries her face in her hands for an instant. Unburies her face.

"Think of Amersham"? I think of him as last I saw him, bounding up the steps of Bains's—and I telling the chauffeur to drive me home. It wasn't till I was almost at my door that I realised my baseness.

TOMMY. But—but—Robbins, do help me! Tell her she seems to be forgetting all about *my* baseness.

ROBBINS, *awkwardly*. I certainly do think——

LADY A. You! Who are you that you should come betwee——

ROBBINS. That's just what had struck me, Lady Amersham.

TOMMY, *under his breath*. Snob!

LADY A., *to* TOMMY. As for your baseness, I glory in it. But for it, my true nature would never have been tested. I thought I was shallow, and a coward, and selfish. I find myself a woman of—of——

TOMMY. Heroic mould. Oh, you're all that, Enid. And that's just why you positively mustn't have anything to do with a pariah like me. . . . Come!

Makes movement towards door.

LADY A., *very firmly*. It is when a man becomes a pariah that he finds out who are his true friends.

TELEPHONE-BELL: "Trr-trr-trr." TOMMY *casts agitated glances at it, snatches up receiver, and babbles.*

TOMMY. Yes—yes—I was so sorry—called away—will you hold the line? I——

LADY A., *darting towards him*. Tommy, I insist on knowing who——

At this moment is heard a loud knocking at the front-door.

TOMMY, *to* ROBBINS *while he himself stands guard over telephone*. Tell Hawkins—quick—not at home—to anybody.

ROBBINS *crosses to door, opens it, starts back, almost closing door.* LORD AMERSHAM'S *voice is heard saying,*

"Mr. Dixon still up? Very well. I'll go straight in."

TOMMY, *to* ROBBINS. Stop him!

ROBBINS, *throwing* LADY AMERSHAM's *cloak behind a chair.*
Hadn't Lady Amersham better——?

Points to screen as he darts out into hall. His voice and
LORD AMERSHAM's *are heard without.* LADY AMERSHAM *has
darted towards screen.*

TOMMY. Don't do that! Only done on stage! Most compromis-
ing thing possible.

LADY A., *with a look of quick illumination.* Exactly! So much
the better!

*She darts behind the screen and, as the door flies open, it
is too late to stop her.*

LORD A., *to* ROBBINS. I tell you——

He sees TOMMY, *who has backed to a corner, and strides
towards him.*

TOMMY, *with faint jauntiness.* Ah—er——

LORD A. Tommy, your hand!

TOMMY *half puts out a wavering hand.*

LORD A. Come! Don't bear malice, Tommy.

Grips the hand and shakes it vehemently.

There! Not another word!

TOMMY, *gazing from screen to card-table.* But——

LORD A. Forget what I said! I'm an impetuous, blundering
fellow. But you must admit—— Hang it, Tommy! I had
some provocation. What you did—it—well, it wasn't playing
the game, *was* it?

TOMMY. No, but . . .

LORD A. *Well,* then . . .

TOMMY. Amersham, it's awfully jolly of you, but—what's the
good of ruining a man and—and then telling him not to
bother?

LORD A. Ruining you? Oh—you mean—Bains's, yes. Well, you
see, when I got there—nobody in the hall. Went into the
coffee-room. Not a soul. Drawing-room deserted. Went up
into card-room. One rubber going on—hard at it. Didn't like
to interrupt. Found myself cooling off a bit. Occurred to
me: worse things in the world than——

Gesture to card-table.

Many a good fellow . . . Awful temptation, those wide shirt-cuffs . . . Went down and had a whisky and a quiet think. . . . Understand all, forgive all. Damned hypocritical world. Pardons any sin but the sin of being found out. Who was I that I should . . . Tommy, old man.

Grips TOMMY's *hand.*

That's all right.

TOMMY. I'm—really, I'm——

LORD A. My only fear is that Enid may . . . you know how difficult it is for a woman not to *talk.* And Enid—between you and me—is the most awful little chatterbox in the British Empire.

At this moment LADY A's *hand appears grasping the top of the screen.* TOMMY *sees it, and, behind* LORD A.'s *back, makes a frantic prohibitive gesture in its direction.*

However, I know how to frighten her, and I'll undertake to——

The screen falls revealing LADY A. *in the act of propelling it.* LORD A. *starts and stares round at her. She instantly folds her hands and stands with downcast eyes.*

LADY A., *in a low, clear voice.* Lady Amersham, by all that's wonderful. . . . Lady Amersham by all that's——

LORD A., *laughing heartily.* Why, little Enid! I *thought,* when I was on the way, I should find you here.

Goes to her with outstretched hands.

My dear child: as if—why, it was a most generous impulse of yours to come and tell our poor Tommy that you—— Just like you! But Lord! what a baby! Running to hide as if . . .

LADY A.'s *expression during this speech has gradually changed from blank amazement to horror and from horror to amusement.*

LADY A., *faintly.* Jack! You don't quite . . . I wasn't . . .

LORD A. You're tired.

Supports her with one arm.

No wonder. Hysteria—the curse of the age. Come! Where's your cloak? By the way, I didn't see our car at the door.

LADY A. No, I told Simpson he needn't——

LORD A. Quite right. Cold night for man or beast. Blamed myself for keeping my taxi.

ROBBINS *meanwhile has furtively produced* LADY A.'s *cloak, and advances to help her on with it.* LORD A., *reminded of his existence, returns down stage to* TOMMY.

LORD A., *sotto voce.* That fellow Robertson . . .

TOMMY. Rob*bins*.

LORD A. There's something about him that . . . Was it he who put you up to——

Gesture to card-table.

TOMMY. Robbins? Good heavens! He's the soul of honour.

LORD A. Well, it would be just like you to shield him, but . . .

Looks round and sees his wife standing cloaked. She has moved away without thanking ROBBINS, *who stands midway between her and her husband.*

. . . I don't like the look of him.

TOMMY. I assure you . . .

LADY A., *querulously.* Jack!

LORD A. Good-night, dear old fellow. And—I'm *glad* it's happened. Only—don't do it again, eh?

TOMMY, *dolefully.* No, 'tisn't a bit of good.

LORD A. *goes to door followed by* TOMMY.

ROBBINS, *holding out hand.* Good-night, Lord Amersham.

LORD A., *ignoring hand.* Good-night.

LADY A. Good-night, Tommy.

TOMMY. Oh, I'm coming down to see you off.

LORD A., *turning on threshold.* Dine with us to-morrow.

TOMMY. No, to-morrow, I——

LADY A. Well, Thursday?

TOMMY. I should love to, but . . . I'm dining with—with H. Robbins.

LADY A. and LORD A. Well, *lunch* on Thursday?

TOMMY. Lunch? Y-yes—delighted——

TELEPHONE-BELL: "Trr-trr-trr." TOMMY *casts agonised glance at it, wavering between it and the* AMERSHAMS, *as he passes out into the hall.* ROBBINS *sits down dejected on a small chair.*

TELEPHONE-BELL: "Trr-trr-trr—*trrrrrrrrr," while the* CURTAIN *falls.*

THE MEASURES TAKEN

by

BERTOLT BRECHT

English version by
Eric Bentley

Characters

FOUR AGITATORS
who are severally seen in the roles of
THE YOUNG COMRADE
THE LEADER at PARTY HEADQUARTERS
TWO COOLIES
THE OVERSEER
TWO TEXTILE WORKERS
THE POLICEMAN
THE TRADER
THE CONTROL CHORUS

A Note on the Form: *The Measures Taken* is a *Lehrstück*—that is, a Lesson or Didactic Play. As such, it is closer to oratorio than to conventional modern drama. Like the soloists in an oratorio, the four actors occupy the front part of a concert platform. Behind them is a chorus of singers.

The term Control Chorus is clearly derived from Control Commission. Martin Esslin writes: "The Control Commissions were first proposed at the All-Russian Conference of the Soviet Communist Party in 1920. The tenth congress of the Party (1921) defined the task of the Commissions as being 'the extirpation of the . . . violation of comradely relations within the Party . . .'"

E. B.

THE CONTROL CHORUS. Step forward! Your work has been successful. In yet another country the ranks of the fighters are joined, and the revolution marches on. We agree to what you have done.

THE FOUR AGITATORS. Stop! We have something to say. We announce the death of a comrade.

THE CONTROL CHORUS. Who killed him?

THE FOUR AGITATORS. We killed him. We shot him and threw him into a lime pit.

THE CONTROL CHORUS. What did he do, that you shot him?

THE FOUR AGITATORS. He often did the right thing. Several times he did the wrong thing. But in the end he endangered the movement. He wished the right thing and did the wrong thing. We demand a verdict.

THE CONTROL CHORUS. Demonstrate how it happened and why, and you will hear our verdict.

THE FOUR AGITATORS. We shall respect your verdict.

1. THE TEACHINGS OF THE CLASSICS

THE FOUR AGITATORS. We came from Moscow as agitators. We were to travel to the city of Mukden to make propaganda, and support the Chinese Party in the factories. We were to announce ourselves at the last Party Headquarters from the frontier and demand a guide. In the anteroom a young comrade came to us, and we spoke of the nature of our assignment. We shall repeat what was said.

Three of them stand together. The other, presenting THE YOUNG COMRADE, *stands by himself.*

THE YOUNG COMRADE. I am the secretary at the last Party Headquarters from the frontier. My heart beats for the revolution. The sight of injustice drove me into the ranks of the fighters. Man must help man. I am for freedom. I believe in humanity. And I am for the measures taken by the

Communist party which fights for the classless society against exploitation and ignorance.

THE THREE AGITATORS. We come from Moscow.

THE YOUNG COMRADE. We expected you.

THE THREE AGITATORS. Why?

THE YOUNG COMRADE. We're getting nowhere. There is scarcity and unrest, little bread and much struggle. Many are brave, but few can read. Few machines, and no one understands them. Our locomotives have broken down. Have you brought any locomotives with you?

THE THREE AGITATORS. No.

THE YOUNG COMRADE. Have you any tractors?

THE THREE AGITATORS. No.

THE YOUNG COMRADE. Our farmers are still harnessing themselves to old wooden plows. And so we have no way of putting our fields in order. Have you brought any seed?

THE THREE AGITATORS. No.

THE YOUNG COMRADE. Have you got munitions at least and machine guns?

THE THREE AGITATORS. No.

THE YOUNG COMRADE. There are just two of us to defend the revolution here. Surely you've brought us a letter from the Central Committee telling us what to do?

THE THREE AGITATORS. No.

THE YOUNG COMRADE. Then you yourselves are going to help us?

THE THREE AGITATORS. No.

THE YOUNG COMRADE. Day and night we never get out of our clothes, in the struggle against hunger, decay, and counterrevolution. Yet you bring us nothing.

THE THREE AGITATORS. Exactly so: we bring you nothing. But over the frontier to Mukden we bring the Chinese workers the teachings of the classics and the propagandists, the ABC of Communism: to the ignorant, instruction about their condition; to the oppressed, class consciousness; and to the class conscious, the experience of revolution. From you, however, we are to demand an automobile and a guide.

THE YOUNG COMRADE. Then I was wrong to ask?

THE THREE AGITATORS. No, but a good question led to a better answer. We see that everything has already been asked of you. But even more will be asked of you: one of you two must guide us to Mukden.

THE YOUNG COMRADE. Then I'll leave my post, which was too hard for two, but which one alone must now learn to handle. I shall go with you. Marching forward, spreading the teaching of the Communist classics: World Revolution.

THE CONTROL CHORUS.

Praise of the U.S.S.R.

Certainly our misery
Was something to talk about.
But seated at our sparse table
Was the Hope of all the oppressed
Who is satisfied with water.
And in a clear voice
Behind the broken-down door
Knowledge taught the guests.
When a door is broken
We only become visible from a little further away
We whom frost does not kill, nor hunger
Untiringly holding in trust
The world's destinies.

THE FOUR AGITATORS. In this way, the young comrade agreed to the general character of our work and we came—four men and one woman—before the leader at Party Headquarters.

2. THE BLOTTING OUT

THE FOUR AGITATORS. But the work in Mukden was illegal, so before we crossed the frontier, we had to blot out our faces. Our young comrade agreed to this. We will repeat the incident.

One of the AGITATORS *presents* THE LEADER *at Party Headquarters.*

THE LEADER. I am the leader at the last headquarters. I have agreed that the comrade from my station should go along as guide. But there is trouble in the Mukden factories. At the present time the eyes of the world are on this city to see if one of us won't be found leaving a Chinese worker's hut. And I hear that gunboats stand ready on the rivers and armored trains in the sidings, ready to attack us at once, if one of us is seen there. And so I am having the comrades cross the frontier as Chinese.

To the AGITATORS.

You must not be seen.

THE TWO AGITATORS. We shall not be seen.

THE LEADER. If one of you is wounded, he must not be found.

THE TWO AGITATORS. He will not be found.

THE LEADER. Then you are ready to die and to hide the dead one?

THE TWO AGITATORS. Yes.

THE LEADER. Then you are yourselves no longer. You are not Karl Schmitt from Berlin, you are not Anna Kjersk from Kazan, and you are not Peter Sawitch from Moscow. One and all of you are nameless and motherless, blank pages on which the revolution writes its instructions.

THE TWO AGITATORS. Yes.

THE LEADER *gives them masks; they put them on.*

THE LEADER. Then, from this time on, you are no one no longer. From this time on, and probably until you disappear, you are unknown workers, fighters, Chinese, born of Chinese mothers, with yellow skin, speaking Chinese in sickness and in sleep.

THE TWO AGITATORS. Yes.

THE LEADER. In the interest of Communism, agreeing to the forward march of the proletarian masses of all lands, saying Yes to the revolutionizing of the world.

THE TWO AGITATORS. Yes. The young comrade said Yes too. In this way he agreed to the blotting out of his face.

THE CONTROL CHORUS. Who fights for Communism must be able to fight and not to fight; to speak the truth and not to speak the truth; to perform services and not to perform serv-

ices; keep promises and not keep promises; to go into danger
and to keep out of danger; to be recognizable and not to be
recognizable. Who fights for Communism has only one of
all the virtues: that he fights for Communism.

THE FOUR AGITATORS. As Chinese, we went to Mukden, four
men and one woman.

THE YOUNG COMRADE. To make propaganda and support the
Chinese workers through the teachings of the classics and
the propagandists, the ABC of Communism: to bring to the
ignorant instruction about their situation; to the oppressed,
class-consciousness; and to the class-conscious, the experience of revolution.

THE CONTROL CHORUS.

Praise of Illegal Work

It is splendid
To take up the word as a weapon in the class war
To rouse the masses to the fight in a loud and ringing voice
To crush the oppressors
To free the oppressed.
Hard and useful is the small daily labor
The grim, persistent tying and spreading of the Party's net
For the capitalists' guns
To speak
But conceal the speaker
To win the victory
But conceal the victor
To die
But hide the death.
Who would not do much for fame
But who would do it for silence?
Yet the impoverished host invites Honor to supper
And out of the tiny and tumble-down hut steps irresistibly
Greatness
And Fame calls in vain
On the doers of the great deed.
Step forward a moment
Unknown ones with hidden faces
And receive our thanks!

THE FOUR AGITATORS. We helped the Chinese comrades in the

city of Mukden, and made propaganda among the workers. We had no bread for the hungry but only knowledge for the ignorant. Therefore we spoke of the root cause of poverty, did not abolish poverty, but spoke of the abolition of the root cause.

THE FOUR AGITATORS. First, we went down into the lower section of the city. Coolies were dragging a barge with a rope. But the ground on the bank was slippery. So when one of them slipped, and the overseer kicked him, we said to the young comrade: "Go after them, make propaganda among them. Say you've seen shoes for barge-workers in Tientsin with wooden soles on them to prevent slipping. Try to bring it about that they too demand shoes of that sort. But don't give way to pity!" And we asked: "Do you agree to it?" And he agreed to it and hurried away and at once gave way to pity. We will show you.

TWO AGITATORS *present* COOLIES, *fastening a rope to a block, and then pulling the rope over their shoulders. One presents* THE YOUNG COMRADE, *one* THE OVERSEER.

THE OVERSEER. I am the overseer. By evening I must get the rice to the city of Mukden.

THE TWO COOLIES. We are coolies and we pull the rice barge up the river.

THE COOLIES.
Song of the Rice Barge Coolies
In the city up the river
A mouthful of rice awaits us
But the barge is heavy that we must pull up the river
And the water flows down the river.
We shall never get there.
> Pull faster
> We want our dinner
> Pull evenly
> Don't jostle the next man.

THE YOUNG COMRADE. It is repulsive to hear how the torture

of these men's labor is masked by the beauty of their song!

THE OVERSEER. Pull faster!

THE COOLIES.

Night will soon fall
A resting place smaller than a dog's shadow
Costs us a mouthful of rice.
Because the river bank is slippery
We are making no headway.
>   Pull faster
>   We want our dinner
>   Pull evenly
>   Don't jostle the next man.

ONE COOLIE, *slipping out of line.* I can't keep going.

THE COOLIES, *while they stand and are whipped till the fallen man is on his feet again.*

The rope that cuts into our shoulders
Holds longer than we do.
The overseer's whip has seen four generations.
We are not the last.
>   Pull faster
>   We want our dinner
>   Pull evenly
>   Don't jostle the next man.

THE YOUNG COMRADE. It is hard to see these men without pity.

To THE OVERSEER.

Can't you see the ground is slippery?

THE OVERSEER. The ground is what?

THE YOUNG COMRADE. Slippery!

THE OVERSEER. What? You claim this bank is so slippery it's impossible to pull a bargeful of rice?

THE YOUNG COMRADE. Yes.

THE OVERSEER. Then you don't think the city of Mukden needs rice?

THE YOUNG COMRADE. They can't pull the barge if they fall down.

THE OVERSEER. Should I provide stones for them to walk on—from here to the city of Mukden?

THE YOUNG COMRADE. I don't know what *you* should do, but I know what *they* should do. They should defend themselves. Don't think a thing can never be just because it never was. I saw shoes among the barge workers in Tientsin with wooden soles on them to prevent slipping. They got them by acting in common. Take action in common: ask for those shoes!

THE TWO COOLIES. It's true: we can't manage this barge without shoes of that sort.

THE OVERSEER. But the rice must be in the city by this evening!

He whips. They pull.

THE COOLIES.
Our fathers pulled the barge from the river mouth
A little farther upstream.
Our children will reach the source.
We come between.
　　Pull faster
　　We want our dinner
　　Pull evenly
　　Don't jostle the next man.

THE COOLIE *again falls.*

THE COOLIE. Help me!

THE YOUNG COMRADE, *to* THE OVERSEER. Are you human? I'm going to take a stone and place it here in the mud.

To THE COOLIE.

There!

THE OVERSEER. Correct! Shoes in Tientsin don't help. I'd rather let our compassionate colleague run ahead with a stone and shove it in front of any worker that slips!

THE COOLIES.
In the barge is rice.
The farmer who grew it received a few cents.
We get even less.
An ox would cost more
Than we do.
There are too many of us.

One of the COOLIES *slips.* THE YOUNG COMRADE *helps him with the stone. He is up on his feet again.*

Pull faster
We want our dinner
Pull evenly
Don't jostle the next man.
When the rice arrives in the city
And children ask who dragged the heavy barge
The answer given is:
The barge was dragged.

One of the COOLIES *slips.* THE YOUNG COMRADE *helps him with the stone. He is up on his feet again.*

Pull faster
We want our dinner
Pull evenly
Don't jostle the next man.
The food from down there
Feeds people up here.
Those who brought it up for them
Have not fed.

One of the COOLIES *slips.* THE YOUNG COMRADE *helps him with the stone. He is up on his feet again.*

THE YOUNG COMRADE. I've done all I can. You must demand other shoes.

THE COOLIE, *to* THE OVERSEER. This fellow's a fool. They all laugh at him.

THE OVERSEER. No, no: just one of those that stir up the workers. Hello there! Hold that man!

THE FOUR AGITATORS. And they at once took hold of him. And they pursued him for two days till he met us. Then they pursued us and him together in the city of Mukden for a whole week. They wouldn't let us get near the central section of the city.

DISCUSSION

THE CONTROL CHORUS.
But is it not right to lend support to the weak
Wherever he suffers?

To help the exploited man
In his daily hardship?

THE FOUR AGITATORS. He did not help him. But he did hinder us from making propaganda in our section of the city.

THE CONTROL CHORUS. We agree to that.

THE FOUR AGITATORS. The young comrade perceived that he had severed his feelings from his understanding. But we comforted him and spoke to him the words of Comrade Lenin:

THE CONTROL CHORUS.
Intelligence is not to make no mistakes
But quickly to see how to make them good.

4 . INJUSTICE GREAT AND SMALL

THE FOUR AGITATORS. We founded the first Party cells in the factories and trained the first functionaries, established a Party school and taught them how to make the forbidden literature secretly available. Then we acquired influence in the textile works, and when wages fell, some of the workers struck. But since other workers went on working, the strike was endangered. We said to the young comrade: stand at the gate of the works and distribute leaflets. He agreed to that. We will repeat what was said.

THE THREE AGITATORS. With the barge workers, you were a failure.

THE YOUNG COMRADE. Yes.

THE THREE AGITATORS. Did that teach you something?

THE YOUNG COMRADE. Yes.

THE THREE AGITATORS. Will you do better with the leaflets?

THE YOUNG COMRADE. Yes.

THE THREE AGITATORS. We will now show the young comrade's behavior with the leaflets.

TWO AGITATORS *play* TEXTILE WORKERS, *one a* POLICEMAN.

THE TWO TEXTILE WORKERS. We are workers in the textile works.

THE POLICEMAN. I'm a policeman, and the ruling class pays me to combat discontent.

THE CONTROL CHORUS.

Come out, comrade!
Risk the nickel that isn't worth a nickel any more
The roof that lets the rain leak through
And the job that you'll lose tomorrow!
Out on the streets! Fight!
It is too late to stand waiting!
Help yourself by helping us: practice
Solidarity!

THE YOUNG COMRADE.

Sacrifice what you have, comrade!
You have nothing.

THE CONTROL CHORUS.

Come out, comrade, and face the guns
And insist on your wages!
If you know you have nothing to lose
Their police don't have enough guns!
Out on the streets! Fight!
It is too late to stand waiting!
Help yourself by helping us: practice
Solidarity!

THE TWO TEXTILE WORKERS. In the early morning we go to the factory. Our wages have been cut, but we don't know what to do about it, so we go on working.

THE YOUNG COMRADE *gives one of them a leaflet; the other stands there doing nothing.* Read it and hand it on. When you've read it, you'll know what to do about it.

THE FIRST *takes it and walks on.*

THE POLICEMAN *takes the leaflet away from him.* Who gave you that leaflet?

THE FIRST. I don't know. Somebody just stuck it in my hand as I was passing.

THE POLICEMAN, *stepping up to* THE SECOND WORKER. *You* gave him the leaflet! We have orders to hunt up the ones that give out the leaflets.

THE SECOND. I didn't give out any leaflet.

THE YOUNG COMRADE. Is it a crime to teach them they are ignorant of their situation?

THE POLICEMAN. These teachings lead to heaven knows what. Teach factory workers that sort of stuff, and they don't know who the owner is any more. This little leaflet is more dangerous than ten cannon.

THE YOUNG COMRADE. What's in it?

THE POLICEMAN. How would I know?

To THE SECOND WORKER.

What's in it?

THE SECOND. I don't know the leaflet. I didn't hand it out.

THE YOUNG COMRADE. I know he didn't.

THE POLICEMAN, *to* THE YOUNG COMRADE. Did *you* give him the leaflet?

THE YOUNG COMRADE. No.

THE POLICEMAN, *to* THE SECOND WORKER. Then *you* gave it to him.

THE YOUNG COMRADE, *to* THE FIRST WORKER. What'll happen to him?

THE FIRST. Could be thrown in jail.

THE YOUNG COMRADE. What do you want to throw him in jail for? Aren't you a proletarian, too, policeman?

THE POLICEMAN, *to* THE SECOND WORKER. Come with me.
Strikes him on the head.

THE YOUNG COMRADE, *trying to stop him.* It wasn't him.

THE POLICEMAN. Then it *was* you!

THE SECOND. It wasn't him.

THE POLICEMAN. Then it was the both of you!

THE FIRST. Run, you fool, run, your pocket's full of leaflets!
THE POLICEMAN *cuts* THE SECOND WORKER *down.*

THE YOUNG COMRADE, *pointing at* THE POLICEMAN. *To the* FIRST WORKER. He's killed an innocent man. You are witness.

THE FIRST, *attacking* THE POLICEMAN. Hired assassin!
THE POLICEMAN *draws his revolver.*

THE YOUNG COMRADE, *shouting.* Help! Comrades! Help! They are shooting innocent bystanders!

THE YOUNG COMRADE *grabs* THE POLICEMAN *by the neck from behind.* THE FIRST WORKER *twists his arm back slowly. The shot goes wild.* THE POLICEMAN *is disarmed and cut down.*

THE SECOND, *getting up, to* THE FIRST WORKER. Now we've knocked off a cop, we can't go back to the works.

To THE YOUNG COMRADE.

And it's your fault.

THE FOUR AGITATORS. And he had to get to safety instead of distributing leaflets, for the police force was strengthened.

DISCUSSION

THE CONTROL CHORUS. But is it not right to oppose injustice wherever it is found?

THE FOUR AGITATORS. He opposed a small injustice. But the great injustice—strike breaking—went right on.

THE CONTROL CHORUS. We agree to that.

5 . WHAT IS A HUMAN BEING ACTUALLY?

THE FOUR AGITATORS. Daily we fought those old associates: Oppression and Despair. We taught the workers to transform a struggle for higher wages into a struggle for power. Taught them the use of weapons and the art of demonstrating. Then we heard there was conflict between the merchants and the British, who ruled the city, on account of tariffs. In order to exploit this rulers' quarrel for the benefit of the ruled, we sent the young comrade with a letter to the richest of the merchants. It said: "Arm the coolies!" We said to the young comrade: "Act in such a way that you get the weapons!" But when the food came on the table, he didn't keep his mouth shut. We will show you.

An AGITATOR *as* TRADER.

THE TRADER. I am the trader. I'm expecting a letter from the coolie organization about the possibility of our getting together against the British.

THE YOUNG COMRADE. Here is the letter from the coolie organization.

THE TRADER. Please come and dine with me.

THE YOUNG COMRADE. It's an honor for me to be able to dine with you.

THE TRADER. While dinner's being prepared, I'd like to give you my opinion of coolies. Please sit down over here.

THE YOUNG COMRADE. I'm very interested in your opinion.

THE TRADER. Why do I get everything cheaper than anyone else? And why would a coolie work for me almost without pay?

THE YOUNG COMRADE. I don't know.

THE TRADER. Because I'm bright. You're pretty bright yourselves or how would you squeeze union dues out of your coolies?

THE YOUNG COMRADE. That's true.—Incidentally, are you going to arm the coolies against the British?

THE TRADER. Maybe, maybe.—I know how to handle a coolie. You must give him enough rice to keep him from dying. Otherwise, you can't get any work out of him. Is that right?

THE YOUNG COMRADE. Yes. That is right.

THE TRADER. I say it is not right. If coolies are cheaper than rice, I can get me a new coolie. Isn't that nearer the truth?

THE YOUNG COMRADE. Yes, that's nearer the truth.—Incidentally, when will you start sending weapons into the central section of the city?

THE TRADER. Soon, soon.—You should see the coolies who load my leather eating my rice in the canteen?

THE YOUNG COMRADE. Yes, I should.

THE TRADER. What do you think: do I pay a lot for the work?

THE YOUNG COMRADE. No, but your rice is expensive, and you insist on the work being well done, and your rice is bad rice.

THE TRADER. You people are quite bright.

THE YOUNG COMRADE. And when will you arm the coolies
   against the British?

THE TRADER. After dinner we can inspect the arsenal. Now
   I'm going to sing you my favorite song.

The Song of Merchandise

Down the river there is rice
In the province up the river people need rice:
If we leave the rice in the warehouses
The rice will cost them more.
Those who pull the rice barge will then get less rice
And rice will be even cheaper for me.
What is rice actually?
Do I know what rice is?
God knows what rice is!
I don't know what rice is
I only know its price.

Winter comes, the people need clothing
One must buy up the cotton
And not let go of it:
When the cold weather comes, clothing will cost more.
The cotton-spinning mills pay too high wages.
There's too much cotton around anyway.
What is cotton actually?
Do I know what cotton is?
God knows what cotton is!
I don't know what cotton is
I only know its price.

Consider men—they need too much food
And so men get to cost more.
To make the food, men are needed
Cooks make the food cheaper
But those who eat it make it cost more.
There aren't enough men around anyway.
What is a man actually?
Do I know what a man is?
God knows what a man is!
I don't know what a man is
I only know his price.

To THE YOUNG COMRADE.

And now we're going to eat my good rice.

THE YOUNG COMRADE *stands up.* I can't eat with you.

THE FOUR AGITATORS. That's what he said. And neither threats nor laughter could bring him to eat with a man he despised. And the trader drove him out of the house, and the coolies were not armed.

DISCUSSION

THE CONTROL CHORUS. But isn't it right to put honor before everything else?

THE FOUR AGITATORS. No.

THE CONTROL CHORUS.

Change the World, It Needs It
With whom would the right-minded man not sit
To help the right?
What medicine would taste too bad
To a dying man?
What baseness would you not commit
To root out baseness?
If, finally, you could change the world
What task would you be too good for?
Who are you?
Sink down in the slime
Embrace the butcher
But change the world: it needs it!
Go on with your story.
We shall not sit listening to it much longer as judges;
Rather, as learners.

THE FOUR AGITATORS. The young comrade saw his mistake before he got downstairs. He suggested that we send him back over the border. We saw his weaknesses clearly enough, but we needed him, for he had a great following among the unemployed, and he helped us a lot in those days to spread the net of the Party for the capitalists' guns.

6. THE BETRAYAL

THE FOUR AGITATORS. That week the persecutions sharply increased. All we had left was a secret room for the hectograph machine and the pamphlets. But one morning there was great unrest in the city because of all the hunger. And news came from the plain, too, of grave unrest. On the evening of the third day, reaching our retreat not without risk, we found the young comrade in the doorway. And there were bundles in front of the house in the rain. We will repeat what was said.

THE THREE AGITATORS. What are these bundles?

THE YOUNG COMRADE. Our propaganda.

THE THREE AGITATORS. What are you going to do with it?

THE YOUNG COMRADE. Let me tell you something. The unemployed are getting pretty excited. Their new leader in the upper section of the city came here today and convinced me we must have action at once. We'll distribute propaganda, and occupy the city hall which will be a lighthouse for the rising in general. He knows for sure that the city hall is unguarded. It wouldn't take many to occupy it. And when the city hall is in our hands, the masses will see that the government is weak. He says the rising is possible tonight, and I take his word for it.

THE THREE AGITATORS. Then tell us the reasons why the rising is possible.

THE YOUNG COMRADE. Poverty is spreading, unrest is growing in the city.

THE THREE AGITATORS. The ignorant are beginning to recognize their situation.

THE YOUNG COMRADE. The unemployed have adopted our teaching.

THE THREE AGITATORS. The oppressed are learning class consciousness.

THE YOUNG COMRADE. The new leader of the unemployed is a real socialist. He makes almost unlimited revolutionary demands. He's a powerful and moving speaker.

THE FIRST AGITATOR. Has he a scar under the right ear?

THE YOUNG COMRADE. Yes. Do you know him?

THE FIRST AGITATOR. I know him. He's an agent of the merchants.

THE YOUNG COMRADE. I don't believe it.

THE THREE AGITATORS. And on our way here we saw soldiers with cannon going toward the city hall. The city hall is a trap. Your new leader of the unemployed is a *provocateur*.

THE YOUNG COMRADE. No, he's unemployed himself, he sympathizes with the unemployed. .
The unemployed can wait no longer
Nor can I
Wait any longer
There are too many paupers.

THE THREE AGITATORS. But not enough fighters.

THE YOUNG COMRADE. Their sufferings are enormous.

THE THREE AGITATORS. It is not enough to suffer.

THE YOUNG COMRADE. Unhappiness doesn't grow on the chest like leprosy, they know that. Poverty won't fall off the roof like a loose tile, no; poverty and unhappiness are man's doing. Scarcity is all the meat in their oven, and their own wailing is all they have to eat! But they know all this.

THE THREE AGITATORS. Do they know how many regiments the government has?

THE YOUNG COMRADE. No.

THE THREE AGITATORS. Then they know too little. Where are your weapons?

THE YOUNG COMRADE, *showing his hands*. We shall fight tooth and nail!

THE THREE AGITATORS. They won't suffice. You see only the misery of the workless and not the misery of the workers. You see only the city and not the farmers of the plain. You see the soldiers only as oppressors, and not as poor men in uniform carrying out oppression. Go, then, to the unemployed, unmask the merchants' agent and his plan of storming the city hall, and persuade them to take part this evening in the factory workers' demonstration. Meanwhile we shall try to persuade the discontented soldiery around the city hall to join the demonstration in uniform.

THE YOUNG COMRADE. I have often reminded the unemployed how often the soldiers have shot at them. Am I to tell them now that they should join in a demonstration with murderers?

THE THREE AGITATORS. Yes. For the soldiers can recognize that it was wrong to shoot their own class. Remember the advice of Comrade Lenin not to regard all farmers as class enemies but to make an ally of the poverty of the villages.

THE YOUNG COMRADE. Let me ask this: is it in line with the classics to let misery wait?

THE THREE AGITATORS. The classics provide methods for dealing with the problem of misery as a whole.

THE YOUNG COMRADE. Then the classics don't advocate helping every poor man at once and putting that before everything else?

THE THREE AGITATORS. No.

THE YOUNG COMRADE. Then the classics are dirt. I tear them up. For mankind cries out. Its misery tears down the dikes of mere teaching. And that's why I'm for action—right now, this minute! For *I* cry out too. *I* tear down the dikes of mere teaching!

He tears the classics.

THE THREE AGITATORS.
Do not tear them!
We need every one of them.
Take a look at reality!
Your revolution is quickly made and lasts one day
And is strangled the morning after
But our revolution begins tomorrow
Conquers and changes the world.
Your revolution stops when you stop.
When you have stopped
Our revolution marches on.

THE YOUNG COMRADE. Hear what I have to say. I see with my own eyes that misery cannot wait. I therefore oppose

your decision to wait. This very night I shall occupy the
city hall at the head of the unemployed.

THE THREE AGITATORS. We know the city hall is full of soldiers.
But even if it were not guarded by a single soldier, what
use is the city hall if the railroads, the telegraph stations,
and the barracks are all in government hands? You have
not convinced us. Go to the unemployed and convince them
that they should not take action by themselves. This we
demand of you in the name of the Party.

THE YOUNG COMRADE.
But what is the Party?
Does it sit in a house with telephones?
Are its thoughts secret, its decisions unknown?
Who is the Party?

THE THREE AGITATORS.
We are the Party.
You and I and you all—all of us.
The Party is in that suit you are wearing, Comrade,
And is thinking in that head of yours.
Where I live is the Party's house
Where you are attacked, the Party fights back.
Show us the way we should take
And we will take it with you
But do not take the right way without us
For without us it is the wrongest way.
Do not cut yourself off from us!
We may be wrong and you may be right.
Therefore do not cut yourself off from us!
No one denies that the short road is better than the long
But if you know the short road and cannot show it to us
What use is your wisdom?
Be wise with us!
Do not cut yourself off from us!

THE YOUNG COMRADE. I am right. That's why I cannot give
way. I see with my own eyes that misery can't wait!

THE CONTROL CHORUS.
Praise of the Party
A single man has two eyes
The Party has a thousand eyes

The Party sees seven states
A single man sees one city
A single man has a single hour
But the Party has many hours
A single man can be annihilated
But the Party cannot be annihilated
For it is the advance guard of the masses
And conducts its struggle
By the methods described in the classics which were created
From acquaintance with reality.

THE YOUNG COMRADE. That's no good any more. Looking at the struggle as it is now, I throw away all that was good yesterday, and do what alone is human. Here is action. I place myself at the head of it. My heart beats for the revolution, and the revolution is here!

THE THREE AGITATORS. Silence!

THE YOUNG COMRADE. Here is oppression. I am for freedom!

THE THREE AGITATORS. Silence! You are betraying us.

THE YOUNG COMRADE. I cannot be silent—because I am right!

THE THREE AGITATORS. Right or wrong, unless you are silent, we are done for. Silence!

THE YOUNG COMRADE.
I have seen too much.
I can be silent no longer.
Why be silent now?
If they don't know they have friends
How are they to rise up?
I shall therefore go before them
As what I am
And state
What is.
He takes off his mask and shouts.
We have come to help you!
We come from Moscow!
He tears up the mask.

THE FOUR AGITATORS.
And we looked and in the twilight saw
His naked face, human, open, guileless.

He had torn up his mask.
And the exploited shouted from their houses:
"Who disturbs the sleep of the exhausted?"
And a window opened and a voice shouted:
"Foreigners! Throw the troublemakers out!"
We were discovered.
And we heard the cannon thunder in the inner city
And the ignorant said:
"Now or never!"
And the unarmed shouted:
"Out of doors! Out!"
And he did not cease to shout in the open street
And we struck him down
And took him up and left the city in haste.

7. THE FLIGHT

THE CONTROL CHORUS.
They left the city!
Unrest grows in the city
But the leadership flees over the city borders!
What measures did you take?

THE FOUR AGITATORS.
Patience!
It is easy to know what is right
Far from the shooting
When you have months of time
But we had five minutes' time
And enemy guns to think of.
When in the course of our flight we came near the lime
pits outside the city, we heard our pursuers behind us. Re-
gaining consciousness, our young comrade heard the thunder of cannon from the direction of the city hall, realized
what he had done, and said: "Our cause is lost." But we
said: "Our cause is not lost." And his face was known. He
couldn't make a getaway. And there were gunboats on the
rivers and armored trains in the railroad sidings, ready to
attack whenever one of us was found. He must not be
found.

THE CONTROL CHORUS.
>If we are found, no matter where,
>The cry goes up: "The rulers are in danger
>Of annihilation!"
>And the cannon fire.
>
>Wherever the starving groan and hit back
>Their tormentors shout
>That we have bribed them
>To groan and hit back.
>
>It is written on our foreheads
>That we are against exploitation.
>And on the wall the WANTED NOTICE reads:
>"They are for the oppressed!"
>
>Who helps the despairing
>Passes for the scum of the earth
>We are the scum of the earth
>We must not be found.
>Your decision!

8. THE MEASURES TAKEN

THE THREE AGITATORS.
>We decided:
>Then he must disappear, and totally.
>For we must return to our work
>And cannot take him with us and cannot leave him behind
>We must therefore shoot him and throw him in the lime pit
>For the lime will burn him.

THE CONTROL CHORUS.
>You found no way out?

THE FOUR AGITATORS.
>The time was short, we found no way out.
>As one animal will help another, we too
>Wished to help him
>Who had fought with us for our cause.

With our pursuers on our heels
For five minutes
We pondered the possibility.
Think of it again now
You think of it.
Pause.
We therefore decided
To cut off a foot from our own body.
IT IS A FEARSOME THING TO KILL.
But we will kill ourselves and not just others if necessary
Since only by force can this dying world be changed
As every living man knows.
It is not granted to us, we said,
Not to kill.
At one with the will to change the world that will not be
      denied
We formulated
The measures to be taken.

THE CONTROL CHORUS.
   Go on with the story
   You are assured of our sympathy
   It was not easy to do what was right.
   You did not pronounce the verdict:
   Reality did.

THE FOUR AGITATORS. We shall repeat our last conversation.

THE FIRST. We are going to ask him if he agrees. For he was
   a brave fighter.

THE SECOND. But even if he does not agree, he must disappear,
   and totally.

THE FIRST, *to* THE YOUNG COMRADE. If you are caught, they
   will shoot you, and, as your face is known, our work will
   have been betrayed. We must therefore shoot you and
   throw you in the lime pit so the lime will burn you. But
   we ask this: do you know any way out?

THE YOUNG COMRADE. No.

THE THREE AGITATORS. Then we ask this: do you agree to it?
   Pause.

THE YOUNG COMRADE. Yes. I see that I always did the wrong thing.

THE THREE AGITATORS. Not always.

THE YOUNG COMRADE. I wanted to help, and I only hindered.

THE THREE AGITATORS. Not only.

THE YOUNG COMRADE. And now it would be better if I were not there.

THE THREE AGITATORS. Yes. Will you do it by yourself?

THE YOUNG COMRADE. Help me.

THE THREE AGITATORS.

Lean your head on our arms
Close your eyes.

THE YOUNG COMRADE, *unseen.*

He then said:
"In the interests of Communism
Agreeing to the advance of the proletarian masses of all
    lands
Saying Yes to the revolutionizing of the world."

THE THREE AGITATORS.

Then we shot him
And threw him down into the lime pit
And when the lime had devoured him
We returned to our work.

THE CONTROL CHORUS.

And your work was successful
You have spread
The teachings of the classics
The ABC of Communism:
To the ignorant, instruction about their situation
To the oppressed, class consciousness
And to the class conscious, the experience of revolution.
In yet another country the revolution advances
In another land the ranks of the fighters are joined
We agree to what you have done.
YOUR REPORT SHOWS US HOW MUCH IT TAKES
TO CHANGE THE WORLD:
ANGER AND TENACITY, KNOWLEDGE AND INDIGNATION
SWIFT PARTICIPATION, PROFOUND REFLECTION

COLD ACQUIESCENCE, ENDLESS PERSISTENCE
COMPREHENSION OF THE SINGLE MAN AND OF THE WHOLE:
ONLY AS TAUGHT BY REALITY CAN WE
CHANGE REALITY.

.

NOTES

Alfred de Musset wrote LORENZACCIO in 1833. He was then twenty-three years old. The work was twice the average length of a play, and was left totally unperformed till 1896 when Sarah Bernhardt put it on—unhappily, perhaps, with herself in the male title role. (The Bernhardt production was reviewed by two great men of letters—Shaw and Anatole France.) There have been other productions since, and the play has been convincingly conveyed to the present generation by the Théâtre National Populaire, with Gérard Philipe as Lorenzo. It was in fact the superb TNP production that commended the play to the editor of this book. The TNP cut the play down to standard length, and Mr. Bruce's version is also cut and "adapted" for the stage, though less drastically. The only complete version to be published in English—in *The Complete Writings of Musset* (1905)—is literal without being accurate.

If Musset's reputation as a dramatist has not changed much in English-speaking countries since Shaw denounced *Lorenzaccio* in the nineties as romantic nonsense,[1] the following brief quotation may serve to indicate what the trend of opinion has been in twentieth-century France: "With the trinity of the seventeenth century and Marivaux, he [Musset] is our fifth great classic."—Lucien Dubech in his *Histoire Générale Illustrée du Théâtre*.

Musset's sources for the play were George Sand's *Une Conspiration en 1537* and Varchi's Chronicles. He is also known to have been reading Schiller's *Fiesco's Conspiracy in Genoa: A Republican Tragedy*. Readers or stage directors who need fuller annotations than are possible in the present anthology would be well advised to consult the standard students' edition of the play in French—edited by Jacques Nathan for the Classiques Larousse.

[1] The *Lorenzaccio* that Shaw witnessed probably *was* romantic nonsense. "Sarah Bernhardt had the play adapted to the theatre by Armand d'Artois, who reduced it to six scenes and left out the two last scenes of the original." (Jacques Nathan)

For the great dramatists of the late nineteenth century a play was a bomb to drop on the respectable middle class. That class retaliated by bans on bombs. SPRING'S AWAKENING, printed at Wedekind's expense in Zurich, 1891, had to wait fifteen years for a production. And the version that Max Reinhardt then put on at the Kammerspielhaus, Berlin, was heavily bowdlerized—a fact our readers can check for themselves, for the only English translation that has recently been in print is the Fawcett and Spender translation of the bowdlerized stage version. Though the play, in Germany, earned itself a regular place in the repertory, on Broadway it seems to have had only a single, matinée performance. It was produced at the Thirty-ninth Street Theatre in 1917 by the *Medical Review of Reviews*. "Slightly before curtain time," writes Mr. Robert McGregor, "the City Commissioner of Licenses arrived and stated that the play could not be performed. An injunction from a Supreme Court judge allowed the curtain to go up at around four." *The New York Times* reported: "With many sniggers, rollings of the eye, and gestures indicating intellectual freedom, a large and strangely compounded audience assembled yesterday afternoon . . . to witness *Frühlingserwachen* at its first performance in what you might call English. . . . Present were Emma Goldman, Geraldine Farrar, and Elizabeth Marbury, who withdrew as soon as possible. . . . There was an elderly gentleman who whiled away the intervals between acts reading *The Birth Control Review*." Three English translations have preceded the present one in print: they are by Francis J. Ziegler (1909); Samuel A. Eliot, Jr. (in *Tragedies of Sex*, 1923); and Frances Fawcett and Stephen Spender (in *Five Tragedies of Sex*, n.d.). The Bentley version was first performed by the University Theatre, University of Chicago, 1958.

In 1911, Frank Wedekind wrote down some notes on his various plays under the title *Was Ich Mir Dabei Dachte* (What I Thought about It). His comments on *Spring's Awakening* follow:

"I began writing without any plan, intending to write what gave me pleasure. The plan came into being after the third scene and consisted of my own experiences or those of my school fellows. Almost every scene corresponds to an actual incident. Even the words 'The boy is no son of mine,' which brought down upon me the charge of gross exaggeration, were really spoken.

"During my work on the play I rather prided myself on never dispensing with humor in any scene, even the most serious. Until it was staged by Reinhardt the play passed for pure pornography. It has now been decided that it is the dryest exercise in pedagogics. Everyone still refuses to see humor in it.

"It went against the grain with me to conclude the play among school children without supplying any image of the life of grown-ups. I therefore introduced a Man in a Mask in the last scene. As model for Moritz Stiefel, the incarnation of death, who has risen from his grave, I chose the philosophy of Nietzsche. . . .

"Did the critics of twenty years ago know what *Spring's Awakening* was? On the contrary: even today they haven't an inkling of the nonpartisan humor to which I gave expression in all scenes of the play except one. I wouldn't like to judge these gentlemen's lack of understanding too harshly. A scoundrel does his best—or even more! What can they do about the frightful lack of humor which is the legacy of our foolish tribe of naturalists? In my theatre, so a famous Berlin theatre magnate told me, the audience may laugh only when laughter on stage gives them the cue to do so. And the humor in which I soaked *Spring's Awakening* has up to now been just as little appreciated by the audience as by the critics. For ten years —1891 till about 1901—the play was generally regarded as unheard-of filth. The exceptional people who set a value on it were few. Since about 1901, above all since Max Reinhardt put it on the stage, it has been regarded as an angry, deadly earnest tragedy, as a thesis play, as a polemic in the service of sexual enlightenment—or whatever the current slogans of the fussy, pedantic lower middle class may be. It makes me wonder if I shall live to see the book taken for what, twenty years ago, I wrote it as—a sunny image of life in every scene of which I tried to exploit an unburdened humor for all it was worth. Only as the peripety of the drama did I insert, for the sake of contrast, a scene that was stripped of all humor: Mr.

and Mrs. Gabor quarreling over the fate of their child. By this time, surely, the joke had gone far enough. The Dismal Day scene in *Faust*, Part One, had served me as prototype."

"Full to bursting with the impressions of thirty-one years of conscious living I sat down at my desk on the 7th of July 1909 and by the 18th of July 1910 had completed my first 'middle-class comedy,' THE UNDERPANTS in Four Acts": thus Carl Sternheim in his autobiography, *Vorkriegseuropa im Gleichnis meines Lebens* (1936). When Reinhardt produced the play in 1911, Carl Sternheim became a national figure. The process of becoming an *inter*national figure was slower and is still far from finished. The attempts to render Sternheim in English were few. Alfred Knopf published his novelette *Fairfax* in 1923. Ashley Dukes translated his *Die Marquise von Arcis* (*The Mask of Virtue*) for a London production in 1935: Vivien Leigh played the lead. In the twenties Eugene Jolas brought out his own version of *The Underpants* in his magazine *transition* (nos. 6-7-8-9). The play is the first part of a trilogy. The second part—*The Snob*—was translated by Winifred Katzin and Barrett H. Clark and included in the anthology *Eight European Plays* (1927). Another version was made by Eric Bentley and included in his anthology *From the Modern Repertoire* I (1949). There exists an unpublished translation of the third part of the trilogy—entitled *1913*—by Professor Francis J. Nock of the University of Illinois. And that (so far as the present editor knows) is that.

A word on the title of the play. The German word *Hose* refers to either the overgarment or the undergarment on either the male or the female body. An English translation has perforce to limit itself to one garment on one sex. But fashions, even in undergarments, change, and words to describe these garments proliferate. Sternheim was born in an age when they were quite often referred to in English as "unmentionables." *Hose* is, by contrast, a four-letter word: hence its shock value in 1909. In 1959 all words have lost their shock value, and Sternheim can no more get his original effect with the word

Hose than Bernard Shaw can get his with *bloody*. One fore-goes fireworks and settles for mere plainness. *A Pair of Drawers* was Mr. Jolas' title in the twenties. But today it is hard to make of *drawers* anything but part of a *chest*. *The Under-pants* was chosen as the most straightforward solution. But it would not work in Britain where a *Hose* for ladies is called a pair of knickers. *The Knickers* would be the British title. . . .

Truly, an inexhaustible subject!

At points where the Aufbau Verlag edition of 1947 differs from the Insel Verlag edition of 1919, the present translator of *The Underpants* has generally followed the Aufbau edition.

A SOCIAL SUCCESS was called to the attention of its present editor by Mr. Edmund Wilson, to whom thanks are hereby extended. The play had been tucked away, since 1928, in a volume of Beerbohm's entitled *A Variety of Things*. And it had existed fifteen years longer than that, having been pro-duced and copyrighted by Sir George Alexander in 1913.

THE MEASURES TAKEN (*Die Massnahme*) was first per-formed at the Grosses Schauspielhaus, Berlin, in 1930. The music was by Hanns Eisler. Both the pro- and anticommunist press was severely critical—a point illustrated at great length by the Communist critic Ernst Schumacher in his book on Brecht. Though no complete English version was available till the Bentley text first appeared at the end of 1956, lengthy summaries appeared in both Ruth Fischer's *Stalin and Ger-man Communism* (1948) and Arthur Koestler's *The Invisible Writing* (1954). Ruth Fischer's synopsis had appeared (1944) in the magazine *Politics,* which was perhaps the reason why Brecht was questioned about *Die Massnahme* by the Un-American Activities Committee in 1947. The records of that encounter suggest that Brecht got the play mixed up with *Der Jasager* (*He Who Says Yes*). "This play," he told the Committee, "is the adaptation of an old religious Japanese play

and is called *No Play,* and follows quite closely this old story
which shows the devotion for an ideal until death. . . ." "I
gather from your remarks," the chairman said, "that he [the
protagonist] was just killed, he was not murdered?"

MR. BRECHT: He wanted to die.

THE CHAIRMAN: So they kill him?

MR. BRECHT: No, they did not kill him—not in this story.
He killed himself."

One learns from a Note appended to Volume Five of the
plays that the *Lehrstücke* require no audience as their purpose
is to teach the actors and that Brecht in his later years forbade
performance of *The Measures Taken* on the ground that "only
the actor who plays the Young Comrade can learn anything
from it, and even he can only do so if he has also played one
of the agitators and sung in the Control Chorus." The German
editions of the play contain several pages of notes, from which
the following is taken:

"Rehearsing *The Measures Taken.* The dramatic procedure
must be simple and sober. Especial emotional punch and especial expressivity are superfluous. The actors must merely
present that part of the behavior of the four that is necessary
for the understanding and judging of the case. (The speeches
of the three agitators can be split up.) Each of the four actors
should have the opportunity, sometime, of showing the Young
Comrade's behavior; accordingly, each actor can play one of
the Young Comrade's four big scenes. The performers (actors
and singers alike) have the task of teaching while learning.
As there are in Germany half a million singing workers, the
question what goes on inside the singer is at least as important
as what goes on inside the hearer. However, attempts to ex-
tract from *The Measures Taken* recipes for political activity
should not be made without a knowledge of the ABC of dia-
lectical materialism. For several ethical ideas like justice, freedom, humanity, etc., which come up in *The Measures Taken,*
what Lenin said about morality holds: 'We derive our morality from the interests of the proletarian class war.'"

    John Willett's *The Theatre of Bertolt Brecht* (1959) con-
tains a photograph of the first production of this play.

As Brecht's plays have been printed in German in versions that differ, sometimes materially, one from another, it will be well to state that the edition used for the present translation was the *Gesammelte Werke*, Malik Verlag, 1938.

APPENDIX

TWO STATEMENTS BY CARL STERNHEIM

1.

Preface to *The Underpants* (1919 edition)

When, in 1908, I brought out a comedy of middle-class life, the German theatre had finished with Gerhart Hauptmann's naturalism and now knew nothing but the old fairy-tale king, the young queen, and the page,[1] who in various guises represented neo-romanticism. Richly clad, they talked (unreal) magnificence and enacted sublimity. In my play a woman of the middle strata lost her underpants, and on the stage the talk—in naked German—was of nothing but this trivial subject.

The world gave its verdict on such simple-mindedness. How could it be literature? Middle-class underpants and five Philistines arguing about it? Where was the accustomed (fake) magnificence? What had happened to the (pseudo) naturalism? The characters, moreover, spoke of this nonsense in language never seen in book or newspaper, never spoken by any well-bred acquaintance.

His intentions being obvious, the author followed up this comedy with several others which added nothing essentially new to the first. There was more talk of banal matters, and insignificant things were discussed with such emphasis and eagerness as never before had been attached to the middle-class world.

This world, however, not wishing to play any part in public life, but leaving the honor and the burden of responsibility to others, grew flustered as it felt upon it the spotlight of an inquisitive eye—caught offguard, as it were, in that bright beam. They accordingly shrieked their denunciations at the

---

[1] Sternheim calls the page "famos," a word which implies both excellence and notoriety. King, queen, and page are all found in Heine's poem *"Es war ein alter König."* E.B.

disturber of the peace. The press dutifully prepared to attack.

Around the year 1910 one could read all the reviewers saying with one voice: We won't stand for such heartlessness! To present backward nobility and modern proletarians was permissible—they are not of this world. The solid, middle-class citizen, however, brings us face to face with the risky reality of business drafts and certified checks, concealed as they may be behind a rampart of agreed ideologies, clouds of gassy apotheoses, and trenches of metaphors.

Between 1908 and 1913, I wrote seven comedies. The last, which bears the name of the year before war broke out, shows, where possible in all naïveté, what effect the solid citizen's business transactions had led to. Reality spoke for itself; there was nothing for the dramatic poet to add.

Despite the many public performances, despite the circulation of my works in print, no one noticed in these works the direction of the author's will. Periodically, it is true, Franz Blei failed to contain his delight and thereby threatened to call a more general attention to me, before in sheer reality the age would exact from the solid citizenry precisely such actions as I had shown their representatives performing upon the stage. In all my comedies of "middle-class heroism," as well as in all the stories that followed and that will soon appear as a *Chronicle of the Onset of the 19th Century,* the whole middle class, its hero included, gets out of step, so to speak, with its own ideology. But the main character in each work, in conflict with society, and seen against the background of the All Too Many, is a man of passionate, heroic will, rooted in himself, in the primitive sources of his being.

He is not overendowed, it is true, with such hackneyed, picture-book virtues as the poets have sung and continue to sing. Instead of the habitat of middle-class decadence painted in pastel colors, he brings us his fanaticism; he is possessed; his point of departure and his goals are alike his own. Schippel and Maske, making a triple appearance, and also Meta and Busekow—these are not the illusion-ridden Germans of former days. They have been awakened to actuality. It did not take long for their peculiar way of taking the world in hand to arouse general astonishment.

Hence, despite the newspapermen and the mob that parrots them, my writings are not to be regarded as irony and satire: they teach a lesson which the public has yet to learn. To preserve his strength, man must not listen to outdated clichés but to his own fresh, individual voice. And if this voice at times has brutal things to say or to imply he must not trouble himself about the public response.

My advice to all who live was to do so according to their distinct and unique nature so that the word "community" may not signify mere numbers but rather the determination of individuals to live their own lives. Only thus can a nation—or humanity—reach a goal. Public announcement of this, my sole intention soon gave me a certain influence. To that influence, resistance was then organized. It is not astonishing that my opponents belong chiefly to the youngest generation of writers, for our youth sees its future less in spiritual allegiances than in incisiveness of attack.

And now, in 1918, a flood of writing in books and periodicals bears witness to an irresistible demand for human feeling, to the existence in every human breast of a daimon that sends us out to see our neighbors. The point is that the whole world is pregnant with some great manifestation of love.

The success of this young generation and the trust that the educated class puts in it will need strengthening by the peace which surely, some day, must come.[2]

(Translated by Eric Bentley)

2.

What all my plays are about

A Word in Advance prefaced to *Carl Sternheim und seine besten Bühnenwerke, eine Einführung,* von Dr. Manfred Georg. Berlin, 1923.

In order to be happy, the human being must not trot on a leash or believe absolutely that 2×2 is four.

That is to say, if one behaves outwardly and adequately in the conventional manner of the good citizen, one can resolutely be oneself, a fellow with the self-will of a Cyclops, and eat

[2] Written early in 1918.

the pastures of life completely bare for one's own pleasure and profit.

It was in 1908 that for the first time in my comedy *The Underpants* I kicked open this door into freedom for the timid plebeian of our day. Whereas up to that time the play-hero whom the dramatist had made responsible paid the penalty for his struggle between the duty to others and his liking for himself by infallibly dying in the last act, at the end of every play of mine the swollen-chested actors took the final step that brought them abreast of themselves.

In a dozen comedies from 1908 to 1920 I established the "heroic life of the middle-class citizen," the avowal of his unique individuality. He *was* a hero, because he played his way out of social and casual compulsions, in the face of opposition, more and more into the personal freedom of his character, into his own incomparable "way of being." So for example, as far back as *Perleberg,* when the hash-slinger Friesecke has his attention called to the unsociable atrociousness which annoys people to death, he announces in victorious accents, "That's the way I am!" Or finally there is Ständer in *Tabula Rasa,* who closes the play with the words, "All I want now is to explore my own breast without dependence on community ideals, and to seek the teachers whom my nature demands, even if I have to find them in China or the South Seas."

Unfortunately the critics, unmanned and maddened by the red rag of freedom, succeeded in gumming up for the public my clear intention with the sweet syrup of their phrases, especially when they could praise my skillful imitators, who copped onto and copied everything except that revolutionary rush toward freedom. Now however the time seems to be no longer distant when the German, whom it takes a long time to talk into anything intellectually out of the ordinary, will take with hook and sinker the food of freedom which I have predigested for him in about twenty books of plays and prose, and will gobble it down and like it.

(Translated by Bayard Quincy Morgan)